$1-

Colorado

An iodors Travel Publications

Compass American Guides: Colorado

Editor: Sarah Felchlin
Designer: Siobhan O'Hare
Compass Editorial Director: Daniel Mangin
Editorial Production: Kristin Milavec
Photo Editor: Jolie Novak
Archival Research: Melanie Marin
Map Design: Eureka Cartography; Mark Stroud, Moon Street Cartography
Production House: Twin Age Ltd., Hong Kong

Copyright © 2003 Fodors LLC
Maps copyright © 2003 Fodors LLC

Sixth Edition
ISBN 1–4000–1204–X
ISSN 1539–3259

Compass American Guides, 1745 Broadway, New York, NY 10019
PRINTED IN CHINA
10 9 8 7 6 5 4 3 2 1

This book is dedicated to my grandparents, Eldo and Gladys Klusmire,
who brought the Klusmire clan to Aspen in the 1940s, and to my Uncle Bob,
a man who never met a shot of whiskey he couldn't drink, a horse he couldn't ride,
or a bull elk he couldn't shoot and haul down a mountainside.

■ PHOTOGRAPHER'S DEDICATION

A special thank you to my parents, Frank and Jean, who first brought me to Colorado with my Brownie camera when I was a young boy. It inspired me to later return and live in Colorado and capture the beauty of my new home state. I also want to thank Carole Lee for her extensive research and organization of the photos.

C O N T E N T S

Maps

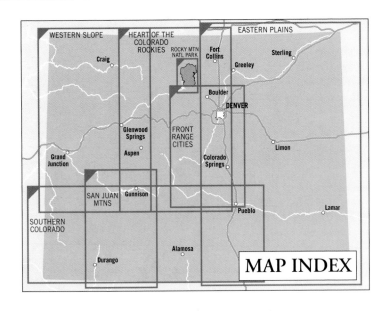

Topical Essays

Literary Excerpts

AUTHOR'S PREFACE

At first blush, I thought writing this book would be a mere finger exercise at the old word processor. I was born here, have lived here most of my life, have a history degree, am a working journalist, have forgotten more about Colorado than most people know, and was more than ready to write the guide of guides: no hagiography here, no sirree, the real stuff, the good stuff, nothing but the truth, babble babble, mutter mutter.

Fired up with enthusiasm and hubris, I started. But something happened to my bluster and bombast as I dug into the state I thought I knew so well.

This isn't another "been everywhere twice, talked to everyone once," Colorado guide. My goal is not to inform you whether lox and bagels are available in Ordway or to rehash the history of the Centennial State and its people. Instead, I have tried to provide an interesting glimpse of a fascinating state, to give you a feel for what made the state what it is and what it wants to be.

But this is also intended to be a guidebook, albeit a more selective guide than some of the encyclopedic offerings already available. Thus, it includes a solid selection of information to help you discover and enjoy a good cross-section of Colorado's famed attractions.

After I uncovered favored and unique restaurants, motels, and fishing holes, I set out to discover how the past helped shape the present, and how the past and present— whether embodied by the Mining Law of 1872 or the high-speed Internet—might combine to signal the future.

It didn't take me long to realize that I had indeed forgotten a lot about Colorado, that some of my assumptions were a bit outdated, that my home state proved to be more interesting and intriguing than I had remembered.

Fortunately, Paul Chesley's photos meant I wouldn't have to keep finding new combinations of words (how many times can you say breathtaking?) to describe Colorado's indescribable scenery. Instead, I'll just let the images speak for themselves.

Tracking good elk hunting and the fastest ski lift while trying to explain the essence of what makes Colorado Colorado proved to be a tremendous challenge. Don't feel too sorry for me, though. It was also a delightful challenge that gave me a grand excuse to tour the state and spruce up, dust off, or throw away my pet theories about how Colorado evolved into the intriguing place it is. I certainly had a wonderful time doing that, and I hope my efforts will provide an entertaining look at a state that holds surprises for any visitor—or even for a once cocksure lifelong resident like myself.

A hot-air balloon ride is a great way to see intriguing, beautiful Colorado.

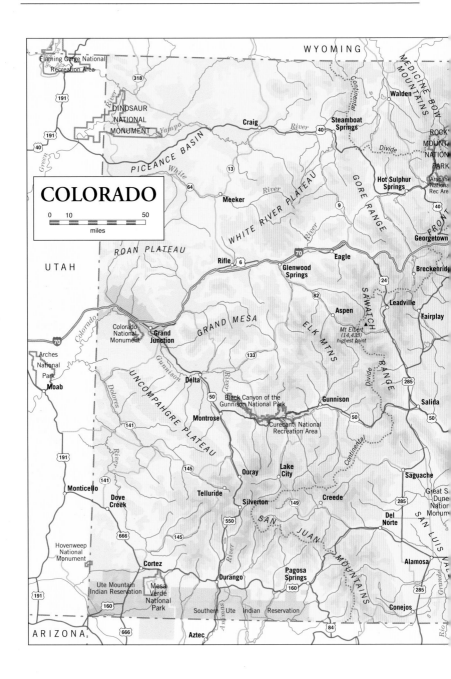

COLORADO

0   10   50

miles

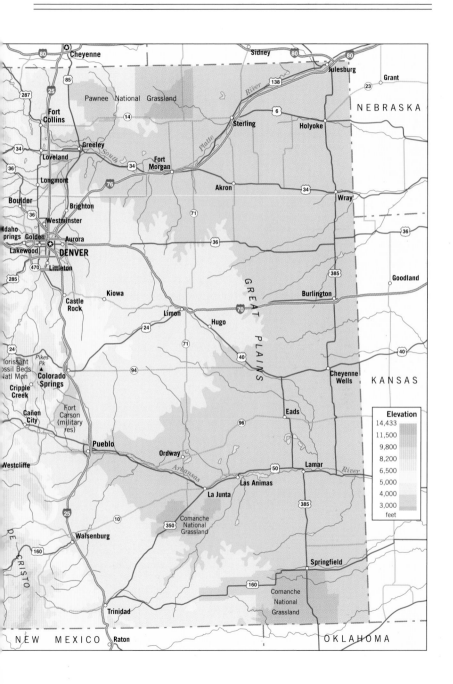

INTRODUCTION

Colorado is a sprawling Western state whose Rocky Mountain spine of towering snowcapped peaks is bracketed by a vast prairie on the east and a dry, windswept desert on the west. To the south, mystery reigns. All of Colorado provides postcard images. If a picture is worth a thousand words, pictures of many Colorado scenes are worth a thesaurus. Yet even these images can't convey the beauty, tranquility, and almost spiritual feel that can overcome mere mortals who escape into the millions of acres of Colorado plains, mountains, and deserts.

Whether it's the stability of small-town life on the plains, a cluster of brightly clad skiers busting through piles of "champagne powder," or a sunrise splashing color across a desert moonscape, nature can provide visitors to Colorado with more than enough goose bumps. Goose bumps aside, there's more to Colorado than postcard images. The state also hosts the Oil Shale Capital of the World, the world's highest town (and railroad, and paved road, and suspension bridge), enough natural hot springs to soak away half the world's fatigue, the world's biggest underground hole filled with military brass (and we're not talking ammo dump), and the sweetest peaches this side of paradise.

Although this book can't reproduce the taste of those peaches, it can give you a feel for the parts that make Colorado a unique whole, while pointing out each area's sights, scenes, and history. As with any story, there are characters, and Colorado is full of them, from optimistic gold miners and silver barons to the current crop of peach growers on the Western Slope.

Before most people get to the Rocky Mountains, they cross or fly over Colorado's eastern plains. Running right up to the mountains, the plains are as flat as a pancake, and full of wheat, tractors, and tornadoes. (If Dorothy and Toto had flown back from Oz and wakened in eastern Colorado, they'd have thought they'd landed in Kansas.)

The string of cities along the Front Range of the Rockies popped to life to supply the booming gold and silver towns deep in the mountains. Once the boom busted, the Front Range cities worked to become bastions of civilization in an

An aspen forest dressed in its finest foliage.

Colorado's mountains, the state's biggest draw, have lured trappers, miners, skiers, and climbers.

untamed land, and then found themselves in the right spot at the right time to become the federal government's western hub.

The Colorado mountains remain the state's biggest draw and biggest bragging point. The mountains first beckoned the mountain men and fur trappers who truly explored the rugged backcountry. Next came the gold and silver miners, who scattered throughout the state, from Boulder to Durango, in search of the minerals of which Victorian-era dreams were made.

Today, millions of acres of national forest, national parks, recreation areas, and public land draw visitors from around the globe. Whether it's to fish, backpack, bike, camp, hunt, or just get back in touch with land that has not been scarred by civilization, they find Colorado more than accommodating. The same is also true of the state's famed mountain resorts.

Entire communities have been created from scratch to satisfy the urge to ski. Towns whose veins of ore had run dry adapted by learning how to mine powder or historic charm instead of minerals. The transformation has been dazzling. Formerly dilapidated Victorian downtowns now offer everything from living history to the latest fashions.

Traveling toward the western side of the Rocky Mountains, it's possible, within a couple of hours, to drive from a 10,000-foot mountain pass down to sprawling farm and ranch land where the myth of the West, with its fiercely independent farmers and ranchers, is still alive and well. From there it's on into a hot desert full of rattlesnakes and wind-carved rock formations.

Turning south, the traveler finds more subtle transformations, in mysteries of the past and mixtures of cultures. It was here that ancient Native American artisans created stunning cliff dwellings, and it was through this area that Spanish explorers traveled during the 16th century searching for the legendary Seven Cities of Gold. Later, a colonial Spanish/Hispanic culture, emanating from Santa Fe, New Mexico, flourished and was eventually challenged by American settlers arriving from the East. Among other things, the Americans decided that southwestern Colorado was just the spot to relocate the state's indigenous Ute Indians. As a result, the area is a true melting pot of people and heritage.

A common bond is shared by all Coloradans: a reliance on natural resources and the surrounding environment for a livelihood. That, in turn, has created another enduring Colorado feature: cycles of boom and bust. First it was gold, then silver, then coal, oil, oil shale, and uranium. Colorado still contains valuable minerals waiting to be mined, but today those hoping to recover them often find themselves in conflict with those whose livelihood depends on the preservation of Colorado's environmental treasures. That the representatives of these two treasure troves collide on a regular basis keeps things interesting, if not downright exciting.

Thanks to its history and its people, Colorado is a state that is used to remaking itself whenever it has to. It is an amazing testament to the state's bountiful natural resources and resourceful citizens that it has been able to adjust and survive in an ever-changing world, while retaining its famous, almost magical reality.

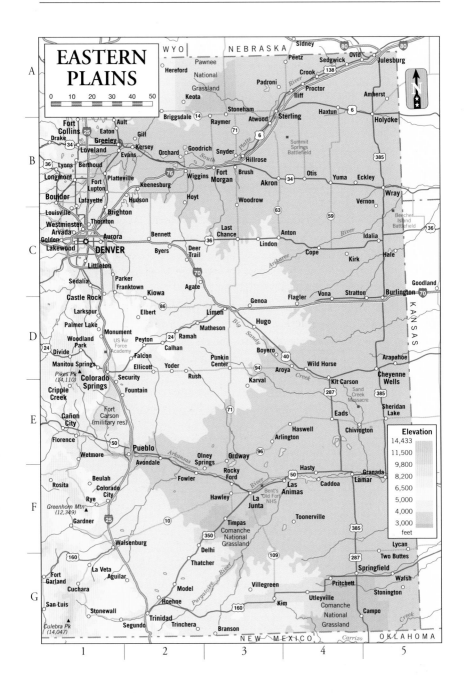

EASTERN PLAINS

0 10 20 30 40 50

EASTERN   PLAINS

The silence is palpable as you travel across Colorado's eastern plains—whether on two-lane, straight-as-a-string state highways; on I-70, which cuts through the middle of the state; or on I-76, which angles across the northern plains from Nebraska to Denver. Acre upon acre of corn, wheat, soybeans, and silence are your only companions.

The first trappers, explorers, and gold seekers who traveled across America's Great Plains probably broke that silence with swear words and vile oaths about this Great American Desert, which was just an obstacle to overcome and appeared to be a totally worthless pain in the butt. (Ride a mule for a month; you'll understand.) Your seating arrangements are probably much more comfortable, but one look at a map might lead you to agree that the plains are to be sped through with a minimum of stops and a maximum of miles per hour.

Don't be so hasty. Not only will you be missing a large part of the state's history and more than a few significant attractions, but you might also bypass some of the last bastions of small-town American life—a life that has survived the frantic freeways, crammed shopping malls, crime, stress, and anxiety that you are speeding away from.

■ BENT'S FORT AND THE SANTA FE TRAIL *map page 16, F-3*

The men who set out into the Colorado Rockies between 1820 and 1840 came in all shapes, sizes, colors, and nationalities. They were the mountain men and fur trappers who, with one horse to ride and another to carry their traps and scant provisions, explored Colorado's mountains. Frenchmen, Americans, Mexicans, and Indians all plunged into the state's frozen streams to supply the beaver pelts that adorned stylish men's hats from New York to Paris.

The trappers would head out into the mountains in the fall, trap all winter, and then, if lucky, return with enough beaver "plews" to sustain them for the rest of the year.

The fickle finger of fashion finished off the beaver trade at about the same time the trappers finished off the beavers. By the 1840s, with silk hats riding high on sophisticated heads, the beaver business was dead. Another animal's shaggy, fashionable head, however, reared up just in time, coating the southern plains with commerce. As buffalo robes replaced beaver pelts in the world of style, the traveling trappers' "rendezvous" was replaced by permanent trading posts and forts that capitalized on the buffalo-robe trade.

Bent's Fort was one of the most successful trading posts in the West during the buffalo-robe stampede. Built in 1833 on the American side of the Arkansas River between present-day La Junta and Las Animas, the fort had thick adobe walls, secure lodging, and a store of trading goods. It was a welcome sight to anyone coming out of Colorado's southern mountains or across the plains on the Mountain Branch of the Santa Fe Trail.

Brothers Charles and William Bent and Ceran St. Vrain operated the original fort and several others for 17 years. They were successful partly because of their innate business sense, but also because they respected the cultures and peoples upon which their trade depended.

This was a heady time. Before the Mexicans had won their independence from Spain in 1821 and freed themselves from colonial domination, the king of Spain had prevented Santa Fe from trading with the United States. Once Spanish rule ended, land and trade opened up, and the effect was electrifying.

Authenticity is the stock in trade at Bent's Old Fort.

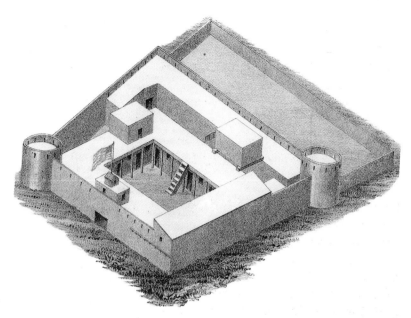

An artist's rendition of the original Bent's Fort. (Colorado Historical Society)

It was a time when skin color didn't matter, paperwork was unheard of, and Spanish and American political shenanigans were old (and irrelevant) news; when you didn't need lawyers and accountants to seal a deal or secure a promise. All you needed was mutual respect for those you encountered, an appreciation of their labors and wares, a little haggling, a firm handshake, and a shot of trading post whiskey—which in its earliest incarnation was grain alcohol flavored with red pepper (hence the term "firewater").

The male Plains Indians killed the buffalo, and the women prepared the robes, so white traders needed good relations with the Indians. The Bents cemented their ties to local tribes with fair trade and the marriage of William Bent to Owl Woman, a Cheyenne; and they offered a respectful welcome to the American, Mexican, and Spanish traders and travelers who plied the Santa Fe Trail.

Once inside the *placita*, the open courtyard inside the fort's walls, nationalities and cultural differences were forgotten and replaced with security, commerce, and companionship.

Maybe that's why, more than 100 years and millions of politicians, lawyers, and bickering bureaucrats later, **Bent's Old Fort National Historic Site** has become one of Colorado's premier tourist attractions. It's also a nice rest after fishing, floating, or hunting along the Arkansas River. (See "Great Outdoors," beginning on page 201, for more on the area's recreational possibilities.)

Within sight of plains and mountains, you can amble through the fort's gates into the *placita* and back into a simpler time. Volunteer interpreters dressed in buckskins and sombreros staff the trading post, which is filled with all the goods needed to refresh the average mountain man or a weary traveler on the way to Santa Fe. You can rest in the shade under the adobe awning that rings the inside of the fort, cuss about the demise of the beaver empire with the bearded trapper next to you, get a tip about a rapid route across the Rockies from a nearby mountain man, or just sit and wonder what life was like when a man's word was his bond, his handshake his seal, his life untroubled by contracts, lawyers, accountants, and politicians. *Six miles east of La Junta on Colorado 194 (Trail Road); 719-383-5010.*

■ COMANCHE NATIONAL GRASSLAND *map page 16, F-2/3*

If that reflective mood remains after a trip to Bent's Fort, you can travel back to La Junta on Colorado 194, then take Colorado 109 or U.S. 350 through the Comanche National Grassland. Here you can see how the Great American Desert looked before the plow turned under the buffalo grass and native plants that were once a part of the plains' barren beauty. Unfortunately, fierce competition, a little war with Mexico, a gold rush in the Rockies, and the arrival of thousands of settlers put an end to the land's raw state—and to the days of peaceful collaboration between the region's white settlers and Native Americans. *U.S. Forest Service office, 1420 East Third Street, La Junta; 719-384-2181.*

The trials and tribulations of the gold-seekers rushing to California, Nevada, and Colorado from the late 1840s to the 1860s were both humorous and tragic. Even those with scant sense realized winter was the wrong time to trek across the prairie, so summer was the chosen traveling season. A few tried it alone. Many were never heard from again. Horses and mules were the preferred beasts of burden, but some humans tried to push wheelbarrows or carts themselves, and a few even tried crude backpacks, a much-ridiculed choice. One enterprising soul decided to make the wind do the work by attaching a sail to a regular wagon. The trick worked for a while, but the vehicle failed well before making port.

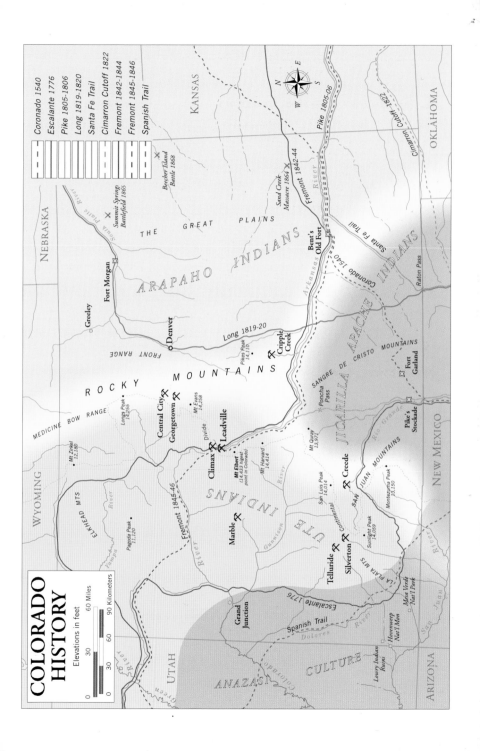

COLORADO HISTORY

Elevations in feet

| 0 | 30 | 60 Miles |
| 0 | 30 | 60 | 90 Kilometers |

Coronado 1540
Escalante 1776
Pike 1805-1806
Long 1819-1820
Santa Fe Trail
Cimarron Cutoff 1822
Fremont 1842-1844
Fremont 1845-1846
Spanish Trail

NEBRASKA

KANSAS

OKLAHOMA

WYOMING

UTAH

NEW MEXICO

ARIZONA

THE   GREAT   PLAINS

ARAPAHO   INDIANS

ROCKY   MOUNTAINS

FRONT RANGE

MEDICINE BOW RANGE

ELKHEAD MTS

SANGRE   DE   CRISTO   MOUNTAINS

JICARILLA   APACHE   INDIANS

UTE   INDIANS

SAN   JUAN   MOUNTAINS

LA PLATA MTS

ANASAZI   CULTURE

South Platte River

Arkansas River

Rio Grande

Yampa River

White River

Gunnison River

Colorado River

Dolores River

San Juan River

North Platte River

Green River

Continental Divide

Coronado 1540

Fremont 1842-44

Santa Fe Trail

Cimarron Cutoff 1822

Long 1819-20

Fremont 1845-46

Escalante 1776

Spanish Trail

Raton Pass

Poncha Pass

Greeley
Fort Morgan
Denver

Central City
Georgetown
Climax
Leadville
Marble
Telluride
Silverton
Creede

Grand Junction

Fort Garland
Pike's Stockade

Bent's Old Fort

Cripple Creek

Becher Island Battle 1868
Summit Spring Battlefield 1869
Sand Creek Massacre 1864

Mesa Verde Nat'l Park
Hovenweep Nat'l Mon
Lowry Indian Ruins

Longs Peak 14,255
Mt Zirkel 12,180
Pagoda Peak 11,120
Pikes Peak 14,110
Mt Evans 14,258
Mt Elbert (14,433 highest point in Colorado)
Mt Harvard 14,414
Mt Quray 13,971
San Luis Peak 14,014
Montezuma Peak 13,150
Sunlight Peak 14,059

■ SETTLERS VERSUS INDIANS

Generally, until after the Civil War, Colorado's plains were just an obstacle to overcome. But the sodbusters—those not seeking quick riches, but merely farmland—saw something else under the buffalo-grass sod: fertile soil. And on Colorado's eastern plains, they saw something even more important: water for irrigation.

As the sodbusters got closer to the Rockies, they noticed a difference from the pancake-flat plains they had crossed. Before hitting the mountains, they encountered waterways—everything from little streams to sizable rivers coming off the eastern side of the Continental Divide. More than 50 smaller streams or rivers feed the Arkansas River, for instance, before it crosses into Kansas. Between the Arkansas and the South Platte, another score of streams flow through the plains, and the South Platte is also fed by dozens of streams, great and small.

In 1860 the federal government squeezed the Cheyennes and Arapahos into a triangular reservation between the Arkansas River and Sand Creek—about 40 miles west of the present-day Kansas border and 30 miles north of the Arkansas River. The once free-roaming hunters got a measly 40 acres per family, along with machinery, money, and instruction on how to pull a plow.

Some younger braves roamed from the unfenced, unguarded reservation, attacked an occasional supply wagon, and didn't quite seem to respect the white

Early Colorado settlers. (Colorado Historical Society)

The Chinook Wind, *by Harvey Dun. (Museum of Western Art)*

folks' generosity or boundaries. Those forays, and the fear of more of them, convinced many settlers that the plains would never be "safe" until even the vaguest threat of Indian attack was removed. That meant removing all the Indians.

The silence of the plains was soon broken with booming cannon fire, crackling rifle shots, chilling war hoops, and the screams of wounded and dying men, women, and children.

The wind has long since swept away the sounds of conflict, though the fighters themselves are recalled today in the names of many counties and towns on the eastern plains: Pawnee, Cheyenne Wells, Kiowa, Arapaho, Comanche, Neeso Pah, and Chivington. Sand Creek and Beecher's Island mark the sites of major "battles" that eventually led to the Indians' final removal from the eastern plains.

But the battles at Sand Creek and Beecher's Island were as different as night and day. The first was the era's equivalent of throwing the Christians to the lions, with a Methodist minister doing the throwing. The second was one of the most astounding displays of stamina and courage during the Indian Wars and an emphatic illustration that superior technology (and specifically firepower) was the key to military victory.

BLACK ELK SPEAKS

We made these little gray houses of logs that you see, and they are square. It is a bad way to live, for there can be no power in a square.

You have noticed that everything an Indian does is in a circle, and that is because the Power of the World always works in circles, and everything tries to be round. In the old days when we were a strong and happy people, all our power came to us from the sacred hoop of the nation, and so long as the hoop was unbroken, the people flourished. The flowering tree was the living center of the hoop, and the circle of the four quarters nourished it. The east gave peace and light, the south gave warmth, the west gave rain, and the north with its cold and mighty wind gave strength and endurance. This knowledge came to us from the outer world with our religion. Everything the Power of the World does is done in a circle. The sky is round…and so are all the stars. The wind, in its greatest power, whirls. Birds make their nests in circles, for theirs is the same religion as ours. The sun comes forth and goes down again in a circle. The moon does the same and both are round. Even the seasons form a great circle in their changing, and always come back again to where they were. The life of a man is a circle from childhood to childhood, and so it is in everything where power moves. Our teepees were round like the nests of birds, and these were always set in a circle, the nation's hoop, a nest of many nests, where the Great Spirit meant for us to hatch our children.

But the Wasichus (whites) have put us in these square boxes. Our power is gone and we are dying, for the power is not in us anymore.

—John G. Neihardt, *Black Elk Speaks,* 1932

The Cheyennes and Arapahos settled into the Sand Creek Reservation, and the Civil War slowed the flow of settlers, so from 1860 to 1863 things went fairly smoothly, except for a little horse stealing and some minor conflicts. In 1864 Indian raiding and rowdiness grew, with roving bands striking along the Arkansas River Valley. In June, some Indians killed the Hungate family a mere 25 miles south of Denver. When the five white, scalped, and mutilated bodies were brought to town for display, terror and outrage struck. The city was certain that complete annihilation by hordes of Indians was imminent.

Arapaho and Cheyenne leaders met with state officials, military leaders, and Territorial Gov. John Evans (Colorado became a U.S. Territory in 1861). The

What an Indian Thinks, *by Maynard Dixon. (Museum of Western Art)*

Indians left the meeting seemingly satisfied and went back to their camps to prepare for a peaceful winter. They hadn't counted on political maneuvering or the power of public opinion. The white officials issued conflicting reports of the meeting and the public and press demanded outright warfare.

■ SAND CREEK MASSACRE

In August, Governor Evans, being a sensitive politician, said that anyone who wanted to fight Indians could volunteer for one hundred days in the Third Colorado Militia. Commanding the militia was Col. John Chivington, a Methodist minister who had served with distinction during the Civil War. With no Indians on the warpath, it appeared that no action would take place before the 100-day enlistment ended, and Chivington's troops began to be ridiculed as the "Bloodless Third."

During the fall, Evans, who was pushing for statehood because as a territory Colorado lacked sufficient resources to defend itself, traveled to Washington. In his absence, Chivington decided it was time for action to satisfy the public demand for a "Bloody Third." He moved his troops into position around the Sand Creek Reservation on November 29, 1864, and, without warning, gave the order to attack.

That's all the citizen soldiers needed to hear. It was a slaughter. The Indians were outnumbered and out-gunned. During an all-day battle, no Indian prisoners were taken. Chivington's men summarily tracked down and killed all Indians, whether armed or unarmed—including the women and children running from the scene.

Some Coloradans thought the move long overdue and applauded the "battle," including the killing of the children. "Nits make lice," was one oft-used quote that justified such cold-blooded action. The nation didn't see things in such glowing terms, however. Congress reprimanded Chivington and called the action "a foul and dastardly massacre which would have disgraced the veriest savages." The famed scout Kit Carson had this to say about Sand Creek:

> The pore Injuns had our flag flyin' over 'em, that same old stars and
> strips that we all love and honor....Well, then here come along that
> durned Chivington and his cusses. They'd bin out huntin' hostile
> Injuns, and couldn't find none no whar, and if they had, they'd run
> from them, you bet! So they just pitched into these friendlies, and
> massacreed them—yes sir, literally massacreed them in col' blood, in
> spite of our flag thar—women and little children even....And ye call
> these civilized men Christians; and the Injuns savages, du ye?

The Indian response to Sand Creek was immediate. Violence broke out all along the frontier, from New Mexico to Montana. More than 20 stage stations were destroyed; the town of Julesburg, Colorado, was burned to the ground; and hundreds of people died on both sides over the following two years.

Today, on Colorado 96, north of the town of Chivington and Chivington Reservoir, a Kiowa County road leads to a small monument marking the Sand Creek Massacre.

■ BEECHER'S ISLAND

The last major Indian battle in Colorado was a far different story. It was a battle in every sense. The Arapahos and Cheyennes had been officially moved to Indian Territory in 1867, but still had hunting privileges. They were also still raiding isolated farms or supply wagons, keeping the public wary of "the Red Menace."

In September 1868, about 1,000 Indians met a patrol of 50 Army scouts under Capt. John Forsyth. The scouts quickly took refuge on an island near the Arikaree Fork of the Republican River, about 11 miles west of the current Kansas border and about 15 miles south of Wray. The scouts delivered withering firepower, thanks to a new weapon: the Spencer rifle. Instead of the old single-shot muzzle-loader of Civil War fame, the Spencer used a single cartridge, and thus could be reloaded and refired much more quickly. After holding off the Indians for nine days and killing famed Chief Roman Nose, the scouts were rescued by the Tenth Cavalry Regiment, an all-black force based at Fort Wallace, and took a place of honor amongst the era's Indian fighters. (The island itself was later named Beecher's Island in honor of a soldier killed in the attack.)

By 1870, the Indians were permanently banished to reservations, the buffaloes were rapidly dwindling, and settlers had begun plowing under the virgin prairie.

■ GREELEY *map page 16, B-1*

In 1872, Colorado set up a Board of Immigration, a forerunner of the modern chamber of commerce, to attract settlers by publicizing the state's virtues. The word "publicizing" doesn't quite express the vigor of the approach taken by the board, which took to screaming to high heaven about what a Garden of Eden this place called Colorado was.

The publicity, combined with the willingness of emigrants to set out for newly opened land and Americans' general feeling that things are better just over the horizon, attracted settlers. Colorado also spawned many "colonies" or "cooperatives," whose members shared in the work, profits, and decision-making process for the whole settlement. These idealists thought the new land, especially the northern plains, was the perfect place to show the world how to run a farming town. Greeley was the most famous, and most successful, of the utopian endeavors.

In 1869, a tour of the West by Nathan C. Meeker, the agricultural editor of the *New York Tribune*, convinced him that Colorado was ideal for a cooperative farm colony. The *Tribune* was owned by the high-profile publisher Horace Greeley, and Meeker took Greeley's advice to "Go west, young man." Followers willing to pay $155 to take part in the effort led by Meeker gathered at a public meeting in New York. (For more about Meeker, see page 156.)

The promised land was purchased near the confluence of the Cache la Poudre and South Platte Rivers. The settlers started arriving in the spring of 1870, imposed a total ban on booze, and established the settlement of Greeley.

(following pages) Irrigation greened "The Great American Desert."

Greeley himself came out to encourage the pioneers—and whether it was because of the encouragement of its namesake, the scarcity of hangovers, or the exceptional land and abundant water for irrigation, the settlement began to prosper. Extensive irrigation led to outstanding crops and an almost unheard of experiment in those days of the open range: fencing cattle off the land. (Of course, a cynic or two thought the $20,000 fence was merely an effort to keep the sinners from other communities away from the saints at Greeley.) Intermingling did take place, however, especially in the "wet" colony of Evans, begun in 1871 just to the south. In its saloons one could usually find a few visiting Greeleyites temporarily testing or tasting whether the grass was truly greener.

Soon Greeley had a buffalo-hide processing plant, a museum, a library, and a lyceum. By 1880, when the colony's charter had expired, the original utopians had created the beginnings of present-day Greeley—which, by the way, retained its anti-booze law until after World War II. Not every colonist thought Greeley was a utopia, though. Many arrived, looked around, and left. Others arrived and tried to live within the rules, but wound up departing for other plains towns or to homestead their own farms.

■ More Utopias Sprout

The Longmont colony, started in 1871 about 30 miles north of Denver, was another success story, in large part because of the support of Elizabeth Thompson, a rich New Yorker. Good management, ample irrigation water, and a cadre of hardworking colonists also contributed to the colony's prosperity.

Fort Collins, 30 miles north of Longmont, was another colony started at this time and still spreading the good word. In 1879 it became the site of Colorado State Agricultural and Mechanical College. Farmers soon reaped the benefits by using information the school's farmer-scientists disseminated about better irrigation and dryland farming techniques, crop rotations, profitable cash crops like sugar beets, and effective mechanization. Today, the school's extension agents still dispense the latest agricultural information and advice to farmers and ranchers throughout the state.

Longmont and Greeley were the exceptions to the rule when it came to colonies. Most colonization efforts were launched by companies in New York and Chicago, pulling cash out of innocents' pockets and sending them to barren stretches of Colorado. Several religious and ethnic groups also tried to start their

Round 'Em Up, Head 'Em Out across the Plains

You'd think anyone with about 30 percent of their brain cells in working order could figure out that the least efficient and most expensive way to get Texas cattle to Eastern markets would be to drive them northwest across the prairie to railheads in Colorado and Kansas, where they would then be shipped back East. Why not angle those herds toward Chicago and be done with it? But there were good reasons Texas cattlemen decided to undertake epic northwest cattle drives from the 1860s to the 1880s.

One reason was that during the Civil War, the Union Army held the northern Mississippi River. In 1863, the fall of Vicksburg, Mississippi, effectively closed off the southern market for Texas cattle. Besides, no self-respecting Texas Rebel would sell anything to those damn Yankees. Thus arrived the great Texas cattle glut. Prices were a joke, even if buyers could be found. Meanwhile, without Texas cattle, beef prices back East soared. That's why Rebel cows started making their way to Colorado in earnest in 1864.

But even after the war, the direct route east from Texas wasn't the most profitable. It was impossible to drive thousands of cows through established, usually fenced, farmland and pay every farmer for every chomp of corn consumed. The great, open plains, on the other hand, featured miles of fenceless range and all the prairie grass a cow could eat. So it was cheaper to start from Texas in March with skinny cows and head north across the plains, letting the cattle arrive at the railhead with plenty of meat on their bones. (Some claim this easy eating started the federal grazing subsidies that have kept the cattle industry fat to this day, at taxpayers' expense.)

Great herds, often in the thousands, kept coming, especially when the railroad reached Denver in 1870. But getting there wasn't always that easy. The drovers had to avoid those pesky homesteaders and their fences, find water every few days, and face truly life-threatening, not to mention profit-reducing, troubles. As usual, as soon as it was apparent money could be made in cattle, large operators and corporations arrived to dominate the scene. Colorado cattle barons accumulated huge acreage and herds along the Arkansas and South Platte Rivers. Some real barons from England and Ireland also invested heavily in the Western cattle industry, and the international connection helped provide the cash to create corporate farming.

By the 1880s, the open range era started to wane. Overgrazing occurred as the cattle vied for less and less grass. More homesteaders were irrigating the plains and fencing their property. In 1874, an effective barbed wire machine allowed farmers to fence on the cheap. To this day, ranchers build fences to keep cattle and sheep off their property—not keep their own herds inside.

By the mid-1890s, the open range was pretty much closed, but with two lingering effects. The first was the mythology of the land: the stories about the open range and cattle drives that still put all Americans' brain cells on hold. Those frontier days are indelibly etched on America's collective vision of the West.

Second, and more important for Colorado, the cattle industry boosted the state's economic standing and solidified Denver's importance as a regional transportation hub. Everyone knows the story: a rancher facing financial ruin turns into a tough but fair trail boss, assembles an unlikely crew of misfits, drunks, and amateurs to herd his thousands of cattle across the plains. They fight the weather, Indians, and each other; finally meld together as a team; make it to the railhead; then get drunk, say their emotional good-byes, and head off into the sunset toward the next drive.

The proliferation of cattle spreads large and small led to the creation of stockmen's associations in the 1880s. Originally started to coordinate roundups and institute a rational branding system, the associations quickly became powerful political forces. And they were instrumental in promoting the idea that cattle had a "right" to graze public land. On the Western Slope, the cattlemen fought not only the railroads and legislature, but the sheep ranchers, too. The name "Night Riders" gives you a pretty good clue to the cowboys' methods when sheepmen were the target.

The sheepmen's and cattlemen's associations, which today display only minor undercurrents of antagonism toward each other, are still kicking and still have the ear of many local, state, and national lawmakers. You can hear them behind the podium, in Meeker, Denver, or Washington, D.C., recalling the heritage of the open range before launching into a biting chant about the vital importance of protecting cattle- and sheep-grazing rights on that huge public trough called federal land.

After all, the open range really is alive and well; today, however, it's described as national forest and Bureau of Land Management land.

own colonies, with limited success. The Mormons (in the San Luis Valley), the German Colonization Society (Colfax), and a Jewish settlement (Cotopaxi) all met the same fate—they failed as utopias but lived on as towns.

Sterling, which straddles I-76 in the middle of the northeastern plains, was founded in 1873–74, but quickly dumped idealism and embraced pragmatism. The townsfolk offered to move lock, stock, and barrel, and toss in 80 acres of free land, if the Union Pacific Railroad would locate a division point for its line 3 miles northeast of the original town. The railroad accepted and the whole town picked up and moved to the new location.

Intensive tillage contributed to dust storms, such as this one outside of Lamar in 1937. (Colorado Historical Society)

Paradoxically, while the utopians were busy trying to use "civilization" to create paradise, they overlooked the type of utopia Mother Nature laid at their feet: the prairie itself. Today, a bit of that natural idyll is preserved in the **Pawnee National Grassland,** located north of Colorado 14, which links Fort Collins and Sterling. No plows slashed through the buffalo grass and other native prairie plants. Creeks still run free, and the wind, rain, snow, and sunshine still play on the natural prairie much as they did when wagonloads of wide-eyed optimists rolled through on their way to their version of utopia. *U.S. Forest Service office, 240 West Prospect Road, Fort Collins; 970-498-1100.*

By the dawn of the 20th century, the colony craze had cooled. Towns had been established, the good land claimed, the bad abandoned, and favorable court rulings resulted in a steady supply of irrigation water. By 1907, about 6 million acres of Colorado farmland had been irrigated, most of it on the eastern plains.

In the decades that followed, the residents of small towns dotting the eastern plains were left with a choice: to put down roots, or leave the serenity and set ways of the eastern plains for bigger, more exciting environs.

(following pages) Cattle raising has been big business in Colorado since the 19th century.

THE REAL AMERICA:
SMALL TOWNS OF THE EASTERN PLAINS

In between the plains' main arteries—the interstate highways and the Arkansas River—are small farm towns sheltering anywhere from a couple dozen to 10,000 residents, and accessible only via those straight-as-a-string blue-line highways. These towns are intriguing, sometimes mysterious, and usually misunderstood. Often they operate under a different set of rules than their urban counterparts, and they can generate deep, almost mystical affection or a cold sneer of contempt.

Along the interstate highways, some plains towns urge motorists to pull off for some gas, a meal, and maybe a night of rest. But most of the plains towns lack the cultural events, upscale eateries, and art galleries to lure tourists off the road.

The eastern plains towns have experienced a natural, slow evolution. They are peopled by those who have found something special, something intriguing in the way of life sustained in an intimate community. The people who choose to live in small towns infuse them with civic parallels of their own personalities.

Fans and foes alike cite common small-town characteristics as the basis for either a passion for such a way of life, or a dread of the same.

WHERE NEIGHBORS STILL CARE

Fans celebrate the small town as a final remnant of "real America"—an America where neighbors still care about neighbors and the good of the community, a community where "values" are more than stock market quotes. These are places where:

▸ If you need to go to the bank you can park in the middle of the street, run inside, do your business, trot back to your car, and wave at the cop driving by, who just waves back and shakes his head a little.

▸ You usually lock your doors at night, but if you wake up at midnight and realize you've forgotten, you don't sit upright in bed and break out in a cold sweat.

▸ The blaring of the fire siren to call out the volunteer fire department sends people racing out of the Elks Club meeting. Or the Rotary Club. Or the chamber of commerce.

▸ You don't have to go to town council meetings because you already stopped the mayor on the street and gave him an earful.

▸ Even without the help of the local newspaper, you know what's happened, what should have happened, and what probably will happen, because that's what always happens.

▸ On most weekday summer nights, the cheering of the spectators at the slow-pitch softball game drowns out the traffic noise on the main drag.

▸ Half the population makes the trek, convoy style, to root for the high school team at the state championships.

▸ You shop downtown, even if it costs a little more than the big mall, just because it's your downtown.

▸ It takes 15 minutes to work your way through the coffee shop because you have to say "hi" to everyone and generally get caught up.

▸ It's easy to appreciate and benefit from a family's roots because they are generations deep.

WHERE LIFE'S TOO SLOW

On the other hand, to the foes of small towns, life seems stifled—stodgy and anachronistic. City snobs see these towns as backwaters, as holding tanks for those who didn't have the talent or gumption to swim in a bigger pond. For these people, small towns are places where:

▸ The police decide on the spot who should spend the night in jail, who should go home and sleep it off, and when a bus ticket to Denver will solve a transient problem.

▸ Playing golf with the town judge or poker with the police chief can keep little "indiscretions" under wraps and tip the scales of justice toward the "right" people.

▸ The same group of men always seems to get elected to the town council. And they include the president of the Elks. And the president of the Rotary. And the president of the chamber of commerce.

▸ There is nothing to do on a weekday summer night but play slow-pitch softball or cruise the main drag.

▸ Everyone who is anyone has played high school sports, and scoring 30 points in a basketball game seems more important than scoring high in academics.

▸ Shopping means filling out catalog order forms and waiting for the UPS truck.

▸ The coffee shop crew knows all about that intimate nightcap you enjoyed with your new flame. And the appearance of a local's car in the parking lot at the Dew Drop Inn informs everyone in town whose spouse is out of town.

▸ If you don't have grandparents buried in the town cemetery, you're going to be a newcomer for quite a while.

So which is it? Shangri-la or living hell? Here's one hint: small-town life must be pretty appealing, or there would be more ghost towns on Colorado's eastern plains than in its mineral-rich mountains, which are full of them.

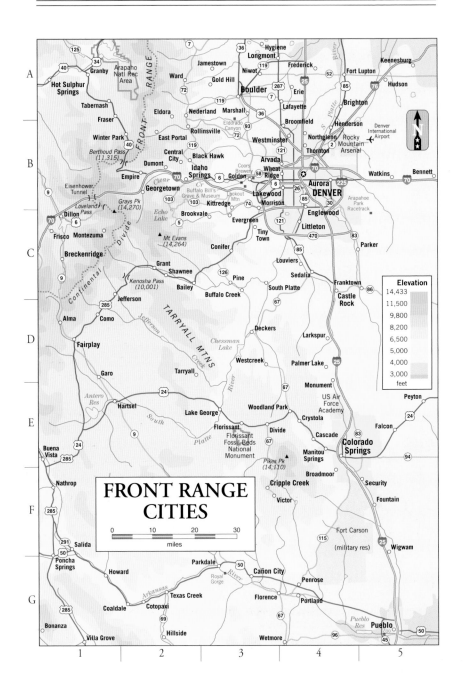

FRONT RANGE CITIES

Elevation
14,433
11,500
9,800
8,200
6,500
5,000
4,000
3,000
feet

0   10   20   30
miles

FRONT RANGE CITIES
DENVER, BOULDER, COLORADO SPRINGS, PUEBLO

When President Dwight D. Eisenhower made his numerous visits to Denver and Colorado during the mid-1950s—to visit the relatives of his wife, Mamie, and do a little fishing—the media followed. Their stories and photos revealed a surprise to the nation: the cities along Colorado's Front Range had evolved from rough frontier towns into unique, modern cities primed to lead the West into the future. That attention also alerted the nation to the Front Range cities' special combination of attitude and natural allure—conditions that later generations discussed under the rubric of "quality of life."

■ URBAN HISTORY

Until World War II, Colorado's Front Range cities—Denver, Boulder, Colorado Springs, and Pueblo—weren't much to talk about. Towns at the base of the Rockies had existed in part to supply mines, miners, and prospectors. Later they supported smelting, minting, and other ways of converting gold and silver into "useful financial instruments" (or of hornswoggling investors eager for easy mining riches). It wasn't bad work, if you could find it.

Despite the best efforts of civic boosters and the newly minted mining tycoons, the urban scenes resembled the squalid, ramshackle slums of older, more established Eastern cities. The gold and silver barons tried to dress up the drab little cities with stately brick mansions and plush hotels, but those bits of Victorian refinement swam against a tide of mud streets and slap-dash buildings. During most of the 19th century, Colorado's "cities" seemed to be frontier outposts at best and muck holes at worst, full of hayseeds, bums, fools, and much of the nation's immoral or otherwise undesirable population. By the early 20th century, urban Colorado, if more respectable, was still a backwater.

■ MOVING INTO THE MODERN ERA

Mining made Denver the state's transportation and financial center, which in turn made it a city to be reckoned with. "Quality of life" was probably an alien term to Robert W. Speer, but as mayor of Denver in 1904, he knew what was lacking. He tackled small

The booming metropolis of Denver, with its historic clock tower in the foreground.

things first, like cleaning up Cherry Creek, building sewers and storm drains, and properly laying out streets and lining them with trees. Bigger items were next, like dotting the town with parks and starting a Greek-style Civic Center Auditorium.

Then came the "Cow Town" days. It was a tag Denver sought during the 1880s, was glad to have during the Depression, and in fact deserved by 1930, when the Monfort family came up with a new way to raise and fatten cattle. Instead of letting cows roam around eating whatever range grass was handy, the Monfort clan penned them up and stuffed them with hay, corn, and grain. Thus was born the modern cattle feedlot, wherein a skinny calf could become a fattened one in no time at all, and in no time, all those cattle were being shipped through the cow town of Denver.

Denver's railroad yards expanded into a spaghetti-like swirl of tracks and spurs to accommodate huge stockyards. Although Denver never matched Chicago's "big shoulders" when it came to stockyards, it wasn't exactly a 98-pound weakling either. The city welcomed the jobs, although the accompanying aroma wasn't listed in chamber of commerce brochures.

By the 1970s, Denver had decided to go upscale, and it's been trying to live down its cow town image ever since.

Cruising into town on I-70, you see the Denver metropolitan region glowing with life at the bottom of the mountains, extending north and south as far as the eye can see. The state's explosive growth in the 1980s and 1990s has blurred the municipal boundaries. Metropolitan Denver is a conglomeration of cities, with Denver at the center and Lakewood, Wheat Ridge, and Arvada to the west; Englewood and Littleton to the south; Aurora to the east; and Thorton, Northglenn, and Westminster to the north. Longtime residents of these towns see them as individual places with a distinct history and character, but to most visitors and residents of other regions of the state, the whole urban pile is generally, and unfairly, labeled "Denver."

The college town of **Boulder,** home of the University of Colorado, spent most of its history just chugging along, relying on the university's ability to lure Eastern "adventurers" who craved a taste of the West along with their beer and Plato. That solid base of youthful activity has been augmented in recent years by an explosion in technology-related enterprises, generated by the university's outstanding research efforts and staffed by a steady stream of CU graduates. Boulder's location at the base of the Rockies has also made it a base camp for outdoor lovers and athletes, among them rock climbers and world-class bikers and runners.

Stockyards fueled the growth of the city after the mining boom faded.

Colorado Springs, thanks to founder Gen. William Palmer and the towering presence of Pikes Peak, was one of the state's first true tourist destinations. With the sprawling Broadmoor Hotel complex, natural wonders such as the Garden of the Gods, and man-made delights such as the Air Force Academy Chapel, Colorado Springs continues to rely on a parade of visitors, rather than natural resources, to keep its economy afloat. Strategically placed military installations, a can-do attitude about business, and a substantial population of retired military types give Colorado Springs a unique personality.

Pueblo, to the south, stayed on an even keel, seemingly immune to the state's famous booms and busts. A steel town, Pueblo's furnaces were fueled by the Colorado Fuel and Iron Company and by the coal and coke fields near Trinidad. As the first fully integrated steel mill in the West, the company owned the mines and rail lines that assured an uninterrupted supply of all the raw materials needed to make steel. This competitive advantage allowed the Pueblo steel works to persist for almost 70 years. The city became home to many immigrants, lured by jobs at the plant.

When steel ran out of steam in the late 20th century, though, this stable, blue-collar city had to make some adjustments. The creation of the Union Avenue Historic District—now an appealing, pedestrian-friendly commercial and historic attraction—was a cornerstone of Pueblo's homegrown revival.

■ THE MILITARY MOVES IN AND OUT

Adobe forts and tent garrisons during the pioneer days began the constant military presence in Colorado, but World War II prompted a full-scale assault on the state's land and economy. Existing military installations were expanded, and the Front Range welcomed new army bases, hospitals, and airfields.

The region also held another type of installation, though not one that is mentioned today with much pride. A relocation camp on the eastern plains near Granada held thousands of Japanese Americans for the duration of the war.

After the war, the boom continued. In 1958, Colorado Springs became the site of the U.S. Air Force Academy, and a few years later, the North American Air Defense Command Center (NORAD) burrowed into nearby Cheyenne Mountain. The Rocky Mountain Arsenal, just outside Denver, became one of the nation's biggest producers of chemical and nuclear weapons.

The peak of the military boom occurred in the early 1980s, when the Air Force Space Operations Center at Colorado Springs was chosen to coordinate and oversee

The front door of NORAD/U.S. Space Command, Cheyenne Mountain Operations, weighs 30 tons and is 3-feet thick. Supposedly, it can withstand a direct nuclear attack.

the "Star Wars" defense program. Colorado's lucrative link to the military pork barrel had many convinced this was one economic boom that would not end with a bust.

The optimists were wrong. When the Iron Curtain came crashing down, Colorado's high-flying defense industry took a nosedive. Military facilities were closed, and the teams at NORAD and the "Star Wars" program scrambled to redefine their missions in the face of drastic budget cuts. The technicians and bomb-makers at the Rocky Mountain Arsenal were sent packing. Cleanup experts attacked the radioactive and toxic residues left behind after decades of careless hazardous waste disposal.

An improbable benefit came to light with the closure of the arsenal. The facility had made use of only a small fraction of the acreage assigned to it. Hundreds of acres of grassland had remained untouched as the surrounding area succumbed to urbanization. The bulk of the arsenal's land was preserved in its natural state and dedicated as a wildlife refuge, with a population that includes deer and bald eagles. The arsenal's transformation puts one of the nation's largest wildlife preserves within easy reach of Denver and Boulder.

■ DENVER *map page 53*

When the nation was suffering through the assorted energy crises of the 1970s and early 1980s, Denver was delighted. In the heart of a region that overflowed with coal, natural gas, oil, uranium, and oil shale, the city was a hub of a monster boom—almost as good as during the gold and silver days.

Skyscrapers popped up so quickly in downtown Denver that people joked that the elevated building crane should replace the lark bunting as state bird. Major energy corporations set up regional offices, independent and smaller companies also flocked to the city, and Denver was riding high. As oil prices rose, rigs popped up, bits drilled down, and Denver's skyline soared ever higher.

The energy bust, of course, eventually came, but Denverites didn't gnash their teeth or whine. Instead, they took stock of their city's assets and set themselves on a new course. Denver was still the biggest city in the inter-mountain West—still a regional transportation, financial, and supply hub, with more federal workers than any city except Washington, D.C. The half-empty skyscrapers presented an opportunity to lure new companies into town with plenty of cheap office space.

Because of Denver's high altitude, baseballs travel farther here than in other major-league towns, making Coors Field, the home of the Colorado Rockies, a hitters' paradise.

Denver: A Major League Sports City

"Rabid" is the word most locals would use to describe the depth of Denver fans' passion for their sports teams. City residents have reason to cheer their city's "big league" status, regardless of how well the home team is faring on the field, on the ice, or at the arena. Denver is among the few American cities that is home to teams in all five major professional sports—football, basketball, baseball, hockey, and soccer. In addition, the teams play in a trio of the finest modern facilities on the sports scene.

One reason for the fans' unabashed love affair with their sports teams—and for their willingness to spend tax dollars on classy stadiums and facilities—is that pro sports came to Denver late and, in the case of football and basketball, through the back door. It wasn't until the 1960s that the Broncos arrived, originally as a charter member of the American Football League, and the Nuggets came to life with the American Basketball Association. Only after the two renegade leagues merged with their more established counterparts, the National Football League and the National Basketball Association, did the city come of sporting age.

In the 1990s, three more professional franchises landed in Denver. The Colorado Rockies baseball team was born as a National League expansion team. A few years later, the Quebec Nordiques hockey team moved from Canada and became the Colorado Avalanche. And after several professional soccer teams had failed to catch on, the Colorado Rapids did so, rounding out the city's professional sports lineup.

With five teams operating here, professional sports is a year-round activity, and even if you're just passing through town you can usually get tickets for whatever game is afoot (the exception being the Broncos, who have sold out every game since the mid-1960s). Or you can watch the game in sports bars and enjoy the detailed dissection of the contest and the fanatic behavior of the local "experts."

Contact the teams for information about schedules, tickets, and special discount and group packages: **Denver Broncos** (303-433-7466); **Colorado Rockies** (303-762-5437); **Denver Nuggets** (303-893-3865); **Colorado Avalanche** (303-893-6700); **Colorado Rapids** (303-299-1599).

The Broncos and Rapids play at **Invesco Field at Mile High** (Federal Boulevard and 17th Street), one of the NFL's newer stadiums. The Nuggets and the Avalanche perform at the **Pepsi Center** (North Speer Boulevard and the Auraria Parkway), affectionately known as "the Can." The home of the Colorado Rockies is **Coors Field** (20th Street and Blake Avenue).

City leaders decided to rejuvenate the downtown core, building a new convention center and expanding and polishing the performing arts center to give it a high sheen. To keep congestion at a minimum, the city installed a light-rail line through downtown and beefed up bus service. Visitors and locals could park their cars and leave the driving to someone else.

Urban renewal, often a quiet, behind-the-scenes effort, evolved into a public and aggressive contact sport. City officials and the business community went on a ferocious recruitment and retention offensive. The economic development team offered tax cuts and alluring partnerships to businesses willing to stay in town or set up shop.

Then lower downtown (known as LoDo) landed two prizes: Six Flags Elitch Gardens amusement park and Coors Field, the home of major league baseball's Colorado Rockies. Fun lovers flocked to Elitch Gardens, baseball fans flocked to Coors Field, developers flocked into LoDo, and a rundown warehouse district blossomed with shops, galleries, and nightspots at street level and large renovated lofts above.

To maintain and expand its role as the region's premier airline hub, Denver, with help from the rest of the state, built **Denver International Airport** (DIA) on 34,000 acres of prairie east of town. The terminal's distinctive tentlike outline is an impressive piece of engineering. Capable of handling more than 1,200 flights a day, Denver International provides a modern, reliable air link to the rest of the world, even during the worst winter weather. When you arrive at DIA, you'll think you're in the middle of nowhere, but Denver is less than an hour away, west on I-70. *8400 Peña Boulevard; 303-342-2000, www.flydenver.com.*

If driving into downtown on I-25, a good option is to park in the garage at Broadway and Kentucky Street and catch the RTD light rail into downtown. For help in getting around town by bus or on the light-rail system call the **Regional Transportation District** (RTD) or stop by one of its information centers. *Colfax Avenue and Broadway, or Market Street and 16th Avenue; 303-299-6000.*

You can also take your chances and drive toward the center until you can't go any farther, and then hope to find space in a garage or parking lot. A glance at the map should convince you to explore downtown Denver by foot. You can walk just about anywhere. When your feet fail you, hop aboard the free shuttle on the mile-long 16th Street Mall and ride from the Civic Center to Market Street, two blocks from trendy LoDo.

Most of the major sights are within about 20 blocks of each other. Driving through the maze of one-way streets, three-way intersections, and triangular buildings requires—or becomes—extensive education. Denver was laid out at the confluence of the South Platte River and Cherry Creek, and the two waterways curve like a wishbone south from 15th Street, making the concept of a grid system a futile joke.

■ **DOWNTOWN DENVER SIGHTS** *map page 47*

Denver is a city of brick homes and tree-lined streets, with a settled, comfortable feel—a place where roots have taken hold. Two decades of urban renewal have spared most of the historic center, spruced it up, and provided new reasons to come for a visit. To learn what the city has to offer, pick up a free copy of *Westword*, the weekly arts and entertainment newspaper.

State Capitol Building

Built in 1894, the capitol has a gold dome and opulent appointments that would make a silver baron blush. The impressive interior makes use of all the rose onyx that quarries could produce during the 18-year construction period. Free tours take place on weekdays. Climb the 93-step staircase and you'll be treated to a stunning view of the Rocky Mountains and the rest of Denver. *Broadway and Colfax Avenue; 303-866-3682.*

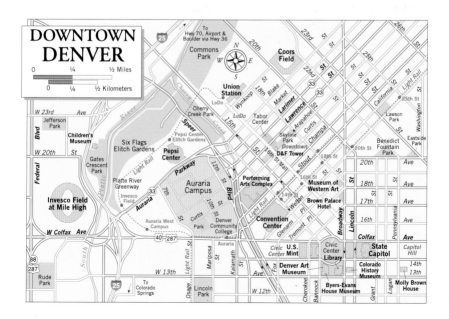

Molly Brown House

Two blocks behind the state capitol, Pennsylvania Street runs atop the slightest of hills, where many of Denver's "sacred 36," the folks who grew rich during Colorado's gold and silver rush, built their mansions. Of the score of elegant 19th-century homes that remain, one that was completed in 1890 stands apart, not only because of the two sculpted lions that guard its opulence, but because of the woman who called it home: the "Unsinkable" Molly Brown, immortalized for her bravery during the *Titanic* catastrophe. The mansion, which Molly and her husband, miner James J. Brown, bought in 1894, has been restored and filled with period furniture, gilt-edge wallpaper and other extravagant flourishes, and plenty of Molly memorabilia. Enthusiastic costumed guides narrate Molly's adventures on tours, which are the only way to see the house. *1340 Pennsylvania Street; 303-832-4092.*

The Colorado History Museum

This museum displays some of the finest examples of Anasazi pottery and contains detailed dioramas that depict frontier forts, buffalo hunts, and mining techniques. On a larger scale are pieces of mining equipment, a covered wagon, a sod house, and a huge model of Denver as it was in 1860, before it was razed by fire. A 150-year time line traces the state's history and the people, places, and events that shaped Colorado. *13th Avenue and Broadway; 303-866-3682.*

Byers-Evans House and Denver History Museum

This house was built in 1883 for William Byers, the founder of the *Rocky Mountain News,* and was later occupied by John Evans, the state's second governor. A guided tour of the home provides a glimpse of the good life in post–World War I Colorado. The carriage house contains exhibits and interactive videos on Denver history. *13th and Bannock Streets; 303-620-4933.*

Denver Public Library

Designed by the postmodern architect Michael Graves and completed in 1995, the public library instantly became a must-see downtown attraction, but the library's renowned Western History collection has long set aficionados of the West to Pavlovian panting. Tours of the architecture and the collection take place daily. *10 West 14th Avenue Parkway; 720-865-1111.*

(top) The State Capitol Building looms over the gardens of Civic Center Park.
(bottom) Downtown's 67-acre Six Flags Elitch Gardens.

Denver Art Museum
The Italian architect Gio Ponti designed this modern 10-story structure, which was completed in 1971 and has since been altered a bit. Windows seem to have been set at random into the building's 28 sides. The windows were placed as they are to reveal "living art"—that is, looking from the inside out. It's eye-catching, but is it art? Inside are what many consider to be the world's finest examples of Native-American art. *100 West 14th Avenue Parkway; 720-865-5000.*

United States Mint
An Italian Renaissance–style monolith with 4.5-foot-thick walls, the mint, an extremely popular tourist attraction, was built in 1904. Weekday tours are free, but you'll have to cough up for samples of its wares, which include the nation's second-largest stash of gold bullion (after Fort Knox, Tennessee). *320 West Colfax Avenue at Cherokee Avenue; 303-527-9500.*

Brown Palace Hotel
Comfortably nestled among the imposing glass and steel skyscrapers of downtown Denver, this now-stubby sandstone rectangle of a building is a living reminder of gold and silver's glory days, complete with Victorian and art deco delights. The nine-story atrium topped with Tiffany stained glass was the talk of its day when it was built in 1892. Now into its second century, the hotel hasn't lost its sheen. *321 17th Street; 303-297-3111.*

Museum of Western Art
This building with a past houses a fine collection of Western art. It includes more than 125 paintings and bronze sculptures that trace the development of the Western frontier from the fur-trapping era through World War II. The building was once a bordello and gambling hall, to which silver barons and cattle kings traveled covertly through an underground tunnel from the Brown Palace Hotel across the street. *1727 Tremont Place; 303-530-1442.*

16th Street Mall
This mile-long pedestrian zone is a commercial center rather than a tourist attraction, but it's a better-than-average way to get from here to there, by foot or free shuttle bus. Along the way, you'll see fountains, trees, shops, restaurants, and espresso stands. *16th Street between Market Street and Broadway.*

The D&F Tower overlooks the 16th Street Mall.

The LoDo, or "Lower Downtown" historic district has become a popular locale for restaurants, galleries, and microbreweries.

D&F Tower on the 16th Street Mall
This bit of history pokes its head into the skyline at a whopping 325 feet. The tallest building west of the Mississippi upon completion in 1910, it was intended to resemble the campanile at San Marco in Venice. *16th and Arapahoe Streets.*

Tabor Center
Also on the mall, the center has three levels of glass, chrome, towering skylights, and a 550-foot-long greenhouse that provide the setting for 70 shops and restaurants. *16th Street between Larimer and Arapahoe Streets.*

Larimer Square
The restored Victorian buildings on Denver's oldest commercial street house an eclectic sprinkling of establishments, from art galleries and outdoor cafés to boutiques and bistros. *1400 block of Larimer Street.*

Lower Downtown (LoDo)
The neighborhood bounded by Union Station, Larimer Square, Coors Field, and Cherry Creek has become one of the hottest spots in town, with dozens of art galleries and scores of shops, restaurants, jazz joints, night spots, and sports bars.

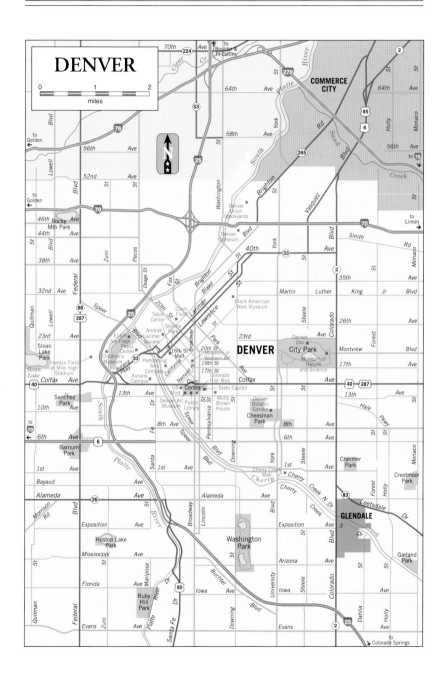

DENVER

0   1   2
miles

Six Flags Elitch Gardens

This century-old institution reopened in 1995 in its LoDo location as a spanking new, cleanly scrubbed, high-speed, modern version of an amusement park. *Interstate 25, Exit 212A, and Speer Boulevard; 303-595-4386.*

■ **GREATER DENVER DIVERSIONS** *map page 53*

Denver is not just a downtown; its many diversions can keep you busy for days. **Rocky Mountain National Park** and several ski areas, such as Arapahoe Basin, Eldora, and Loveland are all within an hour of Denver. And **City Park** (Colorado Boulevard, just north of Speer Boulevard) contains a day's worth of activities for kids and adults, including the zoo and natural history museum, described below.

Denver Zoo

One of the nation's top 10 animal parks, the Denver Zoo is lauded for its innovative natural habitats and fine new exhibits. *City Park, East 23rd Avenue and Steele Street; 303-376-4800.*

Denver Museum of Nature and Science

This popular museum features old Colorado dinosaur skeletons and more than 90 other dioramas that display North America's plants and animals. The museum also hosts national traveling historic exhibitions, as well as a fine mineral display, with "Tom's Baby," Colorado's largest gold nugget. The IMAX Theater, with a screen that is four-and-a-half stories high by six-and-a-half-stories wide, brings everything into sharp focus. The Charles C. Gates Planetarium presents the solar system in multimedia splendor and laser shows that are, shall we say, hot. *2001 Colorado Boulevard; 303-322-7009.*

The Tattered Cover Bookstore

A monument to the written word, Tattered Cover is one of the nation's largest independent booksellers. You can happily get lost among the stacks or just as happily recline on a comfortable chair or couch to check out titles on most any subject. If you want to hang for hours, no problem. To provide enough fuel to keep your book-loving fires burning all day, the flagship Cherry Creek location has a restaurant on the top floor and a coffee shop on the ground floor, and the LoDo store has a coffee shop. *Cherry Creek: 2955 East First Avenue; 303-322-7727. LoDo: 1628 16th Street; 303-436-1070.*

DENVER IN 1865

In that period Denver was appropriately called the "City of the Plains." Situated sixteen miles from the base of the nearest Rocky Mountain peak, and six hundred and fifty miles from Atchison, Kansas, the nearest town to the east, …its population numbered about five thousand souls. Here was to be found the illiterate man—but a grade above coyote—lawbreakers of every kind and from every land, to men of culture and refinement.

Here it stood, a typical mining town, a monument to the indomitable energy of man in his efforts to settle that barren and almost endless plain and open to the world the Rocky's unlimited hidden gold. Here were brick structures modern for that day, the brick being made from the soil of the territory; a United States mint, a church, a school house, large warehouses, stores, and the home of the *Rocky Mountain Daily News*, which kept one partially in touch with happenings in the faraway states. Isolated from the outside world, it was an ideal place of refuge for those anxious to escape the outraged law. Knights of the green cloth held full sway. Men in every walk of life gambled. A dead man for breakfast was not an uncommon heading for the menu card, the old tree on the west bank of Cherry Creek furnishing the man. Society was just a little exclusive and to gain admission the pass was, "Where are you from?" and in some cases, "Your name in the east?"

Desperadoes made one attempt to lay the city in ashes and certainly would have accomplished their purpose had it not been for the timely action of the Vigilance Committee in hanging the ring-leaders. When the guilt of a suspect for any crime was in doubt, he was presented with a horse or mule and ordered to leave between sun and sun and never return.

—Charles E. Young, *Dangers of the Trail in 1865*

Denver Botanic Gardens
Winter or summer, green things are growing and blooming at the Botanic Gardens. Hundreds of trees, from carob to banana, and thousands of other plants, such as roses and orchids and an extensive collection of alpine plants and shrubs, deliver a visual and olfactory blast of beauty. The Japanese garden offers a particularly attractive break from the real world. *1005 York Street, 720-865-3745.*

Coors Brewery
Perhaps the most popular day trip from Denver is the 12-mile drive on U.S. 6 to Golden. Once there, people foam at the mouth to tour the Adolph Coors Brewing

Company, the world's largest single brewing facility. If you're of age, you can sample the company's products—to a point, of course. *13th Avenue and Ford Street, Golden; 303-277-2337.*

Buffalo Bill's Grave and Museum

Buffalo Bill, the West's best-known frontiersman and showman, didn't really want to be buried on Lookout Mountain 20 miles outside Denver. The folks in Cody, Wyoming, and North Platte, Nebraska, where Bill had ranches and lived, remind anyone who asks of this fact. But he died at a relative's house in Denver and, well, civic pride and some fast talking landed Bill atop the hill. The museum contains posters, guns, outfits, and other remnants from Cody's Wild West Show, along with exhibits on frontier life and the Pony Express, which had a station in Julesburg on the eastern plains. *Interstate 70, Exit 256, Lookout Mountain Road, Golden; 303-526-0747.*

Mount Evans and Echo Lake

This is what the Rocky Mountains are all about. Mount Evans is just 40 miles west of Denver, on Colorado 103 off I-70. Once the road is cleared of snow around the end of May, you can drive right to the top of this 14,260-foot peak and breathe the rarefied air usually reserved for those with large lungs and climbing gear. At the base of the mountain, Echo Lake Park has picnic spots, fishing, and views of the surrounding, usually snowcapped, peaks.

Gold-Mining Towns

Some of the West's most famous gold-mining towns are within an hour's drive of Denver. Central City, Breckenridge, Georgetown, and Silver Plume, to name just a few, were once boomtowns and have recently been reborn with their golden history intact. (See "Rocky Mountains" chapter, page 80.)

Arapahoe Park Racetrack

Put two dollars on the bobtail nag and stand at the rail to cheer him home at Colorado's Thoroughbred racetrack. During racing season, the track presents a full day of horse racing that brings some of the nation's top Thoroughbreds down the home stretch. The facility is fairly small, so you can eye the horses and jockeys in the paddock before the race, then step up to the finish line to watch the horses flash past. *26000 East Quincy Avenue, Aurora; 303-690-2400.*

The Unsinkable "Maggie" Brown

Missouri native Margaret "Maggie" Tobin hit Leadville in the early 1880s and in 1886 married James J. Brown, the superintendent of the Little Johnny Mine. Brown's one-eighth share in the mine made him a millionaire and allowed the couple to move to lavish digs in Denver's most stylish neighborhood. Maggie then set out to conquer Denver's close-knit upper crust, but they snubbed her.

That's why April 14, 1912—when the *Titanic* began to sink and she boarded a lifeboat—was an oddly lucky moment for Maggie. Rallying the shivering survivors, she scared the hell out of the helmsman, took a turn at the oars, shared her clothing with those colder than herself, and

"The Unsinkable Molly Brown" afloat in Victorian finery. (Colorado Historical Society)

became a heroine of the *Titanic* tragedy. The newspapers of the day credited her with extraordinary effort and general gutsiness throughout the whole affair, and the doors of Denver society grudgingly swung open for Maggie. We know her these days as "Molly" because the author of the musical *The Unsinkable Molly Brown* thought that name worked better than "Maggie."

Things got messy after her *Titanic* heroics, though. Jim Brown died in 1922, leaving no will, just legal entanglements. Although Maggie's riches began to shrink, her bravado never did. She continued to swagger through exclusive hotels in Palm Beach, New York, and Europe. And she offered to supply Leadville's children with mittens and presents during the Depression, even though she didn't have enough money for the gifts. (Her family members quietly fulfilled the promise.)

Maggie died in 1932. Bills for back rent and legal problems still dogged her, but nothing sank her determination to live the grand life she had created for herself.

■ **BOULDER** *map page 38, A-3 and page 61 for metro area*

When prospectors hit a legitimate mother lode on Gold Hill, just west of town, Boulder found itself leading the state into the 1860s' gold boom. The University of Colorado was a steadier source of employment, however, and over the years has kept the city on an even keel. When the computer age dawned, Boulder was the scene of a high-tech explosion that has made the town one of the nation's top technology startup zones.

Then there's the sports boom. Boulder has long been the home training ground for many of the nation's top-notch runners, cyclists, and triathletes. It has produced runners such as Frank Shorter and Arturo Barrios, cyclists Davis Phinney and Connie Carpenter, and triathletes Mark Allen and Scot Molina—just to get the list started. The town continues to attract young athletes who hope to fill, then pass, their heroes' fast-moving shoes.

Why is Boulder such hot training ground?

Well, the pleasant winters allow for year-round training (with a little spunk and the right gear, that is); the altitude (5,363 feet) makes the air seem thicker almost anywhere else; and a large athletic community provides support, world-class training partners, and, because stars are so commonplace, some anonymity.

Thanks to Eldorado Canyon, Boulder Canyon, and Flagstaff Mountain, all just minutes from town, rock climbers of all abilities consider Boulder a mecca. The climbing community in Boulder is large, supportive, and growing almost daily. Many climbers got their start by scaling a face or wall in one of these climbing hot spots, then deciding that Boulder was the perfect base camp from which to launch wholeheartedly into the demanding sport.

Combine a beautiful setting, university eggheads, computer nerds, a horde of outdoor-loving athletes, and an environmentalist on every corner, and quality of life becomes almost a religion. The "soul" of the community is a little touchy-feely for some, and a bit far out for others; it's extreme by some standards, but jealously guarded and paying off for Boulder, regardless of the snickers from the town's Front Range neighbors.

To some, it's paying off too well. Boulder's expansive public parks, aggressive open space program, and slow-growth political climate give it a well-deserved reputation

The Flatirons rise above Chautauqua Park on the edge of Boulder—a town justly famous for its many recreational areas.

as a city on the cutting edge of urban planning. But those policies cut both ways. Boulder's amenities attract an ever-increasing number of people concerned about quality of life. The city constantly grapples with growing pains and works to ensure that growth will not destroy those qualities that attracted newcomers in the first place.

Boulder has embarked on a long-range plan to limit the type and amount of both commercial and residential growth within its boundaries. In other words, Boulder is in the enviable position of being able to say it doesn't want to grow much more, and it is more than willing to turn people and businesses away so it can give its full attention to making the city a better, and not necessarily bigger, place to live.

A big mall greets those who enter Boulder via U.S. 36, but first impressions can be deceiving. Keep going. Hit Baseline Road, turn off at Broadway, and head for the heart of Boulder.

■ **BOULDER SIGHTS** *map page 61*

University of Colorado
The campus, with its tree-lined walkways and solidly academic-looking brick buildings topped by red tile, is the first attraction. A second is the frenzy of college students trying to look cool while rushing to their next class. By comparison, the lunch bunch at Colorado Springs' Air Force Academy looks a bit rigid. *Broadway between Arapahoe Avenue and Baseline Road; 303-492-6301.*

The Hill
The area where College Avenue and Broadway come together is filled with shops and cafés geared to the college crowd. Cheap eats are offered at pizza joints, sandwich shops, and delis. Music stores keep the crowd listening to the latest hits while funky clothing stores offer everything from CU sweatshirts to hemp sandals. And let's not forget liquor stores, tattoo and piercing parlors, and the second-hand stores offering deals on everything from dinner plates to tools. Food, music, tattoos, booze, and vintage lava lamps: what else does a college student need? This is the place to relive your college days or bemoan the fate of the nation over the sight of our "best and brightest." If you want to check out the current rage among the college crowd, check out **The Sink** (1165 13th Street; 303-444-7465), a legendary CU watering hole.

Pearl Street Mall
This pedestrian mall is always alive and often amusingly bizarre. The entertainment includes sidewalk jugglers, singers, painters, organized concerts, and educational

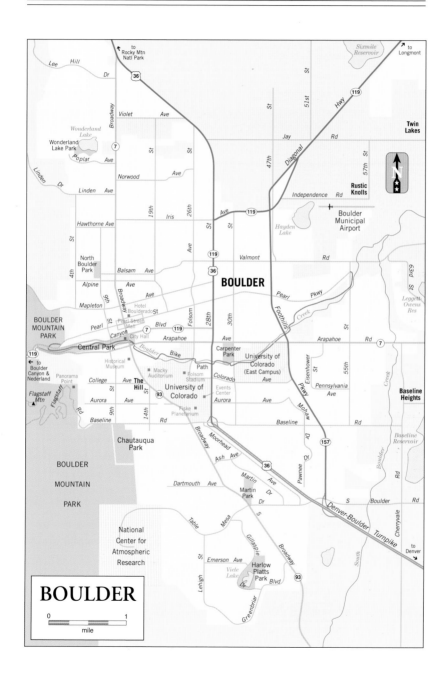

BOULDER

0   1
mile

FIGHTING FIRE WITH PASTA

For most Coloradans, the summer of 2002 will be remembered as a season of fire. Wildfires burned throughout the western and central portions of the state, turning more than 364,000 acres into smoke and ash. Some of the blazes burned for weeks. The Hayman fire, which began on June 8, ended up being the largest inferno in Colorado history, burning about 138,000 acres, killing three firefighters and two civilians and causing $32 million worth of damage in the Pike National Forest, an area 60 miles southwest of Denver.

When Vicki Porter learned that the fire was approaching Buffalo Creek, where she has lived for 23 years, she and the other members of the North Fork Knife and Spoon Auxiliary, a volunteer group, swung into action. For the next 15 days, the group, about 15 strong, made breakfast, lunch, and dinner for hundreds of firefighters and forest workers.

Preparing meals for so many is not without logistical challenges, but the North Forkers know a thing or two about crisis management. "We filled up huge tubs with pasta, and then helicopters lifted the tubs in big pieces of canvas and took them to the firefighters," Porter, the auxiliary's president, said. "Sometimes I'd throw in some broccoli or a different sauce for variety, but it's not like people were complaining about the menu."

They also assembled hundreds of bag lunches filled with Gatorade, PowerBars, granola bars, hard candy, bananas, apples, cheese, and water, *lots* of water—"We went through an 8-by-8-foot stack of water bottles every two days," said Porter, all of it from the local grocery. Sandwiches were mostly made of turkey and chicken, and even tofu. The auxiliary also fielded plenty of requests for nonperishable items like batteries, flashlights, radios, helmets, gloves, wool socks—even Preparation H.

One of the better days of the ordeal, Porter recalls, was when a nearby steakhouse donated 25 steaks, which were promptly cooked and air-lifted to the firefighters along with the regular run of pasta and chili.

Porter and her fellow workers aren't gluttons for punishment, merely firm believers that crisis situations require more than a shoulder to cry on. "The best thing a person can do in an emergency situation is not to ask 'What can I do?'" said Porter. "It's to make a lasagna and ask 'Where do I deliver it?'"

The Hayman fire was the largest inferno in Colorado history.

seminars. Mall restaurants serve everything from burgers to fancy cuisine. The scene here is part Haight Street, part Harvard Square, with a few Bermuda-shorts types thrown in for color. *Pearl Street between 11th and 15th Streets.*

Boulder Creek Bike/Pedestrian Trail

A unique feature of Boulder is that it has brought the outside inside town. The trail winds through town from east to west and delivers a refreshing dose of the outdoors. *55th Street and Pearl Parkway to Arapahoe Avenue and Canyon Boulevard; 303-441-3407 (City of Boulder Parks and Recreation).*

Hotel Boulderado

Cherry-wood trimmings, stained glass, and other Victorian touches make this 1908 building a charmer and worth a peek even if you're not staying here. The ghost on the fifth floor is pretty harmless, as ghosts of murdered guests go. *2115 13th Street; 303-442-4344.*

Chautauqua Park

Close to the heart of town, this park has hiking and walking trails that take you along the bottom of the imposing red-rock walls of the Flatirons, where you can watch rock climbers scale the heights. Also in the park is the Chautauqua Dining Hall, where you can enjoy a fine meal or Sunday brunch inside a historic building or on the veranda. *Trails begin at a parking area at the west end of Baseline Road.*

Boulder Canyon, Flagstaff Mountain, and Eldorado Canyon

Get a real taste of Boulder's outdoor life in the easily accessible mountain parks. They offer challenging climbing routes for rock climbers and trails for mere hikers. You can watch climbers tie themselves to ropes and shimmy up cracks on a sheer rock wall. Strength, grace, awareness, and determination are required to pursue this sport. *Boulder Canyon is west of town on Colorado 119; Flagstaff Mountain is off Baseline Road; Eldorado Canyon is off Colorado 93.*

Farther Afield

Those preferring not to sweat their way into the wilds can take any of a number of scenic drives through the foothills and hit high-mountain scenery on one end, and history on the other. West of Boulder on Colorado 119 is Nederland, an old gold-mining town that has modernized, yet retained its small-town charms. Take Colorado 72 north and you will eventually end up at the resort town of Estes Park and Rocky Mountain National Park (see page 123), or stay on Colorado 119 heading south

An aerial view (looking to the southwest) of the University of Colorado campus.

and you'll find yourself in the revived gold-rush towns of Black Hawk and Central City. (See "Rocky Mountains," page 86, for more on these historic settlements.)

■ **COLORADO SPRINGS** *map page 38, E-4, and page 66 for metro area*

Designed from the very beginning to attract tourists, Colorado Springs has always been a bit different from its Front Range brethren. Broad boulevards, neatly laid out to accommodate the carriages of the rich and stylish of the late-1800s, and the fine Broadmoor Hotel were all part of a plan to turn the town of Colorado Springs into a European-style vacation spa and resort.

Those efforts, as well as proximity to Pikes Peak and the Garden of the Gods—and the first golf links west of the Mississippi—made Colorado Springs the Front Range's original tourist city.

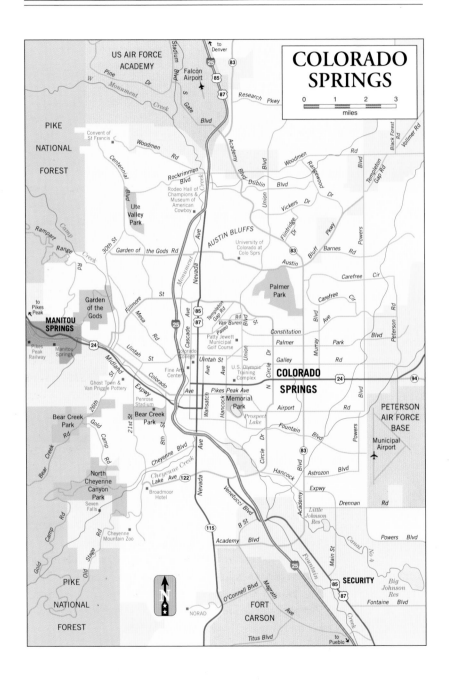

COLORADO SPRINGS

Spirited promotion kept the tourists coming. Pikes Peak became the nation's most famous mountain, even though it isn't Colorado's highest or even its most dynamic-looking peak. The Pikes Peak International Hill Climb—the second-oldest car race in America—was organized in 1915, ensuring the peak's fame. Only the Indianapolis 500 is older, but the Indy lacks 156 hairpin turns up a gravel mountain road. Every summer, some of the nation's top professional race-car drivers hop in their souped-up rigs and roar up the mountain, spewing gravel as they maneuver through the hundreds of turns in controlled, high-speed slides, much to the delight of spectators along the route. Past winners of the challenging race, also known as the Race to the Clouds, include such well-known drivers as Bobby and Al Unser and Mario Andretti. *Pikes Peak Hill Climb Association; 719-685-4400.*

Colorado Springs took its quality of life to the bank for over a century, but it also realized it couldn't rest atop Pikes Peak twiddling its thumbs and waiting for more bankable deliveries. So it began to court the military, and in the post–World War II era, the military delivered. The military brass liked the view of Pikes Peak so much it virtually encircled the town with bases, airfields, and command posts. In 1957, Colorado Springs scored the North American Air Defense Command Center (NORAD). This little enterprise entailed digging a huge cave deep into Cheyenne Mountain from which to command the nation's nuclear wars, come hell or commie nukes. The Air Force Academy came to town in 1958, and those crafty Colorado Springers quickly turned the Academy and its unique chapel into one of the state's largest tourist attractions. A real double-dipper, in other words.

Double back-flips occupied the city as it worked to become the nation's Olympic city. The national governing bodies of 20 Olympic sports now call Colorado Springs home. With Colorado Springs' track record, it seems a safe bet that the city, with its diverse economic base, will keep huffing and puffing along into the future.

■ COLORADO SPRINGS SIGHTS

U.S. Air Force Academy

Visitors aren't necessarily drawn here by a yearning to see young men and women with snappy uniforms and sabers, although that's the scene at lunchtime. The Cadet Chapel, however, with 17 spires pointing 150 feet skyward, is the place's truly inspiring sight. *North of Colorado Springs on I-25; 719-333-1110.*

"America the Beautiful"

Katherine Lee Bates probably didn't give much thought to, or receive much inspiration from, the miles of prairie she traversed on her way to Colorado in the summer of 1893. She was not writing a guidebook and probably hadn't any great interest in the latest grain-producing techniques of the day. A well-respected professor of English Literature at Wellesley College, in Wellesley, Massachusetts, she had made an arduous, cross-country journey to spend a summer as a visiting professor at Colorado College, in Colorado Springs.

Like most visitors to Colorado Springs, she was encouraged by locals to visit the top of the legendary Pikes Peak. The trip was hardly a wilderness adventure or a physical challenge—the carriage road had already been built and the cog railway had been ferrying sightseers to the summit for a few years.

From the mountaintop, she could see miles of planted prairie stretching eastward. Across the top of the Rockies, she saw nothing but beautiful skies. And to the north, south, and west were the dark, brooding Rocky Mountains themselves, jutting almost straight up from the plains to touch the sky with their ragged peaks.

The stunning juxtaposition seemed to sum up not only the West, but the entire nation, and poetic inspiration struck the English teacher that day:

Oh beautiful for spacious skies,
For amber waves of grain:
For purple mountain majesties
Above the fruited plain—
America, America, God shed His grace on thee,
And crown thy good with brotherhood
From sea to shining sea....

The poem "America the Beautiful" did not appear in print until 1911. By then Bates had published 10 other books of poetry; she would eventually pen a total of 15 volumes before dying in 1929 at the age of 70.

As soon as "America the Beautiful" was released, however, it was set to music. It became Bates's most enduring and inspirational work, and many consider it this nation's real national anthem.

Garden of the Gods

This 1,350-acre park lives up to its name with spectacular naturally carved red-rock formations. You can either drive through for a quick look or take one of the many trails to see its mix of strange and fascinating rocks, earth, and plants. Colorado's version of Eden contains windswept rock formations and sandstone towers with names like "Kissing Camels" and "Weeping Indian." *U.S. 24 northwest to 30th Street, or I-25 to Garden of the Gods Road to 30th Street; 719-634-6666.*

U.S. Olympic Training Complex

About 350 inspired athletes sweat out gold-medal dreams here. The 37-acre complex hosts more than 500 programs, including training camps, seminars, clinics, and anything else loosely tied to our nation's Olympic effort. *1750 East Boulder Street; 719-578-4500.*

Broadmoor Hotel

Still Colorado Springs' centerpiece, the original hotel has been augmented by every conceivable type of visitor service and attraction to become a formidable resort complex, which offers everything from a ski hill to three golf courses. *1 Lake Avenue; 719-634-7711.*

Cheyenne Mountain Zoo

Along with NORAD, Cheyenne Mountain is also home to this zoo, notable for its unique setting. The various animal enclosures are tucked into the side of the mountain. A trail meanders up the mountainside, flanked by ponderosa pines and native grasses, shrubs, and undergrowth, and delivers visitors to each animal exhibit. Round a corner, peer through the branches of pines and scrub oak, and discover a snarling mountain lion staring straight at you—it's quite a thrill, even after you make out the fence that surrounds the large-toothed feline's neck of the woods. *4250 Cheyenne Mountain Zoo Road; 719-636-2544 or 719-475-9555.*

Pikes Peak

You can hike, drive, or ride to the top of the most famous of Colorado's "54 fourteeners" (peaks more than 14,000 feet high). To reach Pikes Peak Highway, head west out of Colorado Springs on U.S. 24 for 10 miles to the town of Cascade and look for the well-marked toll road. If you drive, be careful. The road, which starts at elevation 7,400 feet, is paved for 7 miles and then turns to gravel. It takes 156 twists and turns as it heads up the mountain. *For information on road conditions call 719-684-9383.*

(top) Fanatic Air Force football fans jam Falcon Field. Colorado Springs is also home to the U.S. Olympic Committee and its training centers. (bottom) Air Force cadets drilling their honor code.

You can also hike up the **Barr Trail,** a 13-mile march that puts you atop Pikes Peak and affords you views of the Front Range. They'll take away what breath you have left. The trailhead starts just off Ruxton Avenue, above Manitou Springs. Ruxton Avenue is also the starting point for the **Pikes Peak Cog Railway** (515 Ruxton Avenue; 719-685-5401), which operates from early spring until late fall.

Seven Falls
Seven distinct falls cascade along what the local hype types call "The Grandest Mile of Scenery in Colorado." The falls drop 300 feet through the black granite walls of South Cheyenne Canyon. Two sets of stairs head up and down the attraction. During summer evenings, the entire stretch of water and rock is bathed in the glow of more than a thousand multicolored lights, so go during the day if you want a natural look at this wonder. *West end of Cheyenne Boulevard in southwestern Colorado Springs. 719-632-0741.*

■ **MANITOU SPRINGS**
Manitou Springs takes its name from the famous water that flows from 10 springs throughout the town. Brave souls can step up to a pagoda-like public fountain in the middle of town and take a few gulps of the highly touted, "soda spring water" from the Cheyenne Spring. The water's virtues were first discovered and extolled by the Ute Indians, who declared the springs a sacred healing site and named them "Manitou," which translates into "the God of all."

In 1872, Dr. William A. Bell built the town's first water bottling plant. By the early 1900s, a horde of patent medicine men had created one of the first water crazes by bottling the spring water and ascribing to the liquid all manner of miraculous curative powers.

Manitou Springs is also the hub of all the action up Pikes Peak: the road races, marathons, the cog railway, and the plain old drive to the peak in the family car. Manitou also has some cliff dwellings built by the locals, but at best the effort just whets your appetite for the real items, found further southwest in Mesa Verde National Park (see page 178).

Florissant Fossil Beds National Park (map page 38, E-3), on the other hand, is the real thing. About a one-hour drive from Colorado Springs on U.S. 94, the 6,000-acre park provides a glimpse of the tiny, prehistoric world. Insects and plants from the Eocene period are preserved in all their fragile beauty. You can marvel at the delicate wings of long-extinct insects and trace the intricate patterns of fossilized leaves and plants. *Teller County Road 1 off U.S. 24 at Florissant; 719-748-3253.*

PIKE DIDN'T HAVE A PEAK EXPERIENCE

All the fame, notoriety, and mountain naming generated by a little hike through Colorado by a New Jersey–born man named Lt. Zebulon Montgomery Pike is hard to understand if you just look at the bare outlines of his famous 1806 expedition. This was the second of his two major trips. In the summer of 1805, he had been commissioned to lead a group of men, 20 strong, to explore the headwaters of the Mississippi. The next year, in July 1806, he was sent off with a force of 23 men to explore the Arkansas and Red Rivers and, not incidentally, find out what the Spanish were up to at the edge of America's newly acquired Louisiana Purchase.

After successfully crossing the Great Plains and meeting with various Plains Indian tribes, Pike and his crew couldn't seem to get much right once they got inside the borders of present-day Colorado.

When they first sighted the Rocky Mountains, they raised a huzzah for the "Mexican" Mountains. They camped near present-day Pueblo and tried to climb the huge peak that had caught their eye from the prairie. Sorry, wrong mountain. The peak they sought was even farther away, and, they thought, probably couldn't be climbed by anyone. (Wrong again.)

The party moved west and discovered the Royal Gorge, which made Pike think he was near the headwaters of the Arkansas River. He thought the gorge would lead him to the Red River—his ultimate goal. But he headed north and explored South Park; he didn't find the Red River, but did acquire quite a blush on his face when he returned through the gorge to find himself back where he had started.

By now it was the dead of winter. The party kept going south, somehow crossed the Sangre de Cristo Mountains, and landed in the San Luis Valley, on the west side of the Rio Grande. It was Spanish territory—but since Pike's men thought they were on American soil, they built the first fort in Colorado, near the present-day town of Sanford. It was actually a fairly impressive stockade, and flew the stars and stripes. But Pike's Stockade (which has been restored) and his flag didn't impress the Spanish, who in February 1807 pointedly invited him to finish wintering in Santa Fe.

Pike might have missed his mountain count, but he could count muskets, and politely accepted. Convinced that Pike and his men were spies, the province's governor sent the travelers 550 miles south to Chihuahua for more fun in the sun. The governor of that province, however, merely took Pike's notes and sent the crew off toward Texas, which they reached in July.

Pike saved his reputation and etched his name in Colorado history with an amazing feat of memory, penning the story of his trip without notes. The public ate it up. Not only was his book a pretty good adventure story, it also gave the nation its first feel for the southwestern stretches of land, west of the Mississippi, that had been part of the 1803 Louisiana Purchase. (Pike's day-by-day journals of his adventures are still in print, by the way, in *The Expeditions of Zebulon Montgomery Pike,* edited by 19th-century American ornithologist Elliott Coues and published by Dover Publications.)

The mountain that Pike and his men could see, but couldn't climb, became Pikes Peak—although Pike himself had called it "Grand Peak," cartographers tended to call it Pikes Peak on their maps to pin it down more distinctively. "Pikes Peak or Bust" became the rallying cry for the thousands who would cross the prairie in search of Colorado. Of course, they didn't end up near the 14,110-foot Pikes Peak—most were heading for the gold and silver fields hundreds of miles away—but in their own way they were paying tribute to Pike's spirit and his sense of direction.

Pike did manage to avoid putting his well-traveled foot in his mouth—putting him in a historical draw with Maj. Stephen Long, the man who did finally climb Pikes Peak. Like Pike, Long really didn't discover much. His expedition was almost a wander in the woods compared with Pike's adventures.

In June 1820, Long's party, which included a biologist, naturalist, geologist, and other men of learning, spotted the Rockies. Satisfied with the view from afar, they named a peak or two (including the mountain now called Longs Peak, which they gave the inspired name of Highest Peak), then came down the South Platte River and generally took a nice little ride down the Front Range. They did manage the three-day trek up Pikes Peak, but by the end of September the whole thing was over.

It was after the trip that Long blew it. He proclaimed the Great Plains to be "The Great American Desert": he compared them to sandy African deserts, predicted that "vegetable matter" would never grow there, and generally consigned the plains to be forever the domain of Indians, rabbits, and buffalo. The name stuck. For decades afterward, the plains were marked "The Great American Desert" on most U.S. maps.

But the truth about the Rockies—and the region's peaks, rivers and fertile plains—eventually came out. It would take fur-trapping mountain men and prospectors—not the numerous military and government explorers who came after Pike—to traverse the state from top to bottom. And it required a crop of industrious farmers and a sprinkling of water to turn "The Great American Desert" into part of "The Breadbasket of the World."

(above) Before Perrier, there was Manitou soda.
(opposite) A wall fresco in Manitou Springs depicts an Indian weaver.

■ PUEBLO: A STEEL CITY *map page 38, G-5*

The folks in Pueblo, Colorado's "Steel City," have proven that they can be pretty steely-eyed in the face of adversity.

South of Colorado Springs along I-25, and north of the prolific coal fields around Trinidad, Colorado Fuel and Iron (CF&I) steel plants began to stoke Pueblo's economy before the dawn of the 20th century. More than 9,000 workers toiled at the plants during the 1950s, but in the early 1980s new technology cooled the blast furnaces, costing Pueblo 3,300 jobs. After the smoke cleared, the town decided it was time to quit waiting for corporate accountants to decide its future, dusted itself off, and went to work on itself.

The surrounding natural amenities, an entrenched blue-collar work ethic, and an extra effort to spruce up the town assured that it didn't take long for many companies to discover that this was a pretty good place do business. Pueblo lured a diverse batch of businesses and generated enough growth, and new jobs, to more than replace those lost at the steel mills.

Pueblo lies along the Arkansas River, 42 miles south of Colorado Springs on I-25. Even Puebloans admit their city isn't in itself a great tourist attraction, but it does have a few worthy stops.

■ PUEBLO HIGHLIGHTS

Colorado State Fair

Grandmothers with their preserves and peach farmers with their peaches vie for blue ribbons, and eager 4-H kids wash, shave, polish, and preen their animals for judging. The fair, which takes place in late August, is a reminder that from the mountains to plains, ranching and farming still play a key role in the state. Top-name country-and-western singers, carnivals, parades, and professional rodeos are also part of this entertaining event. *719-561-8484.*

Union Avenue Historic District

Downtown Pueblo's historic center has become the focal point for the city's revival. Although the area is tucked in the middle of town, you need only follow the ample signs that start at I-25 and continue through town to find it. Extra wide and pedestrian friendly, Union Avenue is lined with dozens of renovated late-19th-century brick buildings that house shops and restaurants.

Anchoring the historic area is the 1870 Pueblo Union Depot train station. The four-story Romanesque Revival building, topped by a massive clock tower, has been renovated to accommodate shops and offices. The depot's restoration has attracted many new stores and buildings as well. *Union Avenue between the Arkansas River and First Street; 719-542-1704.*

Rosemount Victorian House Museum

Often mentioned as one of the state's finest examples of Victorian architecture, this 24,000-square-foot mansion contains a wealth of period furniture and finery. The exterior is decorated with turrets, chimneys, a sun porch, and just about every other bit of gingerbread ornamentation imaginable. *419 West 14th Street; 719-545-5290.*

Eunice Winkless takes a dive on a dare at the Pueblo State Fair in 1905.
(Pueblo City-County Library District)

Pueblo Zoo

The zoo's claim to fame is the state's largest collection of cold-blooded animals. *City Park, Goodnight and Pueblo Boulevards; 719-561-9664.*

Greenway and Nature Center

On the center's bike and pedestrian paths you can explore the different plants and animals inhabiting prairie, desert, and river ecosystems. *5200 Nature Center Road; 719-549-2364.*

Right next to the nature center is the **Raptor Center of Pueblo,** which is dedicated to rehabilitating injured birds of prey, such as hawks and eagles, and returning them to the wild. Feeding time is always popular, and donations of meat are greatly appreciated. Really. *719-549-2327.*

Pueblo Reservoir

Limestone cliffs border the reservoir's 60 miles of shoreline. Anglers, boaters, and layabouts indulge in their particular pastimes here. *719-561-9320.*

The Royal Gorge

The country's highest suspension bridge arcs 1,053 feet above the Arkansas River at the Royal Gorge, about an hour's drive from Pueblo on U.S. 50 through Cañon City. The canyon itself is stunning, and scary—its steep, solid granite walls flare straight up from the riverbed. To see into the canyon, you can pay to drive across the bridge, take a tramway over the gorge, or loop around the edge on an old-fashioned railroad. Or just park your car and peek over for free.

The Royal Gorge: a great sight if you don't have a fear of heights.

ROCKY MOUNTAINS
GOLD AND SILVER TOWNS

It's the mother lode with a booming tent city with mud streets and miners turned millionaires building opera houses and stores and bars and hotels better start cutting down every tree in sight to build this town into a city for thousands by God let's just keep digging and firing smelters and shipping out the riches yippee the train is here the road is open life can only get better this is the mother lode and it ain't ever gonna end.

What?

The mines are giving out?

Those damn Eastern politicians won't buy silver?

The millionaires are going broke?

Let's get the hell out of here, this place is dead, but there's another mother lode, just over the next ridge, or maybe two mountain ranges west, come on, let's go, the mother lode is still out there, somewhere.

■ GOLDEN BEGINNINGS

From 1859 to 1893, the search for the next mother lode sent miners out from Denver into the Rocky Mountains. First they scurried through the foothills, scratched here, dug there, and panned any stream to be found. Towering mountains that don't lose their snowcaps until midsummer didn't stop the miners' westward surge; nor did the dense stands of pine and fir trees. Determined, prospectors plunged deeper into the Rockies in an arc from Steamboat Springs to Aspen to Cripple Creek. The gold-seekers raced across the huge meadows tucked between the mountain ranges, because gold was in the hills and along the streambeds.

In those moments when their eyes weren't focused on gold, a few must have marveled at the pure beauty of their surroundings—steep canyons, rolling mountains, herds of deer and elk, and a deep blue sky that slowly turned an orange-red at sunset and sunrise.

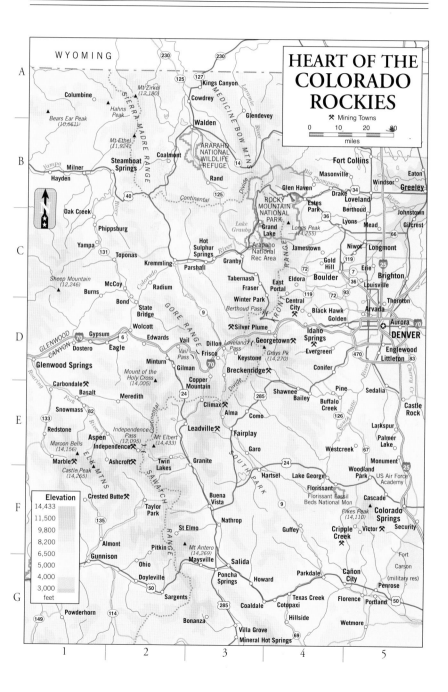

HEART OF THE COLORADO ROCKIES

⚒ Mining Towns

0   10   20   30
miles

WYOMING

Columbine

Bears Ear Peak (10,661)

Hahns Peak

Mt Zirkel (12,180)

230

125

127

Kings Canyon

Cowdrey

Glendevey

Walden

230

Mt Ethel (11,924)

Coalmont

Milner

Steamboat Springs

Hayden

Oak Creek

40

Phippsburg

Continental

Yampa

131

Toponas

Kremmling

Parshall

Sheep Mountain (12,246)

McCoy

Radium

Burns

Bond

State Bridge

Wolcott

ARAPAHO NATIONAL WILDLIFE REFUGE

14

Rand

125

Hot Sulphur Springs

Granby

Lake Granby

Grand Lake

Arapaho National Rec Area

ROCKY MOUNTAIN NATIONAL PARK

Fort Collins

Masonville

Glen Haven

Estes Park

Longs Peak (14,255)

Drake

34

Loveland

Berthoud

36

Lyons

Jamestown

Niwot

Gold Hill

119

Erie

Eaton

Windsor

Greeley

Johnstown

Mead

Gilcrest

66

Longmont

Tabernash

Fraser

East Portal

Eldora

Boulder

Brighton

Louisville

Winter Park

119

72

93

72

7

36

25

Thornton

Berthoud Pass

Central City

9

Silver Plume

Georgetown

Black Hawk

Golden

Idaho Springs

Arvada

Aurora

70

DENVER

Gypsum

6

Edwards

Vail

Dillon

Loveland Pass

Glenwood Springs

GLENWOOD CANYON

70

Dostero

Eagle

Vail Pass

Frisco

70

Keystone

Grays Pk (14,270)

Evergreen

470

Englewood

Littleton

83

Minturn

Gilman

Breckenridge

Conifer

Mount of the Holy Cross (14,005)

Copper Mountain

24

Carbondale

Basalt

Meredith

Climax

Alma

Shawnee

Bailey

Pine

Sedalia

Snowmass

82

Leadville

Fairplay

Como

Buffalo Creek

126

Castle Rock

133

Redstone

Independence Pass (12,095)

Mt Elbert (14,433)

Garo

Larkspur

Maroon Bells (14,156)

Aspen

Independence

Ashcroft

Westcreek

67

Palmer Lake

Marble

Twin Lakes

Granite

Monument

Castle Peak (14,265)

Hartsel

Lake George

Woodland Park

US Air Force Academy

Crested Butte

Buena Vista

Florissant

Cascade

Elevation

14,433	
11,500	
9,800	
8,200	
6,500	
5,000	
4,000	
3,000	
feet	

Taylor Park

135

St Elmo

Nathrop

9

Florissant Fossil Beds National Mon

Pikes Peak (14,110)

Colorado Springs

Almont

Pitkin

Mt Antero (14,269)

Guffey

Cripple Creek

Victor

Security

Gunnison

Ohio

Maysville

Salida

Fort Carson

Doyleville

50

Poncha Springs

Howard

Parkdale

Cañon City

(military res)

Sargents

Texas Creek

Cotopaxi

Florence

Penrose

Powderhorn

114

Bonanza

Coaldale

Hillside

Portland

50

Wetmore

149

Villa Grove

Mineral Hot Springs

69

Valid, modern-day mining claims staked out under terms of the 1872 Mining Act allow gold miners to still "dig" Aspen Mountain.

But what really captured the prospectors' attention was news about a hefty strike in an accessible location. It took transportation, smelters, and capital to make a mining town boom, so once a place like Leadville or Breckenridge boomed, the miners would stream out of isolated cabins high in the Rockies and descend on the town like a swarm of locusts. Today, despite all the mining and excavating, millions of acres of forested slopes and wide-open meadows remain relatively unscarred by the gold boom.

The booms and busts of the mining era remain alive today in the many towns that have retained their Victorian roots. Many mining companies continue to disgorge significant amounts of minerals from the state's mountainous bowels, helping Colorado to maintain its status as one of the nation's top gold- and mineral-producing states.

So you might want to keep an eye on the streambed while you're fishing or hiking, because you might stumble on the next mother lode. Mining has long been considered a reputable occupation in Colorado, even if Mark Twain did claim that a mine is "a hole in the ground owned by a liar."

■ FIBBING IN 1858

Colorado's gold rush had a rather dubious beginning. A Georgian named William Green Russell led a small party to the confluence of Cherry Creek and the South Platte River in 1858. To his party—veterans of the Georgia gold rush—these Colorado streams looked just as peachy and golden as Georgia's. The men panned a little gold, nosed around, assumed there should be more somewhere, and decided to stay the winter and start serious prospecting in the spring.

Even in the 1850s, it was hard to keep any nugget of gold news a secret. Word of their meager find got back to towns like Kansas City and Omaha, which had prospered by supplying the forty-niners on their way to the California gold rush. Stuck in the Depression of 1857, they hated to let facts get in their way, so they declared a full-blown Colorado gold rush based on the meager gold "strikes." Their reports in turn fueled the desperate dreams of the nation's gullible gold-seekers. Sales in the mercantiles picked up dramatically in the spring of 1859, as 100,000 people headed west. Half of them never made it to Colorado. They either suffered prairie paranoia, died, got lost, or came to their senses when they arrived and saw impassable mountains, icy streams, and riverbanks lined with rocks instead of gold nuggets.

■ HEADY YEARS IN GOLD COUNTRY

The first real gold strikes were by George A. Jackson and John H. Gregory, miners who independently discovered veins at Clear Creek in 1858. Two years later, substantial discoveries were also made at Gold Hill, west of Boulder. That was all it took: a boom was on. Of course, the fact that Horace Greeley panned a little Colorado gold, a find he loudly touted in his *New York Tribune*, didn't hurt. (Could someone the night before have dropped a little gold in the spot Horace was supposed to pan?)

It soon became obvious that Cherry Creek, where the hullabaloo started, contained about as much gold as a bottle of watered-down whiskey. The lack of gold didn't mean locals weren't striking it rich, however. Merchants quickly set up shop in the infant towns of Denver and Auraria and started shipping wagonloads of supplies to gold-diggers.

Those first heady years created the myth of a lone prospector who struck gold deep in the hills and came back to town with his burro and a sack of gold nuggets that would make him a rich man. For some, that fantasy became reality. But not for many. Tugging gold out of freezing mountain streams was hard work. As the

GOLD STRIKE AT CHERRY CREEK

Things were looking pretty bleak for gold-hunters in Cherry Creek in May 1858 until a miner came into town and announced that he had discovered gold dirt amid some nearby veins of quartz:

Perceiving a manifestation of incredulity on the part of his listeners, he produced, in corroboration of his statement, a bottle containing about forty dollars' worth of flour gold, and also several fragments of a hard substance which he designated as decomposed gold-bearing quartz....Several persons having, in the meantime, entered the office and showing upon hearing the miner's tale a disposition to doubt its truthfulness, the latter grew rather excited, repeated what he had said, and asserted most emphatically that he would warrant one dollar to the pan of dirt to any number of men that would follow him to the locality in question, and added that they might bring a rope along and swing him up in case he should be found a liar.

This was the first news of the discovery of the Gregory mines that reached us. Its bearer, who had come to the Cherry Creek towns for a new supply of provisions, returned to the mountains on the following day, in company with several others, who intended to sift his story by a visit to the scene of the alleged discovery.

A few more dull days elapsed without throwing any further light on the subject, and the spark of hope kindled by the miner's apparently earnest story had nearly been lost sight of amidst the surrounding darkness, when on the fifth day a Mr. Bates, late of Dubuque, Iowa, made his appearance in Auraria with a vial full of gold, representing a value of about eighty dollars, which he claimed to have washed out of thirty-nine pans of dirt, obtained not far from the spot on which Gregory had made his discovery. Mr. Bates being known as a reliable man, his story was at once credited and he and his bottle taken from cabin to cabin. The sight of his gold forthwith produced an intense excitement, and the news of his luck spread like wild-fire and at once moved the hearts of the denizens of the two towns with gladdening sensations....

On the following day a universal exodus took place in the direction of North Clear Creek. Whoever could raise enough provisions for a protracted stay in the mountains sallied out without delay. Traders locked up their stores; bar-keepers disappeared with their bottles of whiskey, the few mechanics that were busy building houses abandoned their work, the county judge and sheriff, lawyers and doctors, and even the editor of the *Rocky Mountain News,* joined in the general rush.

—Henry Villard, *The Past and Present of the Pike's Peak Gold Regions,* 1932

easy gold along the river banks gave out, the sluice box or the rocker replaced the gold pan. These two-man contraptions were filled with dirt and then rinsed, hopefully to reveal gold.

■ TECHNOLOGY AND CAPITAL

As time went on, more dirt had to be sluiced to produce less gold. This led to new and expensive technology. Coffer dams were unleashed to clean out whole stretches of streambed. Hydraulic mining used hoses and pipes to blast away all the dirt around the stream so it could be set aside and sifted. Lode gold, or veins, quickly became the domain of mining companies that could afford to hire miners, crush tons of ore, and then ship and sell the resulting gold.

The lack of technology and capital didn't stop the solitary miner. Lone prospectors still set out into unexplored territory—but if they did find gold, instead of mining the claim, they would more than likely arrange a friendly corporate takeover with a well-heeled mining company, gilding the deal with a guaranteed percentage of earnings.

By 1865, an estimated 100 million tons of freight were being hauled to Denver by wagon. Getting as far as Denver was the easy part, however; hauling supplies up into the Rockies was something else. It wasn't long before sharp-eyed and deep-pocketed men began to think about building railroads into the booming mining districts.

In 1867, the Union Pacific Transcontinental Railroad hit Wyoming. Three years later a Union Pacific spur reached Denver and the Kansas Pacific made a straight shot across the prairie into town. Then Gen. William Palmer created the Denver & Rio Grande Railroad and pushed its lines south to Colorado Springs, Cañon City, Pueblo, and Trinidad.

Rail links weren't enough to make investors' eyes glow over Colorado gold. A chunk of granite and gold was a tough nut to crack; stamp mills had to pound the ore to break the granite's grip on the gold. Nathaniel P. Hill, a chemist from Brown University, got the gold boom cooking in 1868 when he developed a smelter that would heat the ore, bake away the granite, and attach gold or silver to copper mattes for extraction. Forget smashing high-grade ore; now you could cook low-grade ore and still make money.

■ BLACK HAWK AND CENTRAL CITY *map page 81, D-4*

At the time, Hill's smelter and William A. H. Loveland's Colorado Central Railroad, completed in 1877, made Black Hawk and Central City "the richest square mile on earth." Thanks to legalized gambling, they're booming once more.

To get there, drive due west from Denver on U.S. 6, get off on U.S. 119, and you'll wind through Clear Creek Canyon, where the creek banks reveal piles of rocks left by the placers and hydraulic miners. The closer you get to **Black Hawk,** the more mining debris you'll see, and when you get to town you'll see the rusted leftovers of Hill's inventions.

Just up the road—with the emphasis on "up"—is **Central City.** It's hard to imagine thousands of people living in this steep little canyon. A closer look at the hills, which are dotted, crisscrossed, and covered with tailings piles, roads, and assorted miners' marks, makes you wonder whether the miners could even swing a pick without hitting a fellow prospector. The town's few paved streets quickly give way to dirt roads steep enough to make a mule snort.

It's the buildings, not the roads, that enthrall. After the town burned to the ground a couple of times, a "bricks, or stone, or nothing doing" building code was imposed. Thus Central

The lone prospector in all his "romantic" glory—Pat Lynch, 1910. (Colorado Historical Society)

City probably has the state's best collection of original block, brick, and stone Victorian buildings, and they're all jammed into a couple of easy strolling blocks. The crown jewel is the restored **Central City Opera House** (124 Eureka Street; 303-292-6700), home to a summer opera season unmatched in Colorado. Next to the opera house is the **Teller House** (120 Eureka Street; 303-582-9608), home to the famous "Face on the Barroom Floor." The face belongs to the lovely Madeline and was painted by her jilted lover; he died atop his masterpiece before signing his name. Both the Central City Opera House and the Teller House are open during the summer only.

The introduction of limited-stakes gambling was intended to add tourist appeal to Central City and Black Hawk by reproducing the long-lost feel of the wild silver camps. The quaint vision presented by gambling's backers had the town's existing mom-and-pop businesses, from shirt shops to gas stations, install a few slot machines to augment their income. Local bars and restaurants would also put in a row or two of the one-armed bandits and set up blackjack and poker tables where visitors could idle away an hour or so in a casual card game.

Well, it didn't quite turn out that way. Gambling did create a new gold-rush mentality that more than equaled that of the boom era, but the idea that the towns could retain their low-key charm didn't quite pan out.

Everyone seems to have underestimated the power of gambling fever. The idea of making slot machines another novelty in a curio shop soon gave way to the idea that the big money was in slot machines, not coffee mugs. Hardware stores, T-shirt shops, and even the town's sole gas station were replaced with gambling emporiums.

Then, in an ironic replay of the corporate buyout of the lone prospector a hundred years earlier, the big boys came to the gaming table. Full-blown casinos popped up, with hundreds of slot machines, day-care centers, video arcades, and in-house souvenir shops. Unable to compete, the mom-and-pop shops quickly sold out to the corporate chains.

Historic Black Hawk, which had more vacant land than Central City before the gambling boom, was engulfed and overshadowed by towering, sparkling gambling palaces. Every vaguely vacant parcel in Central City also became home to a big new gambling edifice. The casino-building boom crawled up the narrow valley; now, instead of being two distinct towns a mile apart, Black Hawk and Central City have coalesced into a single gambling conglomerate.

THE FACE ON THE BARROOM FLOOR

"...I was a painter—not one that daubed on bricks and wood,
But an artist, and for my age, was rated pretty good....
And then I met a woman—now comes the funny part,
With eyes that petrified my brain, and sunk into my heart....

"I was working on a portrait, one afternoon in May,
Of a fair-haired boy, a friend of mine, who lived across the way,
And Madeline admired it, and much to my surprise,
Said that she'd like to know the man that had such dreamy eyes.

"It didn't take long to know him, and before the month had flown,
My friend had stolen my darling, and I was left alone....

"Give me that piece of chalk with which you mark the baseball score
And you shall see the lovely Madeline upon the barroom floor."

Another drink, and with chalk in hand, the vagabond began
To sketch a face that well might buy the soul of any man.
Then, as he placed another lock upon the shapely head,
With fearful shriek, he leaped, and fell across the picture—dead.

—H. Antoine D'Arcy

The Teller House's famous "barroom floor" image.

Central City was primitive but pulsating in the 1860s. (Colorado Historical Society)

Today the flashy new casinos present an almost Disney-like facade, where gambling is just good, clean, family fun. It's quite a contrast to the rough-and-tumble image of a 19th-century mining town. The historic brick buildings in downtown Central City have been restored and sandblasted to a rosy sheen. Every Victorian flourish has been accentuated with fresh paint or bronze.

Then there's the noise. In the summer, all doors are open and bells and whistles whine from slot machines that have just paid, say, $8 on a $2 bet. On each casino doorstep, a costumed greeter hails passersby with coupons, spiels, and other tricks of the barker's trade.

Unintended consequences aside, gambling has accomplished two things. First, Central City and Black Hawk are filled year-round with treasure-seekers. Second, and most important for the state as a whole, gambling taxes have put a bulge in the state's historic-preservation coffers. Towns across Colorado have used the money to preserve buildings and attractions.

But for the purists, changing the historic character of Black Hawk and Central City, two of the state's best-known links to its mining heyday, is a heavy price to pay to keep the rest of the state's historic heritage safe from commercialization and exploitation.

As for gamblers: hey, a slot machine is a slot machine, whether it's in Las Vegas or an old Colorado mining town.

■ GEORGETOWN, SILVER PLUME, AND IDAHO SPRINGS *map page 81, D-3/4*

These three towns, which rest one after another about an hour's drive west of Denver on I-70, once swarmed with miners, and the hillsides around them were dotted with gold and silver mines.

The coming of the Colorado Central Railroad in 1877 kept the boom alive. Steep mountains had blocked the line from reaching the prolific mines of Silver Plume. When Jay Gould bought the Colorado Central, he decided to extend the line, creating the **Georgetown Loop Railroad** (1106 Rose Street, Georgetown; 303-569-2403 or 800-691-4386)—an iron train trestle that rises up 638 feet and was considered a great engineering feat of its day (also see page 273).

Argo Gold Mine and Mill in the Idaho Springs area.

As riders peek down from the Loop, many gasp, either in awe of the engineering and the valley's beauty, or from the fear that those tiny little iron sticks couldn't possibly support a passenger-filled, steam-powered train. Atop the trestle (while in the train) is the best place from which to view Georgetown and the surrounding mountains, which are steep, rocky, and still dotted with dozens of yellowish mine tailings among the pines.

Nestled in the valley, downtown **Georgetown** has avoided being ruined by renovation. The back streets and the original brick and wooden Victorian buildings downtown evoke a comfortable, lived-in feel. This is a place where selling T-shirts isn't the only business at hand.

Silver Plume, which once contained some of the richest gold ore in the state, is interestingly Victorian once you get away from the freeway ramps, and many a mining relic is still jammed into the narrow canyon. You can relive some of the good times with a gold mine tour; the biggest is off I-70 at the **Argo Gold Mill** (2350 Riverside Drive, Idaho Springs; 303-567-2421).

■ **CRIPPLE CREEK AND VICTOR** *map page 81, F-5*

Latecomers to the gold rush, these towns were hot spots nonetheless. After a gold strike in 1891, Cripple Creek boomed. By 1900, 475 mining companies were in operation and the town's population had reached 25,000. Labor troubles and falling prices, which began with the financial panic of 1907, combined with devastating fires to end the boom almost as quickly as it started. The gold remains, as do the miners, who now use cyanide leech-field mining techniques to extract the ore.

A new gold rush, based on limited-stakes gambling, descended on Cripple Creek in 1991. The stately brick and stone buildings along Bennett Avenue were converted into casinos large and small. But Cripple Creek hasn't exactly struck the gambling mother lode, because of its relative isolation, lack of large hotels, and distance from the Front Range cities. The town is about an hour's drive west of Colorado Springs on U.S. 24 and Colorado 67.

Bennett Avenue, the main drag, is speckled with casinos and small bars that offer the familiar slot machines and blackjack and poker tables. But plenty of gift shops, coffee shops, and regular small-town businesses help Cripple Creek retain its authentic character. The band of wild burros that has been the town's trademark

(following pages) Sunset in the Rockies (1886), by Albert Bierstadt. (Museum of Western Art)

Downtown Cripple Creek.

for decades still roams the streets, the animals casually munching on lawns or weeds or occasional feed from friends.

On a tour of the **Molly Kathleen Gold Mine** (Colorado 67; 719-689-2466 or 888-291-5689), a mile north of Cripple Creek, you can see how riches were made the old-fashioned way. The mine didn't close until the 1960s. If you take a ride on the **Cripple Creek/Victor Narrow Gauge Railroad** (Bennett Avenue and Fifth Street; 719-689-2640), you'll get a taste of life in Cripple Creek a century ago.

■ BRECKENRIDGE   *map page 81, D-3*

Breckenridge, 70 miles west of Denver on Colorado 9, was a stable producer of gold until 1948, after which many of the original buildings were torn down or modernized. Today, "modern Victorians" line the streets, and Main Street, with its array of tourist-related shops, shows more about the town's reliance on the skiing industry than about its history.

You have to get into the back streets to find the town's 19th-century roots. Large-scale hydraulic mining and dredging of the Blue River, which runs between the ski hill and the town, kept Breckenridge a gold town until just after World War II. It also transformed the Blue's once verdant banks into miles of sterile rock piles, stretching like a white scar along the bottom of an otherwise green valley.

The local historical society has preserved a sluicing and hydraulic operation and a dredge boat—the wooden monster that did the biggest damage. The beast sits a couple of miles out of town in a stagnant lake surrounded by bare river rock. More than 100 feet long and about 30 feet wide, this Bucyrus Erie model and dozens like it chewed through the Blue River and its banks like a giant cockroach through a loaf of bread.

It took a while, but 45 years after the gold dredges left, Breckenridge got its river back. The stretch of Blue River that bisects town is no longer a dry pile of rocks; the town's massive reclamation effort essentially rebuilt the river from the bottom up. The rocks were hauled away, the riverbed was re-created, and now the Blue River sparkles in the sunlight as it courses through town. The revitalized river is flanked by pedestrian paths, "pocket parks," and other public and private riverside attractions that range from restaurants to a performing arts space.

Visit the **Dredge Boathouse and Restaurant** in the middle of the river to enjoy the fruits of the reclamation project and get a feel for what gold dredging was all about. The restaurant serves great seafood, pasta, and grill specialties. *180 West Jefferson Avenue; 970-453-4877.*

■ SILVER BOOMS AND BUSTS

Nevada may have had the Comstock Lode, but thanks to Leadville, Aspen, Creede, Telluride, Ouray, Lake City, Silverton, and the dozens of camps around Gunnison and Crested Butte, Colorado became one of the nation's biggest silver suppliers. The silver boom quickly forced Colorado into the political spotlight, because decisions made in Washington, D.C., hit the state right in the pocketbook.

But silver's demise came as quickly as its rise. The Coinage Act of 1873—called "The Crime of '73" by Coloradans and fought with learned and passionate debate—put the nation on the gold standard and stopped automatic federal purchase of silver. The federal government continued to buy some silver at set prices, but its policy was rudderless and dependent on the political winds in Washington. The Sherman Silver Purchase Act of 1890 drove prices up for a time, but silver's sails drooped again in 1893 when India, a steady international customer, quit coining silver.

The economic depression and tumult following the Panic of 1893 finally did in the silver industry here. Wall Street money men blamed silver for the economic destruction and convinced Congress and President Grover Cleveland to repeal the Sherman Silver Purchase Act, effectively killing the silver royalties that propped up once prosperous towns.

These 30 silver bars from the Black Hawk smelters fetched $45,000 before the silver crash. (Colorado Historical Society)

■ LEADVILLE: MATCHLESS, UNSINKABLE
map page 81, E-2/3

Leadville was Colorado's silver king. Scattered strikes occurred as early as 1870, but by 1877 it was boom time. Thousands descended on Leadville, and between 1879 and 1889 the town produced $82 million worth of silver. It seemed "Cloud City" was set to become one of the state's largest and most prosperous towns.

At its booming peak, Leadville's rich mines, solid brick Victorian buildings, and magnificent opera house gave Denver a run for the money as Colorado's most prominent city. (Leadville residents also boasted that their red-light district was the best in the nation.) The town became a required stop for all of the day's nationally known figures. Feminist Susan B. Anthony raised more than $100 for the cause of women's suffrage with a speech she gave to the miners in Billy Nye's saloon, the biggest building in town, in 1877.

The town itself rests on the first fairly flat spot available at the head of the sprawling Arkansas Valley. The surrounding hillsides, stripped of all timber during the boom, are once again covered with pine trees, but the trees don't hide the scattered mine remains, diggings, and tailings of all sizes and shapes.

To reach Leadville from Denver take I-70 west to Exit 195 and go south on U.S. 24. The town's **Harrison Avenue** provides a glimpse of silver promise and poverty.

■ LEADVILLE SIGHTS

Tabor Opera House
The opera house's original, time-tattered velvet seats remain, as do box seats for the silver barons, a balcony for the masses, a huge stage, and the opulent entry. Here, the town's rough-and-ready populace witnessed performances by everyone from the composer John Philip Sousa to the illusionist Harry Houdini. Even Oscar Wilde lectured here, on the ethics of art. Wilde's most vivid Leadville memory was the presence of a sign above the piano in Pap's saloon that read, "Please do not shoot the pianist. He is doing his best." That little pearl, according to Wilde, was art criticism at its rational best. *308 Harrison Avenue, at the south end; 719-486-3900.*

Delaware Hotel
The unique Queen Anne–style masonry and French mansard design of this carefully restored century-old building gives a glimpse of Leadville's luxurious, glorious past. Walking into the hotel is like stepping back into the late 1800s. The lobby is

an elegant affair, and the rooms are furnished with Victorian antiques. At the hotel bar, you can drink in the feeling of a watering hole that once catered to refined Victorian gentlemen and ladies. *700 Harrison Avenue; 719-486-1418.*

Tabor Grand Hotel
This massive chunk of stonework stood empty for years as a monument to Horace Tabor's grand dreams and lost fortune. The imposing structure has been renovated into an apartment building with a variety of small shops on the ground floor, but it is still quite a sight. *711 Harrison Avenue.*

Matchless Mine
This is where the once-rich and beautiful "Baby Doe" Tabor—trophy wife to local silver baron Horace Tabor—died waiting for the next boom (see pages 102–103). *Seventh Street, 1 mile east of town; 719-486-3900.*

Silver Dollar Saloon
Built in the 1880s, this bustling saloon was one of Western legend Doc Holliday's gambling haunts. *315 Harrison Avenue; 719-486-9914.*

(opposite) The Tabor Opera House was Leadville's cultural jewel.
(above) The century-old Silver Dollar Saloon, built in Leadville in the 1880s.

"String Town"
Heading south you'll pass a collection of plain homes and businesses in the area set aside for the working girls who began their shifts when the miners ended theirs.

Healy House Museum
The Colorado Historical Society brings to life what it meant to be a Victorian lady or gentleman. The dainty main house was home to refined, unmarried school teachers, while the hunting cabin was where married men congregated to drink whiskey and talk about money and women. *912 Harrison Avenue; 719-486-0487.*

National Mining Hall of Fame and Museum
The displays at this facility illuminate mining techniques that range from gold panning to hand-drilling, blasting, and 21st-century procedures. *120 West Ninth Street; 719-486-1229.*

Climax Mine
Around the turn of the 20th century, zinc, copper, and gold discoveries in the old Leadville silver mines kept Leadville alive as a mining town. The most important new find was the huge deposit of molybdenum discovered in 1918 near the top of Fremont Pass. The mine has produced 1.9 billion tons of molybdenum. During World War II it produced about 72 percent of the world's supply.

Unfortunately, the Climax Mine has dumped billions of tons of mill tailings into what used to be Tenmile Valley; today a huge sludge pile completely fills the valley and makes reclamation impossible. The massive mine finally closed in the 1990s, signaling an official and economically painful end to Leadville's century as a mining town. Now, the town is left with the massive tailings piles and other scars of the mining era.

■ **LEADVILLE'S COLORFUL CHARACTERS**
Denver may have been Colorado's biggest city in the 1880s, but it never rivaled Leadville for rags-to-riches stories, colorful characters, and pitiful demises.

Probably most familiar to Coloradans is Charles Boettcher, who arrived in 1879 and started a booming hardware business that he parlayed into a diverse financial empire, which he eventually based in Denver. The family's fortunes increased, and its members have played a prominent role in the city's business, philanthropic, and

Pits and tailings are representative of the debris left over from Leadville's glory days.

civic affairs ever since. The Boettcher Foundation and the Boettcher Concert Hall are just part of the legacy of a man who started out selling nuts and bolts in Leadville.

Retailing also kick-started the good fortunes of Horace Tabor and his wife, Augusta, who arrived in 1860 to open stores in Leadville and surrounding mining camps. In 1877, Tabor grubstaked George Hook and August Rische in return for one-third of whatever they found.

A scandal erupted when Horace Tabor left his wife, Augusta, for the beautiful "Baby Doe." The silver crash hardly affected Augusta, who got millions in her alimony deal, but Baby Doe clung to the Matchless Mine, waiting for another boom she never lived to see. (Colorado Historical Society)

What they found was the Little Pittsburgh Mine's 30-foot-thick vein of silver, which made the mine a multimillion-dollar producer and Tabor a rich man. He kept investing in mining properties, allegedly buying the Matchless Mine with about $100,000 in pocket change. The mine produced $1 million a year during its 14-year life. While Tabor was becoming one of Leadville's richest men and civic stars, bankrolling the Tabor Opera House and other local institutions, he was also becoming an adulterer with the beautiful divorcée Elizabeth "Baby Doe" McCourt. A scandalous divorce from the upright Augusta followed, and Baby Doe became the second Mrs. Tabor.

The silver crash hit the couple hard, and although Tabor did manage to become a U.S. senator, he died virtually penniless in 1899. He told Baby Doe to never give up the Matchless because one day it would again make millions. She honored his request and for 36 years lived in a small shack at the mine, trudging to town for supplies and returning home to wait for a silver boom that would never come. In the winter of 1935, she was found frozen to death in her little cabin.

■ SOUTH PARK *map page 81, E/F/G-3*

Gold and silver prospectors poured into the mountains along the South Platte River, just east of the Continental Divide, but didn't find many good prospects. So the towns in and around the region known as South Park were left to develop, slowly, as small farming and ranching towns. The area contains some of the most spectacular scenery in the state, as well as hot springs and plenty of wide-open spaces. Though not far from Denver, towns here remain unsullied by the tourist rush and retain a small-town charm that has been squeezed out of the more easily accessible Rocky Mountain stops. You can drive for hours and see more cows than condos as you make your way into South Park on U.S. 285 from Denver, U.S. 50 from Pueblo, or U.S. 24 from Leadville.

Away from the major travel arteries, such towns as Fairplay, Baily, Buena Vista, Poncha Springs, and Salida still maintain a quiet life that centers on their main streets. For many, this is the "real" Colorado: the Colorado before the tourist rush, the undeveloped Colorado of uncluttered river valleys ringed by snowcapped peaks. Granted, each summer brings a nice crop of rafters and anglers who ply the Arkansas and South Platte Rivers. Climbers, mountain bikers, and hikers clamber over the region's 14,000-foot peaks. But the short burst of annual activity doesn't disrupt the relaxed feel and unpretentious essence of this swath of high country.

■ ASPEN   *map page 81, E-2*

In 1879, in the dead of winter, some intrepid souls strapped on primitive skis (then called "snowshoes"), headed west out of Leadville, crossed the Continental Divide, and skied down into what would become the town of Aspen. They found what they wanted: huge silver deposits, especially on Smuggler Mountain. Indeed, the largest single silver nugget ever mined, weighing more than two tons, came out of Aspen.

In no time Aspen was racing Leadville for silver and cultural supremacy. In 1883, Jerome B. Wheeler, the first president of Macy's Department Store in New York City, arrived, bought up mining claims, built smelters, and erected the stunning Wheeler Opera House.

By 1892, Aspen had 12,000 residents, making it the state's third-largest city, after Leadville and Denver. It soon began boasting that it had surpassed Leadville

Aside from the fabulous skiing and myriad special events, Aspen also plays host to a multitude of celebrities. The sound of gunfire may mean that gonzo journalist Hunter S. Thompson (opposite) is making a run into town from his enclave in Woody Creek. Actress Jill St. John-Wagner (above) might be seen hanging out at the Aspen Center of Environmental Studies.

in silver output. But what a difference a year makes! Almost immediately after the repeal of the Sherman Silver Purchase Act, most of Aspen's mines shut down and more than 2,000 miners lost their jobs. Even Jerome B. Wheeler, the town's high-flying knight in silver armor, became a penniless stable boy.

By 1930, only 700 hardy souls remained, but thanks to the refinement of those original "snowshoes," Aspen would boom again as an international ski resort. Located 162 miles west of Denver (the drive is longer in winter, when Independence Pass closes), Aspen has developed into a destination resort that is worth the trouble it takes to get there.

Aspen led the way in developing the state's ski industry and took the lead in preservation of both the town's historic character and the valley's natural beauty. In the early 1970s, Aspen and Pitkin County enacted one of the first growth-management programs in the state, a move designed to stop sprawl, preserve ranch land, maintain scenic views, and channel growth to other areas. The road from Basalt to Aspen—unlike the approaches to other Colorado resorts—isn't

Former Aspen mayor John Bennett and friends sample some wine at the annual Aspen Food and Wine Festival.

lined with billboards, cluttered with mini-malls, or marred by the march of condos up the nearby hillsides.

The county's growth policies have produced uncluttered views and huge swaths of hayfields in the upper Roaring Fork Valley, instead of golf courses and housing developments. "Once on the cutting edge, always on the cutting edge," seems to be Aspen's motto. The political debates in town are legendary for their intensity and depth as citizens and elected officials continue to redefine the best ways to enhance Aspen's unique character and world-class charms.

■ ASPEN HIGHLIGHTS

Skiing
Aspen is one of the best and most famous ski areas in the United States, known for its 76 trails, efficient gondolas and lifts, and its proximity to excellent hotels and dining. (For more about Aspen skiing, see page 231.)

(above) Negotiating a reindeer permit, Aspen-style. (following pages) Aspen lies in the Roaring Fork Valley amid some of the West's most spectacular scenery.

Golfing, Hiking, and Biking
Visitors will find numerous 18-hole courses in Aspen and Snowmass Village. More aggressive outdoor recreationists might want to visit the Maroon Bells/Snowmass Wilderness Area, whose numerous hiking/biking trails are just minutes from town.

Historic Buildings
The **Hotel Jerome** (330 East Main Street; 970-920-1000) and the **Wheeler Opera House** (320 East Hyman Avenue; 970-920-5770) stand out as shining reminders of the town's silver days.

Shopping
Try downtown's Cooper Street Mall and Hyman Avenue Mall.

Intellectual Pursuits
Between the **Aspen Institute** (970-925-7010), the **International Design Conference** (970-925-2257), the **Aspen Center for Physics** (970-925-2585), and the **Given Biomedical Institute** (970-925-1057), not a week goes by without an

(left) Snowmass Lake in the Maroon Bells/ Snowmass Wilderness Area, north of Aspen and Marble.

(opposite) Another popular summer event is the Balloon Festival.

esteemed orator or a panel of experts delving into the most pressing political, artistic, scientific, or philosophical questions of the day.

Ghost Towns

Ashcroft gave Aspen a run for its money as a silver camp, and at one time had more than 2,500 residents. But its mines weren't as rich and the town was too far from the railroad to survive. During the 1960s, before all of the town's wooden buildings fell down or faded away, the Aspen Historical Society stepped in and eventually was able to stabilize and shore up a string of buildings along the main street. Ashcroft is about 12 miles up Castle Creek Road, which intersects Colorado 82 about a mile from town.

The first miners in the area thought **Independence** was going to be the place. They didn't count on the horrid winters, though, and soon the mining camp was deserted. The remnants can be seen as you drive up Independence Pass.

Wheeler/Stallard House Museum

The headquarters of the Aspen Historical Society, this 1888 home was built by Jerome B. Wheeler and contains Victorian furnishings, collections of historic photos, and artifacts from the valley's ranching and mining days. Staff members tell great stories about Aspen's past. *620 West Bleeker Street; 970-925-3721.*

Maroon Bells (North and South Maroon Peaks)

Called the most photographed mountains in the state, the stunning Maroon Bells rise from the valley floor and stand tall against the deep blue sky. The lake at the base of the Bells reflects their majesty and adds another element of intrigue and beauty to this classic Rocky Mountain scene. A 1.5-mile trail meanders around the lake. In the summer months, you will have to park your car and take a free **shuttle bus** (970-925-8484) to the Bells, but bikers, walkers, and in-line skaters can approach the Bells under their own steam.

The Maroon Bells are about 10 miles up Maroon Creek Road. The road stops at a visitors center on the edge of Maroon Lake, with the Bells looming just ahead. Hikers and backpackers can take any number of well-marked trails into the **Maroon Bells/Snowmass Wilderness Area,** which surrounds the Bells, and experienced rock climbers can scale the Bells or nearby Pyramid Peak. To get there,

A winter wonderland and spectacular fireworks—the latter illuminating Aspen during Winterskol.

head north out of Aspen for about a mile to the intersection of Colorado 82 and the Maroon Creek Road (not to be confused with Castle Creek Road, which leads to Ashcroft and starts at the same intersection), and follow the signs to the Bells.

■ FESTIVALS AND EVENTS

Aspen Dance Festival
The town's stages fill with performances by some of the most prestigious dance companies in the world. Performances include an eclectic mix of classical ballet, modern dance, and cutting-edge combinations of everything the world of dance has to offer. *970-925-7175.*

Aspen Filmfest and Shortsfest
With these festivals, the spotlight is on cinema. Shortsfest's offerings provoke more thought in 15 minutes than any 15 full-length summer blockbusters. Filmfest features screenings of independent and foreign films that probably will not be coming soon to a multiplex near you. *970-925-6882.*

Aspen Music Festival and School
The School brings top classical musicians and students to town for a summer of lessons and concerts. Weekend performances in the Music Festival Tent and Harris Concert Hall are the highlights of the summer concert season. *970-925-3254.*

Aspen's Winterskol
Five days of midwinter revelry take place every January. The lineup includes fireworks, parades, ski races, and an impressive torchlight descent down Aspen Mountain. *970-925-1940.*

Jazz Aspen at Snowmass
A summer-long stream of top performers culminates in this Labor Day festival, a multi-day jam session starring both the old pros and the young lions who follow in their footsteps. Shows vary from open-air concerts in Snowmass Village to intimate sets performed in Aspen clubs and bars. *970-920-4996.*

Theatre in the Park
Plays are presented throughout the summer on a tent-covered stage in Rio Grande Park. *970-925-9313.*

■ ASPEN'S WINTERSKOL

Because January is generally the coldest month on the slopes, Aspen decided to warm things up with a five-day celebration called Winterskol. "Damn the weather; full fun ahead" is the general theme of this annual event, which started in 1950 as a fairly innocent way for the locals to catch their breath and celebrate a bit after the holiday rush. Today, Winterskol has become a venerable tradition, and an event with enough color and dazzle to attract visitors from around the world.

Did I mention dazzle and color? There is a full-blown fireworks extravaganza launched from Aspen Mountain, followed by a dramatic twisting, turning, torchlight descent down the face. Another nighttime diversion is the famed Bartender's Drink Contest. Anything goes, and usually does, into the concoctions prepared by the town's masters of mixology. Daylight brings all manner of ski races to the town's ski areas. In any given year there's a mix of professional races, charity benefits, local and amateur races, and celebrity slides down the slopes.

You've got to love the parade, which features a cacophony of homemade contraptions that express the eclectic intellectual interests of the locals on issues universal and mundane. (See page 278 for more information about the festival.)

■ ASPEN MUSIC FESTIVAL

Aspen Music Festival and School brings together some of the world's most talented young musicians and experienced players on summer sabbatical from their usual chairs at the country's first-rate orchestras. The young people learn from the professionals, and the professionals, in turn, are rejuvenated and inspired by their young charges. On most days the huge music tent reverberates with spirited symphonic sound.

Renowned musicians hold master classes in the **Harris Concert Hall** (2 Music School Road; 970-925-9042). Brass and string quartets set up shop in the downtown mall, fill the mountain air with well-honed harmonies, and alternately lullaby or bombard passersby with their combined talent and verve.

The historic **Wheeler Opera House** (320 East Hyman Avenue; 970-920-5770) hosts operas, ranging from classical to comical, in addition to a wide variety of other performances that showcase the Victorian building's outstanding acoustics.

Another marvel of the festival is that you don't have to own a tuxedo to attend many of the events. You're out West, remember, so the tidy casual look will do just fine. (See page 282 for more information about the music festival.)

Inside the carefully restored Wheeler Opera House.

■ REDSTONE   *map page 81, E-1*

The past is very much present in Redstone, a quaint little burg tucked into the Crystal River Valley. The handiwork of Colorado Fuel and Iron Company founder John Cleveland Osgood is still apparent everywhere you look. **Redstone Boulevard,** the main drag, is lined with Victorian cottages that Osgood built for his coal miners. The boardinghouse Osgood built has been converted into the **Redstone Inn** (82 Redstone Boulevard; 970-963-2526), which anchors the boulevard with its distinctive design and clock tower.

Osgood's mansion, which he named Cleveholm Manor, is still standing, in all its Victorian splendor, a baronial mile outside of Redstone. Now called the **Redstone Castle** (58 Redstone Boulevard; 970-704-1430), the sprawling, monumental mansion is open to the public for scheduled tours and as a bed-and-breakfast inn.

Outside town, the remnants of the coke ovens that cooked the coal from the Coal Basin mines stand as silent reminders of Redstone's mining beginnings.

Osgood wasn't the last man to seek riches in Coal Basin's black gold. In the 1950s, a group of Glenwood Springs businessmen created Mid-Continent Resources and reopened the Coal Basin Mines. High-grade low-sulfur coal once

Early 1900s shot of coal baron John Cleveland Osgood's home. (Denver Public Library)

again came pouring out of the western mountains, and Redstone was once again a coal-mining town. The mining operation was challenging, to say the least. At about 10,000 feet in elevation, the mines were among the highest in the nation. Unstable rock, methane gas, and a mountain that fought back while its insides were being dug out made the mines dangerous, too. One of the worst underground coal-mining accidents in state history struck the Dutch Creek #1 Mine in 1982. A fire fed by methane gas swept through the mine, killing more than a dozen workers.

High costs and declining markets closed the mines in the 1990s. Just outside the town of Redstone along Colorado 133 stands the **Mid-Continent Miners Monument.** The striking arc is made out of two towering "longwall face shields"—massive bits of modern mining technology that helped hold the mountain in place during the mining operation. The accompanying plaque memorializes the grit and guts of the Coal Basin miners who toiled in the mines, and the ones who lost their lives there.

Redstone today is a pleasant mix of past and present that serves as a hub for visitors to the scenic Crystal River Valley. In the fall, the drive from Carbondale to

Redstone or Marble on Colorado 133 resembles a Technicolor trip through all the colors in fall's impressive palette. Many artists have set up shops and galleries in town, and thanks to the availability of the town's extraordinary marble, sculptors are at the heart of this particular artistic scene.

When winter takes its leave, the town plays host to the full spectrum of visitors, be they climbers, art lovers, kayakers, or just folks who want to spend a few days deep in the Rockies. Redstone is about 35 miles south of Glenwood Springs on Colorado 133.

■ MARBLE *map page 81, E-1*

In the early 1880s, the next logical leap for the silver prospectors spilling out of Aspen was just a couple of ridges west. While digging around for silver, they stumbled on a huge deposit of pure white marble. But at the time, no one knew how to mine it, mill it, or ship it.

The town of Marble came alive in 1885, when a Welsh marble man opened a local quarry. Those first chunks of marble were used in the Colorado State Capitol, but hauling marble with 40-mule pack trains wasn't exactly cheap or easy, so the quarry remained a nickel-and-dime operation.

That changed in 1906 when Col. Channing F. Meek came into town, bought the quarry, and incorporated the Colorado Yule Marble Company. In 1914, the quarry supplied more than $1 million worth of marble for the Lincoln Memorial in Washington, D.C., a fact proudly touted in the firm's 1915 price list. Back then, you could secure an ornamental vase ($16), fruit stand ($7), or Water Kiss Fountain ($250) made from the cuttings of the "beautiful Statuary Golden Vein Colorado-Yule Marble used in the Lincoln Memorial."

In 1930, Marble received the contract to supply the marble for the Tomb of the Unknown Soldier in Arlington National Cemetery. It took 75 men more than a year to carve out the 124-ton block of marble (the largest single piece ever quarried), which was then squared at the mill.

The town has survived the quarry's ups and downs rather nicely. Hearty souls—among them artists, retirees, working people, and folks who just want to get away from it all—live in the cold and secluded valley year-round. The little village comes to life in the summer and fall: in fall, the trees in the surrounding mountains put on a colorful display; and in the warm months, the town serves as the gateway to great four-wheeling and wilderness excursions.

The Crystal Mill, near the ghost town of Crystal, outside Marble.

Just up the road is the ghost town of Crystal and its famous **Crystal Mill,** a tattered but highly photogenic wooden structure clinging precariously to the edge of a cliff above the Crystal River. Marble is about 40 miles south of Glenwood Springs, off Colorado 133.

■ GLENWOOD SPRINGS   *map page 81, D-1*

Historically a hot spot, Glenwood Springs, almost due west of Denver on I-70 and north of Aspen and Marble, didn't have any gold or silver. It became an internationally known resort in the late 1880s, however, with the palatial **Hotel Colorado** (526 Pine Street; 970-945-6511) and what is now the **Glenwood Hot Springs Pool and Lodge** (415 East 6th Street; 970-945-6571). The Denver & Rio Grande Railroad began promoting the "Spa in the Rockies," and soon gangsters, gunslingers, U.S. presidents, and the cream of American society were making Glenwood Springs a stop on their trip through Colorado.

The most famous visitor to Glenwood Springs was President Theodore Roosevelt, who set up a western White House in the Hotel Colorado in 1905. From here he went on a bear hunt in the nearby White River National Forest. While he was out in the wilds he kept in touch with the White House via a telegraph line to the hotel and a messenger who rode out on his horse every day to try to find the president. (For more about Roosevelt's trip and the story of the origin of "teddy bears," see page 217.)

One of the town's more infamous visitors was gunslinger and gambler Dr. John "Doc" Holliday, who died and was buried in town on November 8, 1887. Holliday, a Georgian with a dental degree from Johns Hopkins University, was one of the West's most notorious gunmen, thanks to his friendship with Wyatt Earp.

In 1881, Doc, Wyatt, and the rest of the Earp family were in Tombstone, Arizona, where they took part in one of the West's most famous events: the gunfight at the OK Corral. By the time the shooting stopped, the Earps, with help from Doc's sawed-off shotgun, had summarily slaughtered the Clanton clan. But Doc's fame and proficiency with a firearm couldn't stop the tuberculosis that was slowly killing him; nor could they tame his dangerous appetites for whiskey and card-playing. Unglamorous scrapes with the law involving dead men and fleeced gamblers became his calling cards.

The "healing waters" of the Glenwood Hot Springs Pool. The pool is open from 7 A.M. to 10 P.M. year-round, rain or snow.

When Doc arrived in Glenwood Springs after such trouble in Denver and Leadville, he worked at local saloons to oversee the faro box or play for the house at the gaming tables. Illness forced him to retire to the hotel bed where he died at the age of 35. Doc was buried in Linwood Cemetery, on a hill above town. In the 1960s, the town erected a monument over Doc Holliday's grave. The tools of Doc's trade—six-shooters and playing cards—are etched in stone above his epitaph, "He Died in Bed."

■ GLENWOOD SPRINGS TODAY

Today, Amtrak still promotes Glenwood Springs as a Rocky Mountain spa. It remains the home of the Glenwood Hot Springs Pool, the world's largest natural hot springs pool, which measures more than 300 feet in length and is filled with hot springs water at 89 degrees Fahrenheit in the big pool and a hot tub–like 103 degrees in the therapy pool. You may also want to investigate the natural sauna in the vapor caves.

The city's downtown is a cluster of turn-of-the-20th-century brick buildings, and its residential neighborhoods are an arresting mix of modern split-level and Victorian gingerbread homes. The Colorado River tumbles out of the magnificent Glenwood Canyon to meet the Roaring Fork River right in town, and the White River National Forest attracts hikers, birdwatchers, and hunters.

Glenwood Springs' strategic location between Vail, 60 miles to the east, and Aspen, 40 miles to the southeast, also makes it a regional shopping and supply town. Aspenites and Vailites come here to get their car fixed for a reasonable price or buy underwear that doesn't cost as much as a new pair of shoes. The central location, moderate prices, and huge hot tub attract skiers to the nearby ski hills, where you can buy lift tickets without having to take out a second mortgage.

Whether you're coming or going from Glenwood Springs on I-70, you will be treated to a natural wonder called **Glenwood Canyon**, which has about 15 miles worth of 2,000-foot, sheer granite walls. Trees, cornices, and startling rock formations dot the canyon. Another wonder, this one man-made, is the state-of-the-art, environmentally sensitive four-lane highway that squeezes through the narrow canyon bottom. The highway's features include cantilevered sections of roadway, bridges that crisscross the river, a biking and hiking trail, and easy access for rafters to the Colorado River.

■ ROCKY MOUNTAIN NATIONAL PARK *map page 124*

North of the mining towns of Colorado's central Rockies, and just northwest of the city of Boulder, is Rocky Mountain National Park. The park preserves the pristine beauty and the flora and fauna of the Rockies as they were before settlers began pouring into Colorado during the 1800s.

Trail Ridge Road, one of the highest paved roads in the nation, runs through the park and will deliver a view of the top of the Rockies that cannot be matched. As you quickly climb above timberline, you'll find yourself surrounded by 18 peaks more than 13,000 feet high. The best way to begin the trip is at the headwaters of the Colorado River, which is just a trickle coming down the western side of the Continental Divide.

Granby, east of Kremmling on U.S. 40 and north of I-70, overlooks the Colorado River and is the park's western gateway. As you go north on Trail Ridge Road, you'll pass through Arapaho National Recreation Area and by Lake Granby and Grand Lake itself before hitting the town of Grand Lake. As you might imagine, there are ample high-country camping, hiking, boating, and fishing opportunities amid the forests, glades, and lakes in the area.

Then it's uphill as you mount a charge to the top of Trail Ridge Road. Before you sound the bugle, though, you'd better make sure the road is clear of snow, which sometimes lasts until June and returns by about October; this is definitely

Wildflowers bloom by a bubbling creek high in Rocky Mountain National Park.

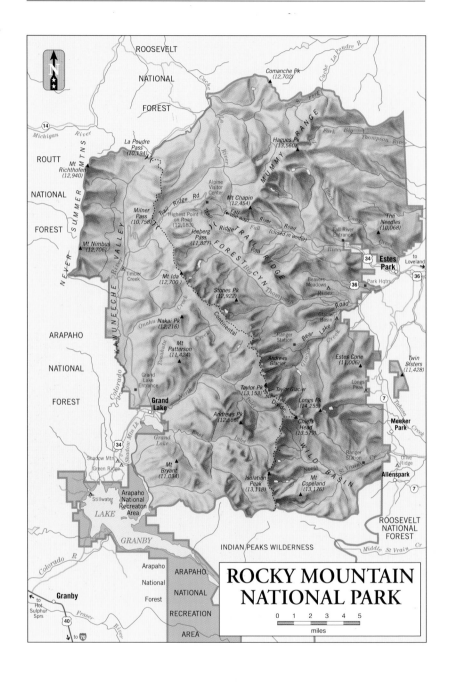

ROOSEVELT

NATIONAL

FOREST

ROUTT

NATIONAL

FOREST

ARAPAHO

NATIONAL

FOREST

14

Michigan River

NEVER SUMMER MTNS

Mt Richthofen (12,940)

Mt Nimbus (12,706)

La Poudre Pass (10,194)

Milner Pass (10,758)

Timber Creek

Mt Ida (12,700)

Onahu

Nakai Pk (12,216)

Mt Patterson (11,424)

Grand Lake Entrance

34

Shadow Mtn

Green Ridge

Stillwater

LAKE

GRANBY

Colorado R.

40

to Hot Sulphur Sprs

Granby

Fraser River

to 70

KAWUNEECHE VALLEY

River Inlet

Colorado River

Shadow Mtn Lk

Grand Lake

Arapaho National Recreation Area

Arapaho

National

Forest

ARAPAHO

NATIONAL

RECREATION

AREA

Comanche Pk (12,702)

Cache

Fork

La Poudre R.

Big Thompson River

MUMMY RANGE

Hagues Pk (13,560)

Alpine Visitor Center

Mt Chapin (12,454)

Highest Point on Road (12,183)

Iceberg Pass (11,827)

Stones Pk (12,922)

Trail Ridge Rd

Fall River (one way)

Fall River Road (closed in winter)

TRAIL RIDGE

FOREST CYN

Big Thompson

Continental

Tonahutu Creek

Mt Bryant (11,034)

North Inlet

Grand Lake

Andrews Pk (12,565)

Taylor Pk (13,153)

Isolation Peak (13,118)

Fall River Entrance

The Needles (10,068)

Fall River

34 Estes Park

to Loveland

36

Park Hqtrs

36

Beavers Meadows

Ranger Station

Glacier Basin

Bear Lake Road

Glacier Creek

Andrews Glacier

Taylor Glacier

Divide

Longs Pk (14,255)

Chiefs Head (13,579)

WILD BASIN

North St Vrain Cr.

St Vrain

Mt Copeland (13,176)

INDIAN PEAKS WILDERNESS

Estes Cone (11,006)

Longs Peak

Twin Sisters (11,428)

7

Meeker Park

Ranger Station

Olive Ridge

Allenspark

7

ROOSEVELT NATIONAL FOREST

Middle St Vrain Cr

ROCKY MOUNTAIN NATIONAL PARK

0 1 2 3 4 5

miles

a summertime undertaking. That short season means you can also expect crowds, and may get stuck behind a tour bus. But those are small prices to pay for the rewards awaiting.

The 410 square miles of park contain abundant wildlife, 700 species of wild-flowers, and 150 secluded alpine lakes. The 13-mile stretch far above timberline is home to alpine tundra that resembles the tundra near the Arctic Circle. Don't stray from the paved paths onto this fragile flora. Your footprint can do serious damage. Do, however, take some time to explore the tiny blossoms that spring out. They seem to be more vivid than any others in the state.

Once you peak out and start down the eastern side of the divide, you'll witness the transformation from tundra to tree-covered mountain valleys to mellow mead-ows. All along the road are numerous pullouts with informational signs describing the ecology and naming distant, snowcapped peaks. The park contains 350 miles of trails that provide access for campers, anglers, mountain bikers, and wildlife watch-ers. The knowledgeable park rangers at Alpine Visitors Center and the Moraine Park Museum can provide more information. *Trail Ridge Road; 970-586-1206.*

Edna Mills, the daughter of the writer-conservationist Enos Mills, holds a photograph of him. Mills fought for the creation of Rocky Mountain National Park. His former cabin-studio (in background) is south of Estes Park.

Melting snow creates a waterfall in one of the many alpine basins in the high country of Rocky Mountain National Park.

The town of **Estes Park** and civilization in all its glory await at the end of the 50-mile jaunt. Estes Park entices visitors with a mélange of services and offers everything from souvenir coffee mugs to restaurants and condos.

The **Stanley Hotel** sits on a hillside above the frantic activity, secure in its glistening white facade and historic roots. Built in 1901 by F. O. Stanley, inventor of the Stanley Steamer, the hotel harks back to the days when touring Rocky Mountain National Park was a genteel undertaking. Today, the sprawling hotel hosts a summer theater program and other musical events to go with the scenery. *333 Wonderview Avenue; 970-586-3371.*

The old mining town of Summitville now sits uninhabited in the San Juan Mountains.

SAN JUAN MOUNTAINS

The great San Juan Mountains of southern Colorado are chock full of minerals, from gold and silver to zinc and copper. They are also rugged and isolated—so isolated they are being considered as one of the few places in the lower 48 states appropriate for the reintroduction of the grizzly bear. The region became one of the state's top mining districts right out of the chute, so to speak, and its mines kept producing into the 1990s. Today, there are still prospectors in the San Juans, but they use chemistry, computer-programmed geologic tracking, commodity-market hedging, and core samples instead of picks and mules, as they scour the area for the next mother lode.

Meanwhile, the area's isolated, historic towns and ski resorts are busy mining a mother lode of skiers, mountain bikers, and scenery seekers.

■ GUNNISON *map page 129, B-4*

Resting at the northern edge of the San Juan mining country, Crested Butte and Gunnison are separated from the Aspen/Marble area by massive mountains that were almost completely impassable in the 1880s. Today, rugged roads head across steep mountain passes. Colorado 133 out of Carbondale carries you to the cutoff for Crested Butte over Kebler Pass—but only in the summer. In the winter you have to keep going, turn off at Hotchkiss on Colorado 92 and take a stunning ride around the Black Canyon of the Gunnison River before hitting U.S. 50 and then Gunnison.

Gunnison was once the supply hub for scattered mining camps (now ghost towns) in the nearby mountains. Set out on the "Scenic Ghost Route," described below, and you'll find them.

■ SCENIC GHOST ROUTE

Want to run over some silver miners turned ghosts and spot the houses of ill repute they frequented after a hard day's work? Head north from Gunnison on Colorado 135 until you hit the small town of **Almont,** turn right on Forest Road 742, and follow the Taylor River Valley to **Taylor Park Reservoir.** Now, take Forest Road 765 to the first ghostly stop, **Hillerton,** which in 1880 had 1,500 residents, a bank, and booming mines. Stay on 765 and you'll find **Abbeyville,** which was

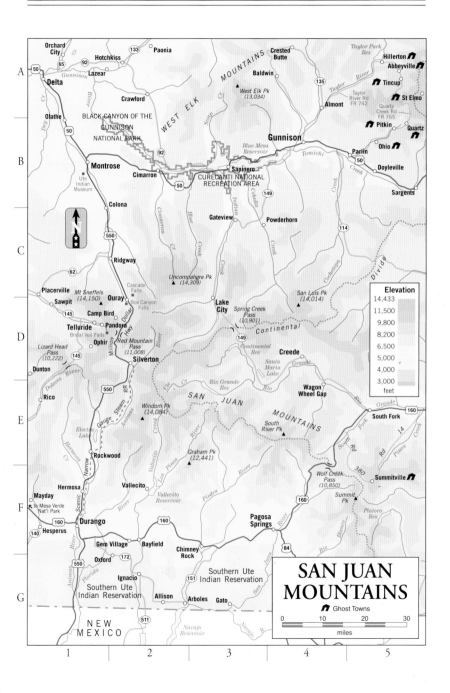

SAN JUAN MOUNTAINS

🏚 Ghost Towns

0   10   20   30
miles

Elevation
14,433
11,500
9,800
8,200
6,500
5,000
4,000
3,000
feet

Orchard City
Hotchkiss
Lazear
Paonia
133
Delta
65
92
50
A
Gunnison River
Crawford
Olathe
50
BLACK CANYON OF THE
GUNNISON
NATIONAL PARK
Montrose
92
Cimarron
50
B
Ute Indian Museum
Colona
550
Ridgway
C
62
Placerville
Sawpit
Mt Sneffels
(14,150)
Ouray
Camp Bird
145
Telluride
Ophir
Bridal Veil Falls
Pandora
Red Mountain Pass
(11,008)
Silverton
D
Lizard Head Pass
(10,222)
145
Dunton
Rico
550
Narrow Gauge Steam RR
E
Electra Lake
Rockwood
Hermosa
Mayday
to Mesa Verde Nat'l Park
F
160
140
Hesperus
Durango
Gem Village
Bayfield
Oxford
172
550
Ignacio
Southern Ute Indian Reservation
G
511
NEW MEXICO

WEST ELK MOUNTAINS
Crested Butte
Baldwin
West Elk Pk
(13,034)
135
Stony Ck
Almont
Gunnison
Blue Mesa Reservoir
Sapinero
Tomichi
CURECANTI NATIONAL RECREATION AREA
149
Cimarron Cr
Blue Creek
Gateview
Indian Creek
Cebolla
Powderhorn
Cebolla Creek
114
Uncompahgre Pk
(14,309)
San Luis Pk
(14,014)
Cochetopa
Divide
Lake City
Spring Creek Pass
(10,901)
Continental
149
Continental Res
Creede
Santa Maria Lake
Rio Grande
SAN JUAN
Rio Grande Res
Wagon Wheel Gap
Dollar Hwy
Million Dollar Hwy
Animas River
Los Pinos River
Vallecito Creek
Windom Pk
(14,084)
Graham Pk
(12,441)
MOUNTAINS
South River Pk
Pinos River
South Fork Rd
South Fork
160
14
Rio Grande
160
Vallecito
Vallecito Reservoir
Piedra River
Wolf Creek Pass
(10,850)
380
Summitville
Summit Pk
Platoro Res
Pagosa Springs
San Juan River
160
84
Rio Blanco
Chimney Rock
151
Southern Ute Indian Reservation
Allison
Arboles
Gato
Navajo R
Navajo Reservoir

Taylor Park Res
Hillerton 🏚
Abbeyville 🏚
Tincup 🏚
Taylor River Rd FR 742
St Elmo
Quartz Creek Rd FR 765
Pitkin 🏚
Quartz 🏚
Ohio 🏚
Parlin
50
Doyleville
Sargents
Quartz

1   2   3   4   5

a silver town in the 1880s. From 1900 to 1912, dredges on local creeks recovered 20,000 ounces of gold.

As you proceed on Forest Road 765, you'll find **Tincup,** in which by 1900 most of Hillerton's and Abbeyville's buildings had been dismantled and rebuilt. (The first mobile homes in the nation? Sure, let's add that one to Colorado's list of firsts.) Unlike many of its neighbors, Tincup is very much alive today. Established in 1880, by 1882 it had twenty saloons, four hotels, numerous stores, and ladies of the night named Big Minnie, Sagebrush Annie, Santa Fe Moll, and (my personal favorite) Pass Out. Gold was mined in Tincup until 1917, then things went downhill until the town's original buildings were restored as a summer resort community.

You'll then have to lug over Cumberland Pass, which at 12,200 feet is one of the highest unpaved roads in the state that you can drive a passenger car over. At the summit, you will be rewarded with views of the Bon Ton and Blistered Horn Mines. Then it's on to **Quartz,** which started as a silver town but, because it had a rail spur from the Denver and South Park Railroad, continued to prosper as a lumber center until 1934, when the train left town and was followed quickly by everyone else.

Pitkin, the next stop, was the first incorporated town on the Western Slope, but its life was brief. The Alpine Tunnel brought the Denver and South Park Railroad to town in 1882, but when the area's biggest silver vein played out after 75 feet of mining, things got pretty grim. Many of the old buildings remain, however. The red schoolhouse contains a historical exhibit of Pitkin's fast past.

Ohio had luck on its side, because its mines disgorged both gold and silver, so when the Silver Panic of 1893 hit, the town continued as a gold camp. The Raymond Mines still produce gold, off and on, and the town has a small number of year-round residents who mix in nicely with the solitude, the surrounding mountain scenery, and the ghosts.

Parlin, the final stop, isn't really a ghost town, but it sure is old. It started as a stage station in 1880, and then both the Denver and Rio Grande and Denver and South Park Railroads used it as a supply station and stopover. Today, it is a fully functioning supply center for area ranchers.

As you continue down County Road 765 you'll hit U.S. 50 just 12 miles east of Gunnison, where this whole ghostly trip started.

Fall color in the remote and magnificent San Juan Mountains.

■ **CREEDE** *map page 129, D-4*

Deep in the heart of the San Juans lies the last great silver town, Creede. Its mines weren't tapped until 1889, but for the next four years it became the boomtown of boomtowns, where millions were made. Creede hosted such sure-shooting legends as Marshal Bat Masterson, Bob Ford (who killed Jesse James), and Calamity Jane and her pal, Poker Alice. The city never slept and turned out 80 million tons of silver during its short life as a silver city.

A long slumber began with the repeal of the Silver Act in 1893. Then five separate fires and some mudslides pretty much destroyed the tangible reminders of its glorious past. Today, Creede has become a regular small town buried deep in the San Juans; it doesn't mind the occasional tourist, but its real attraction is a slow, somewhat isolated lifestyle in the middle of the Colorado Rockies. Creede is about 100 miles south of Gunnison on Colorado 149. If you visit, try getting tickets for a performance at the **Creede Repertory Theatre** (124 North Main Street; 719-658-2343).

■ **OURAY** *map page 129, C-2*

Ouray's first visitors and residents were the Ute Indians who venerated the numerous hot springs bubbling out of the ground in the Uncompahgre River Valley. In honor of the Ute's link to the land, the area's first white settlers named their town after Chief Ouray. The dignified leader of the Utes diplomatically brokered a peaceful resolution to the clashes between his tribe and the swelling masses of white settlers laying claim to the Utes' ancestral lands.

On the western side of the mountains, Ouray is squeezed into a stunning canyon from which it seems there is no escape. Ouray's present mix of hot-spring spas, Victorian buildings, and modern conveniences overshadows its mining past. The Camp Bird Mines and others in the surrounding mountains first produced gold in 1898. Those mineral-laden mountains are now crawling with jeeps full of sightseers, hikers, mountain bikers, and rock and ice climbers.

The **St. Elmo Hotel,** a Victorian delight on Main Street, stands as a reminder of Ouray's colorful past. The St. Elmo was built in 1898 by "Aunt" Kitty Heit, who earned her big-hearted reputation by rarely turning hungry miners away from the hotel's restaurant, the Bon Ton. Fun fact: the St. Elmo was once bet and lost in a

Exploring an ice cave in Box Canyon, one of the San Juans' treasures.

Sightseers, hikers, mountain bikers, and climbers head to the mountains near Ouray.

poker game. Today, the establishment is a B&B with a good-natured ghost who seems content merely to rattle nerves by rattling a few dishes. *426 Main Street; 970-325-4951.*

Ask for directions to the spectacular **Box Canyon Falls,** a short walk up Box Canyon. When the passage becomes very, very narrow, take a quick step back to avoid being given a massive shower by the falls. For a shorter hike to water, head to the east end of Eighth Avenue and venture onto the Lower Cascade Falls Trail, a half-mile hike to the base of the **Cascade Falls.** The riverbanks just outside of town also harbor little hot springs. Don't be shy; jump right in. The water's lovely.

Come winter, Box Canyon and Cascade Falls don't fall anymore; they freeze, which makes them ideal for ice climbing. The area has become a magnet for the ice-climbing crowd and highlights the sport every winter with a full-blown ice-climbing festival. The **Ouray Ice Festival** (970-325-4746 or 970-325-4981) heats up the town during its three-day run every January, and attracts some of the world's best ice climbers.

If you'd rather see the sights while seated, Ouray is situated in the middle of a veritable spider web of four-wheel-drive roads in the surrounding hills. You can

Real cowboys still populate places like the San Juans.

play it safe and let an experienced driver take the wheel, or you can grab a map, crank up your courage, ditch your fear of heights, and head for the high country in your own rig or a rental. (Yes, you'll need insurance.)

For a spectacular drive through the San Juans, take the Million Dollar Highway, a vertiginous stretch of U.S. 550 and the start of a 236-mile scenic loop that runs from Ouray to Silverton, then on to Durango, Cortez, and Telluride. (See page 144 for the route.)

■ SILVERTON *map page 129, D-2*

Set in a magnificent, isolated valley, this little Victorian hamlet enjoys about eighty days a year of summer tourists, delivered directly to town via the Durango & Silverton Narrow Gauge Railroad. The expansive and ornate **Town Hall** (1360 Greene Street) recalls Silverton's rich mining history, which lasted for 100 years, thanks to the prolific production of the Sunnyside Mine.

Another shiny edifice from Silverton's boom days is the **Grand Imperial Hotel,** which was the classiest in town when it was built in 1882. The building's many

RACING RAILS AND ROADS TO SILVER

When silver began to outpace gold as king of Colorado's mineral court, silver mines and mining camps started popping up throughout the state quicker than they could be marked on a map. Unlike the gold country, which was relatively close to Denver and the Front Range, silver strikes were made in the generally inaccessible high country of the central and southwest Rockies. The coming of a railroad or even a wagon road could turn a simple mining camp into a booming silver city and the road builders into millionaires. So conditions were ripe for more than one high-stakes railroad race and several extraordinary displays of high-country road building.

Leadville was the first jewel lusted after by competing railroaders. Coming from the south, both the Rio Grande and the Santa Fe crews laid tracks right up to the mouth of the narrow Royal Gorge. Before rail crews decided with fist and sledge which track would fit through the canyon, a deal was struck. The Santa Fe's effort came to a halt when the Rio Grande paid for the privilege to build into Leadville, and reached town in 1880. One railroad wasn't enough to serve Leadville, however, so the Denver and South Park line kept plugging away, and via a more circuitous route, reached town four years later.

The Rio Grande was involved in two other races, and won both. It was the first to hit Gunnison in 1881 and beat the Colorado Midland to Aspen in 1887. The Colorado Midland, though, was a gutsy little line. Starting in Colorado Springs, it ran through South Park and topped the 11,500-foot Hagerman Pass (replaced in 1890 by the Busk Ivanhoe Tunnel) on the way to Aspen.

While most attention focused on Leadville and Aspen, Otto Mears attacked the rugged San Juan Mountains, whose gold and silver would have been no more than piles of shiny curiosities if they couldn't be shipped out of the isolated valleys. The jagged peaks didn't deter Mears, an immigrant Russian Jew, who set out to connect the isolated mining camps with a series of toll roads. In all, Mears built more than 300 miles of toll roads in the San Juans, linking the area to the outside world and earning the sobriquet "The Pathfinder of the Southwest." Many of Mears's original roads later became rail lines, and his work is still evident today in the road from Ouray to Silverton—now part of the famed "Million Dollar Highway."

But the days of home-owned railroads were doomed by one man: Eastern financier Jay Gould, one of the slickest and most ruthless operators of capitalism's heyday. Gould was insatiable. He already held significant interests in the Missouri Pacific, the Rio Grande, the Union Pacific, and the Denver Pacific Railroads, and he had operating agreements with the Santa Fe and Rock Island lines. He then bought

Toll station on Bear Creek Road from Ouray to Silverton.
(Colorado Historical Society)

the Denver and South Park, the Kansas and Pacific, and the Colorado Central. Thus not only did faceless corporations come to dominate Colorado mining, but Gould came to control most of the state's railroads, which were lifelines to its remote regions.

The result was predictable. Once the booming silver towns went silent, the screech of the steam whistle, the clickety-clack of iron wheels, and the steady chugging of a steam locomotive also receded into silence—all victims of the bust. The trains would have to wait decades for historical nostalgia to fire up the engines, blow the whistles, and let the steel wheels roll once again. (See "Historic Railroads," pages 271–274, for a list of the state's historic steam-powered train rides.)

elegant Victorian touches include the finely crafted cherry-wood bar, complete with a bullet hole. It was made in London and shipped around Cape Horn before making the land journey to Silverton. The three-story hotel impressed Diamond Jim Brady, Lillian Russell, and other late-19th-century high rollers; as the biggest building in town, it is still an impressive part of Silverton's landscape. *1219 Greene Street; 970-387-5527.*

From Silverton you can only go down, but it's a great ride regardless of which side you decide to descend.

■ **DURANGO**   *map page 129, F-1*

If you drop off the hill south of Silverton, this is where you'll end up. If you take the trek by car on U.S. 550, you'll wind through the rusted remains of many an old mine and mill, and pass the **Durango Mountain Resort** (970-247-9000 or 800-525-0892), 19 miles north of Durango on U.S. 550. Or you can ride in comfort on the **Durango & Silverton Narrow Gauge Railroad** (479 Main Avenue; 970-247-2733 or 888-872-4607); an authentic steam-powered locomotive makes daily runs during the summer. A towering plume of steam tips off locals to the train's whereabouts.

Durango is an interesting old town that keeps itself new. Because of its location, it became the supply center for the San Juans' mining camps and the surrounding Indian reservations, as well as for the area's farms and ranches. With Mesa Verde National Park about an hour's drive to the west on Colorado 160, and with all the old silver mining towns, camps, and roads to the north, Durango is a good spot to set up camp during a stay in the San Juans. That stay can include a full agenda of outdoor fun: rafting the Animas River; fishing and boating on the crystal waters of Vallecito Reservoir; heading into the backcountry via the jeep trails in the surrounding national forests; or getting a true dose of wilderness in the massive Weminuche Wilderness Area.

Stroll down Main Avenue to the historic **Strater Hotel** (699 Main Avenue; 800-247-4431) to catch a little honky-tonk piano or a melodrama. Then journey past restaurants, ice cream parlors, and shops with all manner of Western paraphernalia, from bandanas to beaded belts. Along the way you'll also pass blue-collar bars where you can rub elbows with Native Americans and real cowboys who continue to live a modern version of the Western lifestyle.

Steam rises from the locomotive of the Durango & Silverton Narrow Gauge Railroad.

■ TELLURIDE *map page 129, D-1*

The problem here wasn't a lack of good gold, which was abundant, but that the veins occupied the bottom of a sheer box canyon with just one rough road in and out. The precious metal languished until the Rio Grande Southern Railroad chugged to town in 1890, touching off gold boom days.

Isolation and bad labor relations between the miners and the mining companies—strikes were frequent and sometimes led to violence—combined to stifle Telluride by 1930. But "To-hell-you-ride" was brought back to life in 1953, when the Idarado Mining Company bought old mining claims and began mining gold, zinc, and silver—which it did until 1978.

It still takes a bit of trouble to get to Telluride, even though it's just an inch west of Ouray on the map. Don't be fooled: it's a rough inch, though it's well worth the roundabout trip. For sheer dramatic effect, the first glimpse of the striking box canyon that holds Telluride is hard to beat. On both sides of town the mountains appear to bolt straight up into the sky. At the end of the canyon, another sheer wall of rock and pine trees soars above the town, its rugged outline broken by the shimmer of Bridal Veil Falls. You have reached a dead end, but you've also ended up in a spectacular setting in the heart of the Rockies. Stop and enjoy the view.

The classic **New Sheridan Hotel** has seen nearly all of Telluride's past. Opened in 1895, the Sheridan was the very picture of late-19th-century elegance. William Jennings Bryant gave an impassioned version of his "Cross of Gold" speech (which argued against the gold standard) here, before a receptive, radical audience of free-silver union men in 1903. Today, the restored hotel stands out among the neat Victorian buildings that line Colorado Street in the center of town. *231 West Colorado Street; 970-728-4351.*

Bridal Veil Falls, at the head of the canyon, is a dramatic sight, as are the rainbows that reach from one mountaintop to the other at any hint of moisture.

Telluride became the first electrified town in the world in 1891, when the first power plant producing alternating current began operating here. Local historians credit electricity with saving the area's mining business by reducing the cost of running the mining machinery.

On most summer weekends you'll find something going on; Telluride is home to a number of festivals featuring film, dance, and folk, bluegrass, and jazz music. (See "Festivals and Events," beginning on page 278, for details.)

Bridal Veil Falls cascades from the canyon wall east of Telluride.

ALFERD THE CANNIBAL

If you happen to be strolling along the sidewalks in Lake City, and you see the following community announcement—"Annual Alferd Packer Community Dinner: MEAT PROVIDED"—you've arrived at a special time. Here's the story of Alferd.

In 1874, Los Piños Indian Agency, south of Gunnison, wasn't used to many white visitors arriving at springtime on foot. By all accounts that winter had been a doozey, complete with deep snows, chilling winds, and short supplies of deer and elk. The agency was about halfway between Saguache and Lake City, in the middle of the San Juan Mountains, so walking there from about anywhere was quite a feat.

Alferd Packer—not a man to do lunch with. (Colorado Historical Society)

That's why the Los Piños folks were a bit suspicious when Alferd Packer arrived that April asking for whiskey, not food. In such nasty weather it would have taken him weeks, if not longer, to make it to the agency, yet he didn't look even a little bit puny. In fact, Packer looked pretty healthy, even rosy-cheeked.

When the springtime prospecting rush arrived, suspicions about Packer's winter paunch started popping up. Miners on the Lake Fork of the Gunnison River, a few miles below Lake San Cristobal, came upon the bodies of five men whose flesh had been carefully carved from their bones. Folks at Los Piños remembered Packer's rosy cheeks, and the day's primitive grapevine soon linked the five men to Packer.

Suspicions led to questions, which led to first some information and then some excuses from Packer. Packer said he and five other prospectors from Utah had set out in January from present-day Delta for the Los Piños Indian Agency. Ute Chief Ouray had warned them not to go; and in truth, the snow was too deep, they hadn't brought enough food, there was no game, and they were starving. They started eating their boots. Then they started eating each other.

First Packer said his feet froze and the others left him behind. Then he said one man died of natural causes and was eaten by the rest, so it became a case of eat or become tomorrow's cold cuts.

Packer was jailed in Saguache, but escaped and remained at large for nine years. Finally captured in Wyoming, he was brought back to Lake City in 1883 for trial. After finding Packer guilty of murder and cannibalism, Judge M. B. Gerry uttered (according to the poem by Stella Pavich, titled "Packer the Cannibal") the following sentence and rationale:

There was seven Democrats in Hinsdale County!
But you, you voracious, man-eating sonofabitch,
You ate five of them, therefore I sentence you
To be hanged by the neck, until you're dead, dead!
As a warning against reducing the Democratic population
of this State and Nation.

Packer managed to escape the noose, however. The killings had taken place on Ute land when Colorado was a territory, so Packer was originally charged under territorial laws. But between the killings and the first trial, Colorado became a state, so he was tried under state law—a procedural misstep. At Packer's second trial, in 1886 in Gunnison, the proper legal formalities were observed, and Packer was sentenced to 40 years in prison. His case had drawn considerable attention from supporters who believed his side of the story, however. In 1901, the governor paroled Packer. He died in April 1907, and was buried in Littleton.

Such a story couldn't rest in peace. In one of the best excuses ever conceived for a scientific field trip, a group of scientists literally dug up the Packer case in 1989. Forensic expert James Starrs gathered a gang of anthropologists, forensic experts, and a geophysicist/engineer, and set out for a summer dig in the San Juans.

The team located the five bodies on a bluff above the Lake Fork River. They found skulls that had probably been crushed when the men were asleep, signs that some of the men had tried to defend themselves, and bones chipped as if they had been coolly butchered. The scientific evidence proved that Judge Gerry was right to proclaim Packer a "voracious" man-eater. The damage to the area's Democratic Party appears to have been permanent, moreover: from statehood onward, Hinsdale County has been a Republican bastion.

■ SAN JUAN SKYWAY   *map page 129, C/D-2*

If you were to glance up Red Mountain from Ouray, you might think there was no way to drive to the top of that hill without cardiac or carburetor arrest. Calm your beating heart: the 11,000-foot mountain pass was born more than 100 years ago when Otto Mears carved a wagon road up the hill, and not too many travelers have fallen off it since.

Mears's gutsy road-building feat laid the base for U.S. 550, more commonly referred to as the **Million Dollar Highway.** This is just the beginning of the **San Juan Skyway,** a loop of state roads that takes you to almost every delight southwestern Colorado has to offer. To take full advantage of this trip you're going to need a couple of days, but once you get rolling you'll see that a day or two on "the most beautiful drive in the nation" is well worth the time and effort.

Don't be alarmed if your car doesn't exactly roar up Red Mountain Pass; this is one steep puppy, so just take your time. There's plenty to look at, anyway. Once you peak out, you'll next drop, slightly, into the Victorian mining town of Silverton (see page 135).

Several peaks within the rugged San Juan Mountain Range top 14,000 feet.

As you head south toward Durango, the roadside is littered with ghost towns, tailings, and old silver mine buildings. You'll travel through Colorado high country at its finest, and top two mountain passes more than 10,000 feet high before reaching Durango.

Turn west on Colorado 160, and you'll head into Indian country, both past and present. To the south is the Southern Ute Mountain Indian Reservation, and just past Mancos is the entrance to **Mesa Verde National Park.** As you scan the seemingly endless mesa you'll understand why it took so long for white men to discover the park's magnificent cliff dwellings and other archaeological wonders (see page 178).

Farther west, you hit **Cortez,** the largest town in the region and the center of today's Indian culture and politics. Straight north on Colorado 145, then 4 miles north of Dolores, is the **Anasazi Heritage Center** (27501 Highway 184; 970-882-4811), a trove of ancient Indian artifacts and information about the Escalante-Dominguez Expedition of 1776 (see page 182). Over Lizard Head Pass is Telluride, nestled in a box canyon with ski hills on the right, towering mountains on the left, and Bridal Veil Falls in front.

You're actually due south of Ouray right now, but to get there you'll have to take Colorado 145 to Placerville and then Colorado 62 to Ridgeway. Right past Ridgeway is U.S. 550, which will take you back to Ouray. One final tip: if you do take the entire loop, stop in Ouray when you're finished and spend some time in one of the town's natural hot springs.

■ **SUMMITVILLE** *map page 129, F-5*

The things that go bump in the night in the once-booming gold-rush town of Summitville don't have to rely on the same old ghost stories to entertain themselves. Summitville, due south of Del Norte and just east of Wolf Creek Pass at more than 10,850 feet, experienced its first boom from 1872 to 1874. But the area's gold didn't pick up and leave as quickly as the early prospectors did, so the town has experienced a number of gold-driven rebirths, keeping the ghosts hopping in and out of the old miners' cabins.

In its first boom, Summitville was the state's third-largest gold producer. About 50 mines on South Mountain disgorged a grand total of 257,000 ounces of the shiny stuff. When a Canadian firm reopened the mines in 1986, gone were yesteryear's gold pan, pick and shovel, sluice box, and hydraulic hoses. Also gone were

the nuggets or flakes of gold easily spotted by the naked eye. Modern miners search for microscopic flecks of gold. Instead of crushing or smelting gold ore, the miners sort the microscopic gold from the dirt by using a weak mix of cyanide and water held in large processing ponds called leaching fields.

Like the miners of old, those at the 20th-century Summitville operation made hay while they could; the Canadian operation left after six years. Unlike the old-timers, however, the high-tech miners left behind a gaping wound in the earth that leaked a watery toxic stew. Then a new mining crew went to work: the cleaners. After several years of lawsuits, threats, and bureaucratic back and forth, reclamation crews spent another couple of years cleaning up the mess by rearranging the disturbed landscape and putting the toxic genie back in the bottle.

The ghosts roaming the tattered, weather-beaten old buildings in Summitville once again had the place to themselves.

(opposite) A leisurely ride in the San Juans.
(above) Summitville's George Popovich still prospects for the mother lode.

WESTERN SLOPE

It was a homemade T-shirt, but its message came through loud and clear. The design featured the red international "NO" symbol, with the slash cutting through a carton of milk and a slice of toast, with the words, "U.S. National Hang Gliding Championships Dinosaur, Colorado"—an event that, as far as the T-shirt wearer was concerned, automatically disqualified the milquetoast crowd.

Dinosaur is the perfect example of a small town. It boasts a slim batch of modest homes, a city hall, and a scattering of motels and cafés on streets that cut and jut in random order. Fresh paint and street signs don't overwhelm a visitor, so you have to feel your way around, but it's a short feel.

Dinosaur's isolation and steady winds have made it a regular stop for hard-core hang gliders and parasailors. The sky fliers routinely hop off Cliff Ridge, confident they can ride the wind for up to 100 miles in any direction. They know that the chances are slim that they'll land in a shopping mall parking lot or on a suburban rooftop.

If a hang glider hit one hell of an updraft and went circling around northwest Colorado, he would be treated to a variety of sights far more interesting than shopping malls or suburbia. Floating north out of Dinosaur, he could gaze into the gorges made by the Green and Yampa Rivers as they cut through Dinosaur National Monument. As he headed west, he would peer down on mile after mile of untouched brown-hued hillsides splattered with sage and piñon.

Then abruptly, around Craig, the pine- and spruce-covered western flank of the Rocky Mountains would rise up in greeting. Continuing south, he would cruise over the densely forested, dark green White River National Forest, southeast of Meeker. Cutting back to the west, he would zip over the Piceance Basin, where the land alternates between blocks of green, irrigated hay fields, and gray-dry chunks of land thirsty for water. Amid the rolling hills of spruce and piñon he might spot hundreds, if not thousands, of the deer and elk that make the basin one of the finest places in the state to view wildlife.

Swooping back northward along the Utah border, toward Dinosaur and the desolate desert, he'd again see a mottled mixture of reds, grays, and browns. His head spinning with images ranging from desert to forest to mountain to pasture, our hang glider would return to the isolated burg of Dinosaur and coast to a stop.

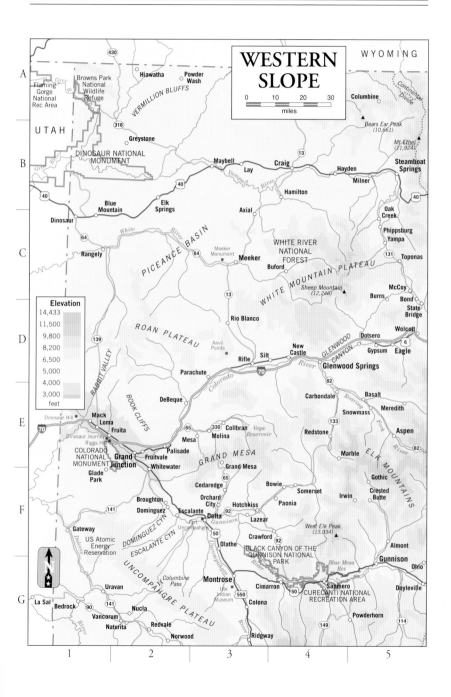

WESTERN SLOPE

0   10   20   30
miles

WYOMING

Continental Divide

UTAH

Flaming Gorge National Rec Area

Browns Park National Wildlife Refuge

Hiawatha

Powder Wash

Columbine

Bears Ear Peak (10,661)

VERMILLION BLUFFS

Greystone

Mt. Ethel (11,924)

DINOSAUR NATIONAL MONUMENT

Maybell

Lay

Craig

Hayden

Steamboat Springs

Milner

Blue Mountain

Elk Springs

Hamilton

Dinosaur

Axial

Oak Creek

Phippsburg

Yampa

Rangely

White River

Meeker Monument

Meeker

WHITE RIVER NATIONAL FOREST

Buford

Toponas

PICEANCE BASIN

WHITE MOUNTAIN PLATEAU

Sheep Mountain (12,246)

McCoy

Burns

Bond

State Bridge

Elevation

14,433
11,500
9,800
8,200
6,500
5,000
4,000
3,000
feet

ROAN PLATEAU

Rio Blanco

Wolcott

Anvil Points

New Castle

Dotsero

GLENWOOD CANYON

Gypsum

Eagle

Rifle

Silt

River

Glenwood Springs

RABBIT VALLEY

Parachute

Colorado

DeBeque

Carbondale

Roaring Fork

Basalt

Meredith

Snowmass

Dinosaur Hill

Mack

BOOK CLIFFS

Collbran

Vega Reservoir

Redstone

Aspen

Loma

Fruita

Dinosaur Journey

Riggs Hill

Mesa

Molina

COLORADO NATIONAL MONUMENT

Grand Junction

Fruitvale

Palisade

Whitewater

GRAND MESA

Grand Mesa

Marble

Gothic

ELK MOUNTAINS

Glade Park

Cedaredge

Bowie

Somerset

Irwin

Crested Butte

Broughton

Orchard City

Hotchkiss

Paonia

Dominguez

Escalante

Delta

Lazear

ESCALANTE CYN

DOMINGUEZ CYN

Gunnison

Fort Uncompahgre

West Elk Peak (13,034)

Gateway

US Atomic Energy Reservation

Crawford

Almont

Olathe

BLACK CANYON OF THE GUNNISON NATIONAL PARK

Blue Mesa Res

Gunnison

Ohio

UNCOMPAHGRE PLATEAU

Columbine Pass

Montrose

Ute Indian Museum

Cimarron

Sapinero

CURECANTI NATIONAL RECREATION AREA

Doyleville

Uravan

Colona

La Sal

Bedrock

Vancorum

Nucla

Powderhorn

Naturita

Redvale

Ridgway

Norwood

Dinosaur is the far northwestern outpost of Colorado's Western Slope, which can be broken into two distinct regions. The northwest, generally referred to as the Piceance (PEE-aunce) Basin, contains one of the nation's largest storehouses of valuable minerals. This real estate, most of it under federal control, faces Utah to the west, Wyoming to the north, and the Rocky Mountains to the east, bottoming out along I-70. South of I-70, the mountains still loom to the east with Utah to the west before you head into the San Juan Mountains and southern Colorado.

The basin's natural resources have created a diverse legacy—one that includes extensive ranching and farming; the development of oil, coal, uranium, and natural gas; and wilderness areas, two national monuments, and a national recreation area. The different users come with different demands, fueling an endless debate over who should come first: the miner/oil driller/rancher or the hiker/hunter/camper. Because huge chunks of the basin are federally controlled, most decisions affecting the region are made by people who don't live there.

■ DINOSAUR NATIONAL MONUMENT   *map page 149, B-1/2*

Whether you head toward Dinosaur National Monument from Steamboat Springs, Meeker, or Grand Junction, it takes hours of two-lane driving to get there. As you meander through this somewhat desolate landscape of red, tan, and white rock, it's hard to imagine that this was once a tropical landscape, where giant vegetarian dinosaurs roamed through clumps of conifers, ferns, mosses, and cycads.

Today, hang gliders cruise through the up- and downdrafts in the Piceance Basin sky. This sight isn't unprecedented: about 140 million years ago, a winged dinosaur called the Rhamphorhynchus sailed the skies during the Jurassic Period and peered down on the huge walking dinosaurs that have captured the imagination of children and the curiosity of scientists. Herds of Rhamphorhynchus, brontosaurus, and other dinosaurs once called the region home, and their fossilized remains are scattered throughout northwest Colorado.

After the first dinosaur fossils were discovered around 1900, tourists and paleontologists began to pick up bones and lug them away. The bone boom got going full bore in 1909 when a Carnegie Museum paleontologist arrived and was stunned to see eight brontosaurus tail bones sticking out of the ground. The cash of steel magnate Andrew Carnegie assured that many a museum would become a dinosaur depository. Fifteen years after the first discoveries, more than 350 tons of dinosaur bones had been dug up and shipped to museums across the country.

COLORADO'S AGE OF DINOSAURS

Dinosaur National Monument provides us with a grand view of the Jurassic landscape of 145 million years ago, when the earth's continents were joined together in a single land mass now referred to as "Pangaea." As you look about you at the subtle grays and browns of the desert, try to imagine the brilliant green ferns, conifers, and mosses which once grew here, and the behemoth dinosaurs that wandered among them. One of these was Apatosaurus (also known as the brontosaurus), a long-necked and long-tailed vegetarian—measuring over 70 feet in length and tipping the scales at 35 tons. Because Apatosaurus's brain was smaller than ours, but was given the job of directing a body as big as eighteen station wagons, some people assumed it was dull-witted and spent most of its time sloshing around in swamps. Yet, now we know from studying rock strata in such places as Dinosaur National Monument that Apatosaurus galloped around in herds, probably with its young in the middle, kicking up dust and trampling trees. The smell must have been awful, but they may have been fairly smart. After all, Apatosaurus belongs to one of the most successful groups of animals ever to live on the earth.

Other smaller dinosaurs shared Jurassic Park with these monsters, among them the comely Stegosaurus ("roofed reptile"), known for the bony knobs and bumps all over its body, the upright plates on its back, and its tail spikes. These animals grew to 20 feet in length and weighed about one-and-a-half tons. Early researchers thought that the back plates served as a defensive weapon, but more recently scientists have suggested that they served as solar panels and radiators regulating Stegosaurus's body temperature.

Roaming around with these oversized vegetarians were meat-eating carnosaurs, who packed their weight behind large heads, powerful necks, stout hind limbs, and small forearms. These included Allosaurus ("strange reptile") and Ceratosaurus ("horned reptile"). The adult Allosaurus was close to 40 feet long with a skull that reached nearly 3 feet in length; it had sharp, recurved daggers for teeth—serrated on both sides—lining its jaws. Possibly, it sped around Jurassic Park on its long, powerful hind limbs and grabbed its prey in the claws on its small, muscular forelimbs. Allosaurus probably fed on whip-tailed Apatosaurus.

As you climb into your two-ton station wagon to leave Dinosaur National Monument, you may feel relieved to return to the 21st century, where the descendants of Allosaurus (birds) prey on insects and worms.

—Mark Goodwin, U.C. Berkeley Museum of Paleontology

(following pages) Life among the dinosaurs, as depicted in the Rudolph F. Zallinger mural Age of Reptiles. *(Peabody Museum of Natural History, Yale University)*

The wholesale grave robbing came to an end in 1915, when 80 acres of the diggings were designated as Dinosaur National Monument. In 1938 another 326 acres were added. Therein lies the town of Dinosaur's real claim to fame: it's the gateway to Dinosaur National Monument. Well, sort of. **Rangely,** about 18 miles south of Dinosaur, also claims the title; and since it bears some resemblance to a real town, with a community college and a downtown, it's hard to argue the point. Actually, the entry and the original portion of the current monument are more than 20 miles to the west in Utah, and feature the much publicized **Visitors Center** (970-374-3000), where paleontologists chip bones out of a real dino dig.

■ GREEN AND YAMPA RIVER VALLEYS *map page 149, A/B-1/2*

Between 1950 and 1955, the nation's eyes focused on Dinosaur National Monument. They weren't peering in awe at 200-pound dinosaur bones, but rather glaring at a proposal to dam the Green and Yampa Rivers.

Thanks to some serious shenanigans, which set the tone for the "mainstream" environmental movement from then onward, the dam wasn't built and the Green and Yampa River Canyons were preserved. The deal struck in 1955 was to dam Glen Canyon and, in return, allow the Green and Yampa Rivers to run free by making them part of the national monument—even though the canyons run through juniper and piñon country that contains nary a dinosaur bone.

These two staggeringly abrupt cracks in the windswept desert can make a viewer feel insignificant. Standing at the edge of the Yampa River Canyon, miles of unspoiled desert surround you; a trail along the rim lets you gaze into the deep canyon at the snake-like river below. The same feeling of insignificance hits you as you raft or fish the Green River and peer up, between bursts of whitewater, at its towering canyon walls.

■ WILDLIFE IN THE PICEANCE BASIN

The best way to get a feel for the Piceance Basin is to drive Colorado 64 between Rangely and Meeker. Thousands of animals feel quite comfortable ambling across the land and picking their way through stands of sagebrush, cedar, piñon, juniper, and Douglas fir. Towns and motels are nonexistent, so if you'd like to spend the night along the way, bring a tent and sleeping bag.

There aren't any towns in the middle of the basin because in the 1880s, white men didn't think the place was worth a damn. The basin lacked the gold and silver resources of Central City or Leadville, so prospectors quickly abandoned their original mining claims; of the basin's 804,500 acres, about 675,000 acres eventually landed in the lap of the Bureau of Land Management (BLM). But centuries ago, people lived a pleasant life here, as evidenced by the **Dutch Creek Wickiup Village,** a prehistoric site listed on the National Register of Historic Places. About 35 other sites may be eligible for the same honor. For information about access to the Piceance Basin's public lands, call the BLM's Meeker office (970-878-3800).

As you travel the two-lane road, you'll see timber-covered mountains, rolling hills, and small streams. The streams have been channeled and tamed into irrigation works that created 82,000 acres of farmland and another 400,000 acres of open range. Ranches dot the landscape, as do herds of cattle and sheep. The forested hills are also harvested for local lumberyards, which produce thousands of cords of piñon and juniper firewood and hundreds of thousands of board-feet of Douglas fir.

It's almost impossible *not* to see wildlife on the ground or in the sky. The area contains one of the largest migratory mule deer herds in North America—numbering more than 25,000 head—along with more than 1,200 head of elk. In all, there are more than 350 species of wildlife in the basin, including 22 species of raptors, ranging from owls to eagles, and a wild horse herd.

■ TREASURE CHEST OR PANDORA'S BOX?

Piceance Basin embodies the many-faceted debate over how the West should manage and develop its ample natural resources. This corner of northwestern Colorado is a veritable treasure chest. For one hundred years, the urge to unlock this treasure has inspired scams, booms, and busts that make the opening of Pandora's box seem like a minor mishap.

Beneath the rolling countryside lie the world's largest deposits of oil shale, the largest untapped natural gas fields in the lower 48 states, and more than 400 million tons of coal. Huge reserves of gravel, oil, asphalt, and nacholite also rest beneath thousands of acres of timber and grazing lands.

The boom-bust cycle these riches inspired began in 1872 with a diamond scam. A pair of swindlers "salted" the land with diamonds, scored $600,000 from a San Francisco bank for their "mine," and unleashed a frenzy of fortune seekers.

One look at the alleged diamond territory by a U.S. government geologist quickly ended that boom.

Around the same time, as legend has it, settler Mike Callahan arrived on the basin, built a cabin, and fired up his shale-rock fireplace, which was immediately set aflame: oil shale, for the uninitiated, is "the rock that burns." The discovery set off dogged efforts to transform oil shale rock into oil.

Small shale booms erupted at irregular intervals thereafter, but every boom turned to bust as the discovery of huge new oil fields made shale seem less worth the bother. Sky-high oil prices in the late 1970s and early 1980s sparked the biggest boom of all, with four major oil companies working on oil shale projects. But as prices dropped again, the companies abandoned their plans.

Natural gas, too, has had its cycle. In the late 1960s, the federal government tried to extract this resource with the help of an underground nuclear bomb. That literal boom was a bust: pools of natural gas failed to form in the void left by the bomb. Today, gas-drilling rigs pop up in the middle of hay fields and forests and on the edges of towns. This industry hasn't been welcomed by the area's many newcomers, who have seen their vistas blotted by drilling rigs, their country roads cluttered with truck traffic, and their quiet nights shattered by the roar of diesel engines.

The oil and mining companies still covet the basin's underground wealth. Loggers covet the forests that cover the ground. Hordes of hunters covet the game animals that roam the forests. Ranchers covet the animals' grazing rights and irrigation water. And environmentalists want to preserve this massive "bioregion" and its full complement of flora and fauna. The result? A cacophony of voices screaming in the wilderness, espousing divergent views, goals, and priorities.

"Resource issues" continue to face the Piceance Basin and its various landowners, including the federal government, rancher families, and multinational corporations. As the debate rages about managing public lands for the benefit of all, only one clear theme emerges: the Piceance Basin is both a treasure chest and a Pandora's box, and you can't open one without opening the other.

■ MEEKER: WHERE WILDERNESS WAS BORN
map page 149, C-3

In 1919, a federal employee in Meeker looked at the pristine beauty of the forests east of the mineral-laden Piceance Basin and decided there should be a way to assure that the public interest would come first, foremost, and forever. That radical idea would eventually rock the Western Slope, rattle Colorado, and reshape the nation's public lands.

The employee in question, Arthur Carhart, was a Forest Service landscape architect working in the **White River National Forest,** east of Meeker. The tranquil beauty of Trappers Lake was being threatened by plans for summer homes, guest ranches, and "civilization" in general. Carhart's radical idea was that certain places should forever be preserved as wilderness, untouched by man.

Nationally known conservationists of the day, such as Gifford Pinchot, Bob Marshall, and Aldo Leopold, picked up and pushed ahead Carhart's idea for "wilderness areas," where homes, roads, mines, farms, and other "civilizing" tendencies of humans would be banned. So it was that the idea of setting aside vast sections of public land began west of one of the state's largest mineral storehouses.

As Aldo Leopold wrote: "We abuse land because we regard it as a commodity belonging to us. When we see land as a community to which we belong, we may begin to use it with love and respect."

Participants in action in the Meeker Classic Sheepdog Championship Trials.

In 1964, Carhart's radical idea was codified as the U.S. Wilderness Act, which was fought tooth and nail by most Colorado politicians. Today, although wilderness areas attract a steady stream of tourists, creating more wilderness is still a hot topic. Old ideas and ways die hard, especially in ranching country.

Meeker, which rests between Rifle and Craig on Colorado 13, was originally named after Nathan C. Meeker, who arrived in the area in 1878 to head the White River Indian Agency, charged with changing the Ute Indians from hunters and horse racers to solid Protestant farmers. (For more about this disastrous enterprise, read the "Utes" essay in "Southern Colorado," pages 188–189.) Today, a simple farm implement is prominently displayed at the **White River Museum** (565 Park Street; 970-878-9982) near downtown Meeker. It's a plow, the one Nathan Meeker planned to use to turn the Utes' horse track into a cornfield.

Two miles west of Meeker on Colorado 64 is a plain wooden sign and stone monument that pinpoints where the White River Ute Indian Agency used to be. Behind the sign you can see the broad valley that the Utes called home, now tamed into pasture and farmland. But turning to the east, you can see the hidden valleys, hot springs, and peaceful retreats that the Utes will always remember as "the land of shining mountains."

■ **PREDATORS VERSUS LIVESTOCK**

Meeker is a small ranching community that gets some mineral-based glory and grief but is sustained by the surrounding cattle ranchers and sheepmen. (Their motto: "Eat Lamb, 100,000 Coyotes Can't Be Wrong.") Meeker's old brick downtown buildings; mellow, small-town ambiance; and quiet, well-kept residences make it easy to believe the town spawned the idea of tranquil wilderness. Yet the town is also home to the **Meeker Classic Sheepdog Championship Trials** (970-878-5510), which brings sheepdogs and their owners from as far away as Scotland every September. The event's popularity—and the fact that there are still plenty of sheep for the dogs to chase—provides a clue as to why the area is home to one of the West's most contentious debates regarding predators and livestock.

Every year or two, Meeker finds itself in the spotlight over the intertwined issues of livestock grazing on public land and "predator control." For the ranchers who run sheep and cattle, the ability to turn their herds loose on public land for summer grazing at a nominal fee is regarded as a right. "Predator control" means being able to shoot any coyote, mountain lion, bear, or stray dog that might threaten the herds.

To environmentalists, the low grazing fees are a publicly funded subsidy they liken to "agricultural welfare." They see herds of cows and sheep as damaging to grasslands and streams, and regard "predator control" as government-sanctioned murder of animals that keep the local ecosystem in balance.

Grisly scenes of dead sheep, poisoned bears, and coyote hides inflame passions on both sides. Well-meaning efforts by federal and state land managers to reach some middle ground are resisted by both sides, which prefer to dig in their heels and stand their ground. The debate, and the killing, continues.

■ GRAND JUNCTION: PEACHIEST TOWN AROUND

map page 149, E-2 and page 160 for metro area

As soon as they were fairly certain the Utes would be removed from the Western Slope, land speculators and farmers went right to work. It is not stretching the truth to say that fruit trees and crops were being planted, mining claims staked, and hot springs turned into spas before the Utes' footprints had disappeared.

Grand Junction was the apt name speedy speculators chose for a grand town to replace the Ute camps at the confluence of the Grand (Colorado) and Gunnison Rivers. Between desert plateaus on the west, and mountainous, pine-covered mountains to the southeast, and with water readily available, Grand Junction was able to take advantage of every leg upon which the Western Slope economy rests. This city is the slope's largest town and commercial hub, supplying everything from transmissions to tricycles. Tourism and agriculture also bring business to Grand Junction, and in both cases variety provides the spice of economic life.

The city is uniquely situated between an alpine wonderland and the arid, wind-carved beauty of the desert. On the western fringe of the Grand Valley rests the **Colorado National Monument,** featuring stunning rock formations in a desert-like setting. The eastern side of the valley is defined by **Grand Mesa** (see page 163). A trip to the top of the mesa reveals the full strata of high-country scenery: desert sagebrush; piñon, and juniper forests in the foothills; aspen and pine at higher elevation; and barren peaks poking above the timberline.

Consuming the fertile floor of the Colorado River Valley between these two natural wonders are acres of orchards and vineyards, representing man's efforts to order nature around. In the early spring, visitors driving on I-70 can see two seasons at a glance: Fruit trees decked with bright blossoms cover the valley floor, while the Grand Mesa looms over it, crowned by the snows of winter.

As spring passes into summer and fall, the carefully planted rows of fruit trees deliver a bountiful harvest, the most notable of which is the Grand Junction peach. The combination of cool nights and hot days creates a robust, definitive peach bursting with flavor that is craved by connoisseurs and hoarded by Coloradans, who travel for miles at harvest time to buy peaches by the crate.

But there's more than peaches on those trees. Apples, cherries, and plums are also mouth-watering homegrown products. A newcomer to the valley is the wine grape. In the early 1980s, vintners started to grow wine grapes and announced the birth of the Colorado wine industry. The move was looked upon by traditional fruit farmers as either a nice hobby or a waste of time.

They quickly changed their tune. The same growing conditions that produce peachy peaches also produce distinctive wine grapes. Innovative wine makers took it from there, and Colorado wines have progressed from a regional oddity to a credible contender in the American wine market. More than a few Grand Junction wine makers proudly display prizes garnered in wine competitions, and the future looks bright for the valley's latest agricultural undertaking.

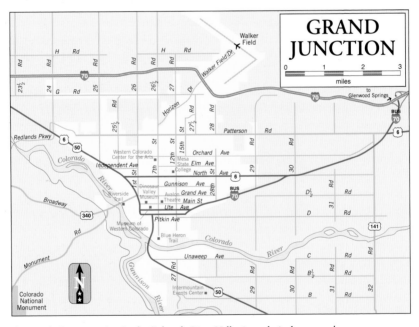

(opposite) Grape-growing in the Colorado River Valley is a relatively recent phenomenon.

Grand Junction itself is an interesting mix of what's old, brick, and stable, and what's new, gleaming, and hopeful. Coming off I-70, you'll be greeted by a gleaming strip of new motels, office buildings, and commercial space—development sparked by nearby **Walker Field Airport** (Horizon Drive Exit off I-70; 970-244-9100). The airport's modern glass-and-chrome design is a solid benefit of the 1980s shale boom; the oil companies were soaked for most of the bill.

Downtown Grand Junction has been working on renewing itself for a long time. This is evident in its trees and flowers, serpentine lanes, pedestrian-friendly stoplights and crosswalks, and brick stability. In 1962, Grand Junction became the second city in the nation to take a chance on reviving its downtown by creating a more relaxing, "shopper-oriented" atmosphere, featuring ample parking and locally owned shops.

The community has added two new highlights to downtown. First is the renovated **Avalon Theatre** (645 Main Street; 970-242-2188), built in 1923. The former vaudeville house, later a movie theater, has been spruced up and remodeled to

Gayla and Jackie Hawks are a mother-daughter barrel-racing team from the Grand Junction area.

become the city's premier performance space. Second, years of work have transformed an abandoned industrial zone on the banks of the Colorado and Gunnison Rivers into a family-friendly stretch of urban greenway accessible via numerous trails. The **Riverside Trail** takes off at the end of Grand Avenue, and the **Blue Heron Trail** starts at the end of Seventh Street. For information on the ever-expanding trail system, call the **Colorado Riverfront Trail Commission** (970-245-0045).

Of particular interest downtown is the **Dinosaur Valley Museum,** a special exhibition of the Museum of Western Colorado, whose other displays include a great gun collection—from muzzleloaders on up—and loads of other Western Slope memorabilia. Dinosaur Valley features half-size replicas of several dinosaurs, which move, stomp, and roar, as well as a working paleontology lab and other educational exhibits. *362 Main Street; 970-242-0971.*

Since Grand Junction sits astride I-70, it's a good launchpad from which to explore the region's attractions.

■ A TASTE OF THE WESTERN SLOPE

Come harvest time, getting a taste of the Western Slope is easy. Roadside fruit stands start to sprout along highways and county roads throughout the Grand Valley in midsummer. Roadside vendors run the gamut, from a couple of kids with a cooler full of cherries (the rural equivalent of the street-corner lemonade stand) to full-blown market stands with rows of just-picked fruits and vegetables.

Palisade, west of Grand Junction, offers up peaches, plums, and apples. A trip up the North Fork Valley between Delta and Paonia along Colorado 92 yields prize Paonia cherries, peaches, and apples, and vegetables from potatoes to squash.

The king of the vegetable dynasty, however, is Olathe sweet corn. You'll never be satisfied with regular ears of corn after one bite of Olathe sweet corn. Its kernels are big and juicy and bursting with a full-bodied, sweet taste that takes your taste buds way beyond any previous corn-related experience.

■ GRAND MESA AND COLORADO NATIONAL MONUMENT   *map page 149, E/F-1/3*

Grand Mesa, which at more than 12,000 feet in elevation is the nation's highest flat-topped mountain, is east of Grand Junction. Hunters, fishermen, campers, and nature lovers flock to the surrounding forest and its hundreds of streams and lakes via Colorado 65 and county and four-wheel-drive roads.

Colorado National Monument, which can be reached off I-70 from either Fruita or Grand Junction, is a dramatic dose of desert wind-carving, jolting color juxtapositions, and unanticipated arches. A good introduction to the monument is the 23-mile Rim Rock Drive. The road's tunnels are punched through the same red sandstone the wind has carved into arches and gentle curving formations. The red of the rock is accentuated by stands of bright green juniper and piñon trees, some seeming to grow right out of the rock. Lonely sandstone spires stand sentinel in the steep 2,000-foot canyons. Various spots along the canyon rims afford a quick view of the Colorado River Valley below.

■ RABBIT VALLEY DINOSAUR DIGS

You don't have to make the long, desolate drive to Dinosaur National Monument to satisfy your children's fascination with dinosaurs (or yours—come on, admit it). Right off I-70 near Grand Junction, where the Western Slope's northern and southern halves meet, you can avail yourself of guided tours and supervised digs minutes from civilization.

At Rabbit Valley, 24 miles west of Grand Junction in the middle of a dusty, desert landscape, you can take an unsupervised stroll or guided tour through actual, scientific dino digs. Also of interest to dinosaur buffs are the self-guided tours through **Riggs Hill** and **Dinosaur Hill,** near the town of **Fruita.** The **Museum of Western Colorado** (462 Ute Avenue, Grand Junction; 888-488-3466), offers various tours and dino-related activities and fun.

Across the interstate from Fruita is **Dinosaur Journey.** The 26,000-square-foot building is filled with robotic dinosaurs that move (and even spit) and more than 20 interactive educational activities, ranging from a dino-digging pit to a simulated earthquake. *550 Crossroads Court, Fruita; 970-858-7282.*

■ DELTA AND MONTROSE *map page 149, F-3 and G-3*

Driving south of Grand Junction on U.S. 50, you may get the feeling you're lost in the middle of the desert. If you dote on the desert and have some extra time, turn west on Colorado 141 at Whitewater to get a taste of the type of slick-rock desert country that appeals to mountain bikers, dirt bikers, and backpackers seeking desert solitude. The highway eventually runs into and follows the **Dolores River,** which is fed by a number of small streams pouring out of an isolated

Dinosaur National Monument.

chunk of the Uncompahgre National Forest to the east. It's desert, river, and forest all in one bundle.

Eventually, Colorado 141 takes you to the old uranium towns of **Nulca** and **Naturita,** where you can head east to the San Juan Mountains. If your desert thirst hasn't been quenched, continue south along the Utah border all the way to Cortez.

If you think a desert is as exciting as a litter box, stay on U.S. 50 out of Grand Junction, and watch the desert quickly give way to some of the state's most productive farmland. The key to the region's productivity is the Gunnison River; keep an eye out for roadside markers pointing out its beautiful canyons. Among the most magnificent are Escalante and Dominguez Canyons, named after Franciscan priests who tromped through western Colorado in 1776 and claimed the whole place for God and Spain.

The Spaniards didn't try to oust the Ute Indians from their homes. It took settlers from the East another 100 years to accomplish that task. Being forced to leave the mountains they had roamed for generations brought the Utes bitterness, anger, shame, and pain. Many of the newer settlers couldn't have cared less or were delighted to be rid of the natives.

URANIUM: THE UNFORGETTABLE BOOM

When the Ute Indians created war paint from a yellowish rock found throughout Colorado's Western Slope, they could not have imagined what the white men who displaced them would create from it. The rocks that supplied the Utes with yellow pigment were a form of uranium ore, and the atomic bombs that destroyed Hiroshima and Nagasaki owed their existence, in part, to Colorado uranium.

Between the Utes, the atomic bomb, and the uranium boom, Colorado can claim another atomic link. In the middle of the Rockies, along the banks of the Colorado River, is a little town named Radium. It was here that famed French chemist Madame Marie Curie came near the end of the 19th century to collect uranium samples for her pioneering radiation experiments. Her work allowed physicists to create the theories upon which the atomic bomb was based.

As World War II raged and the Manhattan Project sped toward the creation of atomic bombs, attention focused on Colorado's uranium country. The area's mill tailings were reworked for their uranium; more than 70 percent of the Manhattan Project's domestic uranium came from Uravan and neighboring Vancorum.

After the shooting war stopped, the Cold War really heated up the uranium business. More than 100 uranium companies set up shop in Grand Junction, and the boom was on. By 1955, Colorado led the nation in uranium and vanadium production, with some 400 mines feeding more than a dozen processing plants.

Uranium towns like Uravan prospered, but the workers took no special precautions against radiation exposure, because little was known of its long-term effects.

Occasionally, time heals emotional voids and provides perspective. Delta and Montrose have asked the Utes back, honored them with a museum, and preserved some of their powerful symbols.

Delta, located at the junction of the Gunnison and Uncompahgre Rivers, about 40 miles south of Grand Junction on U.S. 50, is a farming community that also delivers a real taste of Ute tradition.

A small sign near the entrance to Delta points travelers toward the **Ute Council Tree,** a Colorado historic landmark. Because of its central location, this huge cottonwood (85 feet tall and 7 feet in diameter) was a meeting place for several Ute bands, whose leaders would gather to discuss common affairs. As time passed, these discussions centered more and more on the pros and cons of staying to fight the white pioneers, or ceding territory in return for peace and promises that some

Mill tailings, which everyone assumed didn't contain enough uranium to be a problem, were blown about by the wind and used as fill dirt and in concrete in hundreds of Western Slope buildings.

The residents of Uravan, like thousands of other Coloradans who had worked the uranium mines and mills, had an unwelcome surprise coming. First, the uranium and vanadium market slowly shrank, forcing many plants and mines to close. Vanadium was still processed at several mills into the 1980s. Then it became clear that uranium exposure could cause cancers and other deadly side effects. In addition, it turned out that even slight amounts of uranium, such as those in the tailings piles, emitted radon gas, which could cause lung cancer. By the 1990s, the federal government agreed to compensate workers whose health had been affected by job-related uranium exposure.

The end of the Cold War doomed the uranium industry on the Western Slope. But the yellow ore had one last boom to bestow. In the late 1980s, the federal government decided huge pilings of uranium mill tailings resting in the middle of towns and along riverbanks were unsightly at best, a health hazard at worst. Bulldozers and dump trucks came rolling back to uranium country to complete a $366-million effort to cover up, seal off, destroy, or hide all the leftover traces of the state's uranium industry. Workers tore down old processing mills and hauled off or stabilized 25 million cubic yards of radioactive waste. This last atomic boom, which lasted about 10 years, is now over, the final chapter of the Western Slope's red-hot, heartbreaking love affair with uranium.

part of the Western Slope would remain theirs. The Ute Council Tree sits in between two houses at the end of a small lane lined by homes. So much for the string of early treaties promising that the Western Slope would be Ute land "for as long as the grasses grow."

The once stately tree is showing its age. Its branches are battered, some look almost dead, and the huge trunk is starting to split. But while that powerful symbol withers, cooperation between the Utes and the people of the Western Slope is growing. Under a landmark agreement, the U.S. Forest Service allows Ute elders to roam their former homeland once again to identify and preserve ancient Ute holy sites, historic trails, and burial grounds. The Utes are working to inventory the tangible remnants of their former lives in the millions of acres of national forests stretching from Durango to Meeker.

Henry Farney's 1902 painting captures the nomadic ways of Indians. (Museum of Western Art)

In the town of Delta, one sign points the way between a McDonald's and a Kentucky Fried Chicken outlet to **Fort Uncompahgre,** a living-history museum that springs to life every summer when it is filled with mountain men, Indians, and displays illuminating Colorado's fur-trapping days. The fort provides a summer setting for summertime productions of "Thunder Mountain Lives Tonight," in which Ute Indians in full regalia perform ceremonial and traditional dances. Interpreters trap beavers, make buckskins and arrowheads, and maintain the forge. At the visitors center are books about the fur trade, along with fur-trading supplies. *Gunnison River Drive; 970-874-8616.*

Delta proudly proclaims itself "the city of murals." A quick trip down Main Street proves the point. Colorful scenes of the region's historical roots, natural wonders, and agricultural bounty greet the eye at almost every corner.

The muralists have incorporated Indians, mountains, peaches, apples, and pears in their various works of art. You can see the inspiration for the murals everywhere you look—from the massive Grand Mesa to the east, to the desert just beyond the western horizon. In every direction are the orchards, farms, and ranches that provide the region's economic backbone; the resilient population's pride and ties to the land have survived gyrating commodities markets and an occasional killer frost.

A comprehensive view of Ute life is provided by the **Ute Indian Museum,** 2 miles south of Montrose. The museum, run by the Colorado Historical Society, occupies the former farm of famous Ute Chief Ouray and his equally famous wife Chipeta, who is buried there. Ute beadwork, ceremonial objects, and clothing are on display, as well as photos dating from the 1880s. Other exhibits illuminate Ute religious and ceremonial life. *17253 Chipeta Drive, Montrose; 970-249-3098.*

■ **BLACK CANYON OF THE GUNNISON AND BLUE MESA RESERVOIR** *map page 149, G-3/4*

The **Black Canyon of the Gunnison National Park** and **Blue Mesa Reservoir** stretch almost the full length of U.S. 50 from Montrose to Gunnison. The canyon's black, jagged, granite walls tower thousands of feet above the Gunnison River and make the Black Canyon both spectacularly beautiful and almost inaccessible from the rim—but a great place to raft or fish. Here the river is deeper for its width than any other river in North America, almost a half-mile straight down. The canyon is also the highest vertical climbing face in Colorado, towering in places more than 1,800 feet above the valley floor. Look up and you'll likely see climbers on it. The wild canyon and fish-filled river are just part of the action here.

Ute Indian scouts crossing the Los Piños River. (Denver Public Library)

Ute Chief Ouray stressed negotiations, not battle. Neither saved his people's independence.
(Denver Public Library, Western History Department)

Blue Mesa Reservoir, Colorado's largest body of water, also has great boating and fishing. (For more information about Blue Mesa Reservoir, see page 213.)

The huge reservoir, which ends abruptly at an awesome wild canyon, supplies water to farms and ranches. The planning for the reservoir prompted all the questions about water that have been debated since the attempt to dam the Green and Yampa Rivers near Dinosaur: Are all rivers to be managed for irrigation, growth, and hydroelectric power? Is a wild river a wasted resource?

Agriculture has sustained the area from day one and will not go away. Logging is another mainstay, and there always seems to be a new plan cropping up for increasing the "harvest" from the surrounding national forests to feed sawmills and fireplaces. But recreation and tourism are also vital to the Colorado economy. The final question still being debated is how to accommodate and generate wealth from everyone: farmers, lumberjacks, miners, hunters, fishermen, and campers.

■ HERDING SNAKES

Trying to build some sort of consensus about how best to use and preserve the Western Slope's natural resources is an exercise akin to herding snakes. Everyone is heading in his or her own chosen direction. Although the so-called New West and remnants of the Old West are on different paths, they can't avoid colliding on a regular basis.

The New West ideal, in a nutshell, is a West whose economic lifeblood is in its natural beauty and its ability to combine a rural lifestyle with modern convenience. Newcomers drawn by those attractions will keep the economy moving, as will the free-spending, non-polluting tourists for whom the natural world can be presented as a huge theme park. Computers and communications technology have allowed individuals and companies to leave the urban jungle and head for the high country. Some of these newcomers view the area's forests as a natural playground and the wildlife as ornaments. They rail against efforts that would sully their bucolic surroundings, but they would prefer that nature not impose on them—hence the cry for compensation when deer and elk invade a newcomer's 35-acre "ranchette" and treat the garden like a salad bar. Newcomers even complain about "agricultural odors"—the ever-present smell of cow dung that offends the sensibilities of those who'd prefer a sanitized version of rural life.

But there's a flip side to the New West coin. Grappling with industrial-strength tourism, the region's resorts and communities are focused on decidedly urban issues, such as public transit, traffic gridlock, growth control, and subsidized housing for the working class.

Environmentalists jump into the fray about anything that concerns the use of public lands. All the big issues are being aired out in present-day Colorado: the protection of endangered species; the expansion of wilderness areas; the protection of wetlands; the decline in logging; and the control over grazing on public lands.

Close quarters in the early mining days called for compromise,
a term still being defined on today's Western Slope.
(Colorado Historical Society)

But the Old West, which believes in reliance on the individual and that nature's bounty is worth something only when it is converted to cold, hard cash, has no intention of giving up without a fight. "You can't eat scenery," is a common snarl from loggers, who view trees as stands of money ready to be harvested.

Hunters see wildlife as potential trophies or pot roasts, and some town governments see hunting season as a time to make a killing at the cash register. Farmers and ranchers alike still want irrigation water, and if it takes a dam or two to keep this high-country desert green and growing, so be it. Grazing cows and sheep on public forests? Been doing it for generations and won't stop just because the "tree huggers" think cow pies dirty up a creek. Got it? The defiant attitude that "this is my land and I'll do what I damn well please with it" still holds sway in many a small town, where land-use planning and zoning laws are seen as illegitimate infringements on individual freedom.

■ BOUND TOGETHER

On the surface, it appears the herd of snakes will never point in the same direction. But several threads bind everyone on the Western Slope together.

First there is the land itself. Towering mountains, sweeping forests, fertile cropland, and wild, raging rivers invoke respect and awe from old-timers and newcomers alike. Land is sacred, and if you don't take care of it, it won't generate cash from either crops or tourists.

Second, despite their personal convictions, most people now realize that everyone is partly right about everything. Acres of tidily tended ranches and farms provide the scenic rural greenbelts that attract newcomers. Forests are living organisms that need to be literally pruned of deadwood to thrive. Too many deer and elk can overgraze the land as quickly as too many cows and sheep. Thus, hunting is a valid "wildlife management tool."

Finally, it doesn't take long to become attached to the hearty lifestyle and people of the Western Slope. Newcomers respectfully ask for, and old-timers gladly impart, their considerable wisdom about how to treat the land and its animals. Grudging respect is afforded those who decide to sacrifice the comforts of the city to be in a beautiful place where living the life you love is more important than making a good living.

Common ground is not in such short supply as one might suppose.

SOUTHERN COLORADO

In some flash of unintended intelligence or semiconscious consistency, the U.S. Congress made the right move when it created a single congressional district combining the Western Slope and southern Colorado.

Both areas have much in common: a dependence on natural resources, stunning scenery, and isolated communities that don't take to orders from outsiders. Once you drop south out of the San Juan Mountains or head west from Salida, a change starts to take place that sets southern Colorado apart from the rest of the state.

Around Cortez and the Four Corners region, the desert starts to take on the bone-dry, reddish, windswept look found in Utah and New Mexico. Farther east are forested mesas and very few towns. If enough water is available, green hay fields thrive to feed the area's cattle and sheep. Where there's no water, the land is gritty and covered with sagebrush. The triangular San Luis Valley of south-central Colorado is one of the largest level basins in the state's mountainous regions. Ringed by mountains, its streams keep the area lush by Colorado standards.

In a bizarre twist of nature, at the northeast end of the valley is Great Sand Dunes National Park, a veritable white ski hill made of sand and tucked between the green fields of the valley and the towering peaks of the Sangre de Cristo Mountains. This sight may be even more inspiring than anything up north.

But it's more than the scenery that makes southern Colorado distinct. There's also the history: ancient Anasazi cultures and cliff dwellings, the Spanish conquest, and the arrival of traders and settlers, who came in the 1800s by horse and covered wagon. In today's southern Colorado there's a unique ambiance with a slower pace and an old-fashioned grace. The area is steeped in time, rather than racing furiously toward the future. Southern Colorado tends to look south to Santa Fe for inspiration, rather than north to Denver, and since the Ute Indian Reservations straddle and dip into New Mexico, perhaps the whole area's in the wrong state. Certainly, the area retains and heartily embraces its Indian, Mexican, and Spanish roots.

■ FOUR CORNERS, CORTEZ, AND THE ANASAZI

No one knows if it was a mapmaker's joke, a fluke, or just something that happened, but barely a mile off U.S. 160 is the only place in the nation where the

Four Corners: a desolate spot where four state boundaries meet.

borders of four states meet. At one time, only a circular bronze plaque set in concrete informed you that, if you got down on all fours, you could be in Colorado, Utah, New Mexico, and Arizona all at the same time. Today, the plaque is circled by plywood booths filled with Ute, Navajo, Apache, and other Native American artwork, crafts, artifacts, and rugs. If you happen to be in the neighborhood, it's worth a stop to touch all the states and to see what real Native American arts and crafts look like, and cost.

Looking into Colorado, past the surrounding desert, you can see the outline of the San Juan Mountains. As you continue into Colorado on U.S. 160 toward those mountains, you enter the Ute Mountain Indian Reservation. **Towaoc,** nestled against the hills off U.S. 160, is the only substantial town on the reservation. Towaoc's **Ute Mountain Tribal Park** (970-565-3751) has a pottery showroom, ancient Anasazi dwellings, and 125,000 acres of backcountry you can hike through.

As you leave the reservation, the barren land, with just a sprinkling of native shrubs and bushes, gives way to verdant hay fields, pastures, and ranch land. The reason for this has to do with the availability and politics of water. More on this later.

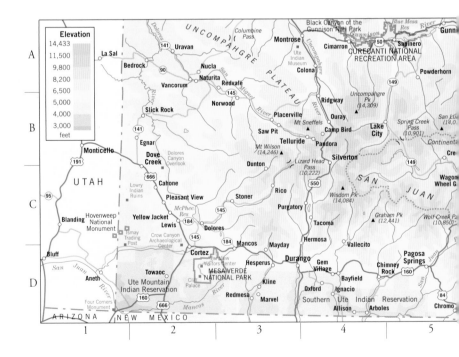

Cortez, this region's largest town, contains many arts and crafts galleries that exhibit works of Ute, Navajo, Apache, and other Native American artisans. The town and surrounding area are excellent places to get a feel for Anasazi culture.

The **Anasazi Heritage Center,** 9 miles north of Cortez in Dolores, houses educational and participatory exhibits on the Anasazi. It is also the storehouse for two million artifacts that, without some political arm-twisting, would have been drowned by the McPhee Reservoir, constructed in the 1980s farther north. *27501 Highway 184, Dolores; 970-882-4811.*

Crow Canyon Archaeological Center, 4 miles outside of Cortez, offers lectures and tours of current digs. The center stresses "do it yourself" archaeology by teaching amateur diggers where and how to dig for artifacts. *23390 Road K; 970-565-8975 or 800-422-8975.*

Hovenweep National Monument lies west of Cortez, through desert country reminiscent of innumerable car commercials. Tall towers still guard some of the deserted ruins (*Hovenweep* is Ute for "deserted valley"), which have been preserved in part because of their inaccessibility (even today, you can only drive to one set of

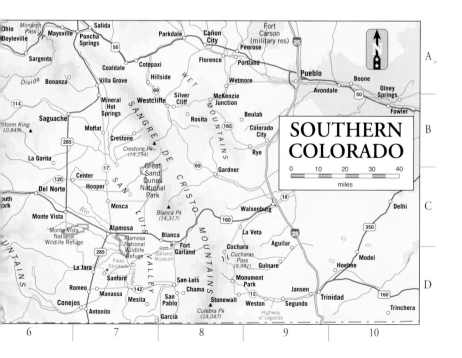

ruins) and partly because they were designated a national monument in 1923. *From Cortez take McElmo Canyon Road; or from U.S. 666 take County Road 9 at Pleasant View; 970-562-4282.*

Lowry Pueblo, built around A.D. 1000 and uncovered in 1928, has the largest ceremonial room, or kiva, discovered to date. More accessible than many of the nearby ruins, the pueblo was restored in 1965 and designated as a national historic landmark in 1967. The visitors center is just across the border in Utah. *From U.S. 666, take County Road 9 at Pleasant View; 970-247-4082.*

Hard-core Anasazi buffs, who will need several days to hit all these sights, can set up camp in Cortez, which has a relaxing, small-town atmosphere.

■ MESA VERDE NATIONAL PARK   *map pages 176–177, D-2/3*

The entrance to Mesa Verde National Park is 10 miles east of Cortez on U.S. 160. Paved, winding roads provide panoramic views of the landscape and take you into the heart of the 52,122-acre park. About 20 miles past the entrance, you come upon the Cliff Palace, which contains some of the most enthralling ruins of the region's ancient civilization.

The National Park Service's **Far View Visitors Center,** about 15 miles from the entrance, has information and directions, and is the only food stop on the way—so pack a lunch or pack your wallet if you want to eat. *970-529-4465.*

After the visitors center, you will enjoy an uninterrupted drive through piñon-covered hills and mesas where the ancient Anasazi long ago (and almost unbelievably) grew corn, beans, and squash. Streams are no longer visible, nor are there any remnants of irrigation works. In the mesa area, you will see numerous half-ruined pit houses and other structures that belonged to Anasazi ancestors, whose cliff dwellings you're on your way to see.

After driving those miles, most people seem to conclude that the Anasazi chose this spot to live in for purposes of defense or hiding. It would have taken some serious seeking to find these folks, just to make a little war and plunder their pottery.

■ ANASAZI HISTORY

A rudimentary Anasazi culture first got under way about the time the Western world went from B.C. to A.D. This first Anasazi group is now called the "Basketmakers," and for about 450 years they eked out a meager existence, foraging for desert plants, hunting with spears, and making baskets. Eventually this era evolved into what is now called the "Modified Basketmaker Period" (A.D. 450 to 750), identified by the use of the bow and arrow, pottery, beans, corn, and underground pit houses. From A.D. 750 to 1100, the Anasazi built houses and communal buildings from stone and adobe.

The people who moved into the cliffs didn't just pop up from behind some sagebrush with all their spiritual and cultural refinement. Rather, they were taking advantage of centuries of history and experience. And they used every shard of it in such monuments to their culture and skill as the Cliff Palace.

■ CLIFF PALACE

When the Ute Indians first migrated into this area, they looked at the Anasazi ruins, decided they were haunted, and afterward avoided them. Indian tribes farther south in New Mexico also had seen evidence of the vanished culture as they'd migrated through southern Colorado into New Mexico. They were the ones who first referred to these ancient people as "Anasazi," or "enemy ancestors."

After that, no one thought much about the ruins at Mesa Verde for a long, long time. In the winter of 1888, two cowboys out in the middle of nowhere, looking for stray cows, suddenly stopped in their tracks in a state of shock. What Richard Wetherill and Charlie Mason had caught sight of was an intact, abandoned stone city. We don't know whether they found their cows, but the world quickly learned what they did find: the Cliff Palace, a complex of about 200 individual homes and 23 kivas, with towers rising as high as four stories.

The world came to see what the cowboys found, and every clod in a pith helmet came away with something, be it a stone or a pottery shard from the surrounding area's estimated 800 cliff dwellings. Congress got off its duff in 1906 to stop the random looting and created Mesa Verde National Park, the first national park designed to preserve archaeological treasures.

Tucked underneath huge overhangs, built from A.D. 1100 to 1300, then abandoned almost as soon as they were completed, the cliff dwellings still stun and mystify. Some of the stone dwellings, such as the sturdy and imposing Cliff Palace, could accommodate up to 400 people. The masonry walls were not just rocks and mortar slapped together, but were crafted with care, plastered, and in some cases decorated. The fact that many of these buildings are still standing 700 years later is testimony to the masons' skill.

(following pages) The stunning Cliff Palace at Mesa Verde National Park remains an architectural triumph and retains an air of mystery.

The mystery of Mesa Verde revolves around two basic questions: Why did these people come here, and why, after barely 100 years, did they start to leave? Every Southwestern archaeologist in khaki shorts tries to answer those questions, and most visitors arrive at their own conclusions after a tour.

The pros speculate the dwellers departed for one or more of these reasons: drought, over-intensive farming, which ruined the land, or fear of nomadic raiders.

Same goes for the move to the cliffs: the Anasazi may have feared an attack; they may have been trying to protect what were the state's first irrigation systems; or they may have just stumbled on the caves' natural protection and built from there.

■ SPANISH EXPLORERS

The Catholic kingdom of Spain entered the New World to reap both riches and souls. By 1521, with the aid of guns, horses, and armor, Mexico had become a Spanish colony, and its silver and gold mines began their prodigious production, via the natives' slave labor. But like other gold- or silver-crazed prospectors, the Spaniards lusted after the big bonanza, the quick strike somewhere over the next ridge or just north of the next river where gold was resting in piles for the taking. In the Spaniards' case, they thought that bonanza was the legendary "Seven Cities of Gold," or "Cibola." Throughout the 1600s and 1700s, expeditions, some going as far north as Colorado, set out from Spanish territory to find cities rumored to be built of gold.

The most famous Spanish explorers to reach Colorado were two Franciscan priests, Silvestre Escalante and Francisco Dominguez. In 1776, when the newly formed United States of America began its battle for independence, the Franciscans set out on a trek that would make winter at Valley Forge seem like a Boy Scout weenie roast.

Embarking from Santa Fe, they headed northwest, then bounced around the San Juan Mountains until they came to the Dolores River. They followed it to the Gunnison River, then onward to the White River, stopping here and there to pray a bit and officially claim all they crossed for God and Spain. They then headed due west into Utah, in an effort to find a trail to California, until heavy snows and inhospitable desert forced them back to Santa Fe.

What the desert-dwelling Native Americans thought about being "discovered" by Spanish explorers is unrecorded, but they may have thought they themselves had just discovered something: a new breed of pale and pretty peculiar men. What

KIVAS, THE CROSS, AND CRESTONE

There's a voice in the wilderness crying,
A call from the ways untrod:
Prepare in the desert a highway,
A highway for our God!
The valleys shall be exalted,
The lofty hills brought low;
Make straight all the crooked places,
Where the Lord our God may go!

—Isaiah 40:1-11

From kivas to Catholicism to Crestone, southern Colorado has witnessed and been a testimony to an unrelenting faith in powers greater than those mere mortals possess.

For centuries the Pueblo peoples turned to their kivas to seek in solitude the power of their gods and spirits. Starting as a rude hole in the ground, the kiva evolved into a standardized, circular pit that provided symbolic structure to honor

The cliff-dwellers went into underground kivas for ritual ceremonies.

nature's four elements—wind, water, fire, and earth—or other supernatural elements in the ceremonial life.

Most of the kivas are silent now, but a sensitive traveler can descend into one at Mesa Verde, for instance, and still get a tingle—a tremor of feeling that something special and unexplainable but still powerful can occur when people slow their hurried pace and listen to the earth around them.

The Spanish conquerors who brought the Catholic faith and its churches to southern Colorado also brought a unique offshoot of Catholicism: the societies of flagellants known as the Penitent Brothers, or Los Hermanos Penitentes.

This rare photograph captures Penitentes flagellating themselves in 1896. (Museum of New Mexico).

Begun in the 13th century to honor St. Francis of Assisi, the Penitente societies, which died out everywhere in Europe except Spain, met in *moradas,* or lodges, and practiced self-torture as part of their devotions. From the early 1800s on, these exclusively male societies filled a void in the isolated towns of northern New Mexico and southern Colorado, many of which had no priests or others willing to undertake charitable work and maintain a sense of spiritual community.

Penitentes obeyed the tenets of the Catholic Church, but during Holy Week they dressed in black hoods and white breechcloths to perform a painfully honest reenactment of the Passion of Christ from the capture and trial through the crucifixion. The Penitentes would issue forth from their lodge and, stripped to the waist, would march in procession through the streets to the church, all the while engaging in self-flagellation (called the *disciplina*) with whips or cacti. They would be accompanied by the faithful, singing hymns, and by a few of the brothers carrying heavy crosses (the *maderos*). On Good Friday, one member of the brotherhood would be bound to the cross and left on it until he fainted.

The societies and their grisly ceremonies were eventually banned by the church, but that just made the Penitentes societies secret instead of open. Hundreds of Penitentes continued their unique devotions well into the 1900s, and some portions of the groups' ritual self-torture are still practiced today. Their moradas remain scattered throughout southern Colorado.

In Crestone, at the top of the San Luis Valley on the edge of the San Isabel National Forest, earthly calls of another nature beckon to the spirit of a new breed of believer. This little summer hideaway has become the focal point for many New Age spiritualists.

The area, allegedly sacred to the Indians, is supposed to be the center of a cosmic earth wart, where all manner of earthly, unearthly, spiritual, and transcendental planes and energy sources converge, coagulate, reincarnate, cross-mutate, and commingle. Doubters dub it a reincarnation of the Age of Aquarius, and wait for the new spirituality of Crestone to endure the test of time. Believers come to rest, refresh themselves in the natural surroundings, listen to the vibrations from earth, wind, and trees, and soak in powers unknown but felt all the same. (Some also buy real estate, but that's another story.)

No one knows why southern Colorado has become home to such a sustained sprouting of spiritual outburst. The spirits who provoke such shows of faith aren't saying. Maybe if you climb into a kiva, feel the passion of a Penitente, or commune with a Crestoner, you will receive a glimmer of the grace that fuels such faithful fire.

kind of fool would come to the desert wearing heavy clothing, a helmet on his head, and armor over his clothes that turned him into a miniature kiln? The new breed's "big dogs" and "booming sticks," however, did get the natives' attention. Although the Indians themselves became expert horsemen and riflemen, a combination of warfare with Europeans and exposure to their diseases would cause the ultimate destruction of their culture and their people.

By the late 1700s, southern Colorado was just a hop, stagger, and donkey ride from Santa Fe, in relative terms, and was claimed and settled quickly in the Spanish era, courtesy of land grants direct from the king of Spain himself. Thus, the area retains some of Colorado's deepest Spanish/Mexican roots and an identification with New Mexico and Mexico.

■ SOUTHERN UTE INDIAN RESERVATION
map pages 176–177, D-3/5

As you travel along U.S. 160 you can see the mineral-laden mountains to the north. The Spaniards didn't explore them thoroughly, but white prospectors swarmed all over. Their persistence led to huge discoveries around Durango, Silverton, and Lake City and also prompted the removal of Ute Indians from those mountains.

South of U.S. 160, as it makes its way from Durango to Pagosa Springs, is the **Southern Ute Indian Reservation** (566 Ute Road; 970-563-0270). The tribe is headquartered in **Ignacio,** about 20 miles southeast of Durango on Colorado 172. Amid rolling hills and ranch land is the **Piño Nuche Purasa Tourist and Community Center,** where you'll find a motel, a restaurant, an arts and crafts shop, and a museum. During the summer and fall you can take guided trips into Ute country.

It would seem, what with all the Ute cultural centers, the national park, and the historic sites and preservation actions taking place from Cortez to Ignacio, that the federal government was right on top of things in southern Colorado.

Nice try.

Before Colorado became a territory in the mid-1800s, it always seemed that the same white men who gloried in the myth of the rugged individualist got the government handouts first. In the 1880s, the leftovers blew south to the reservations that the whites thought consisted of worthless land. After a century of reservation life, broken promises, and patience, members of the Ute Mountain and Southern Ute tribes are still fighting a two-front battle—for land rights and for respect.

Flute playing was an important Ute courting ritual.
(Center of Southwest Studies, Fort Lewis College, Durango, Colorado)

Modern prospectors have found water, coal, and natural gas in abundance on the "worthless" land, and the Utes are still struggling for the right to shape decisions about how and when to develop the natural resources.

As for respect: Until relatively recently, the Bureau of Indian Affairs' "treaty room," in Washington, D.C., was decorated with a melodramatic 1880s painting depicting a "bloodthirsty savage" scalping a white man. No one knew where the

UTES: EXIT FROM THE LAND OF SHINING MOUNTAINS

The Ute Indians who roamed Colorado could always rely on one thing: a safe haven in the mountains and valleys they called "the land of shining mountains." Ute bands roamed from the Great Plains into Utah, Arizona, New Mexico, and southern Colorado. Whether seeking refuge from other raiders or a quick escape after a raid of their own, the mobile Utes could lose their pursuers in the mountains they knew so well.

Before the Spanish brought horses into North America, the Utes scratched out a living much like the Paiutes, Navajos, and Apaches, with whom they shared their far-ranging domain. They relied on small-game hunting and gathering of desert and mountain plants for subsistence.

Physically, the Utes were stocky and powerfully built, with dark, bronze-colored skin. They would move their camps into the high country for summer hunting, but retreat to gentler climes to wait out winters. Their women's beadwork was, and still is, intricate, colorful, and refined into an art.

The Utes also developed a rich ceremonial and spiritual life. They "knew" the bear and how to coax him from hibernation with the Bear Dance that signaled the beginning of spring. The Sun Dance, initiated in the middle of summer, was to ensure good hunting.

The Utes were a playful people, and many of their dances—the Circle Dance, Coyote Dance, Tea Dance—were strictly social in nature. Social, but more serious, were the melodies from handmade flutes that a man used to attract his true love. All sorts of games occupied idle time, including stick dice, archery, ring spearing, juggling, wrestling, and foot racing. Horse racing was the most popular sport and, unfortunately, contributed to the ultimate removal of the Utes from Colorado.

Spaniards spotted the Utes as early as the 1600s, and eventually arrived at an uneasy peace with them. The Spanish also provided the Utes with the horse, although that certainly wasn't their intention. The Utes became one of the first tribes with extensive herds, something that greatly increased their mobility and heightened the respect given them by other tribes.

The Utes had few squabbles with the mountain men who arrived from the East in the 1830s. Many of the early explorers married Ute women and appreciated the Utes' knowledge of the land. But things changed when gold was discovered in the 1860s. The gold and silver seekers wanted control of the land, and the farmers who followed saw potentially productive land being "wasted." As Colorado became first a territory and then a state, the desire to drive the Utes off their land intensified.

That desire was fulfilled by a series of treaties. The Utes ceded the San Luis Valley (in southern Colorado) in 1863, were moved west of the Continental Divide in 1868, and gave up their claim to other mineral-rich land in 1873. Thus, northwest and west-central Colorado became their home. Its advantages were plentiful game, natural mineral hot springs with their spiritual and healing powers, and, for a while, lax federal supervision.

That paternalistic neglect, however, came to an end in 1878, when Nathan C. Meeker arrived to head the White River Ute Indian Agency. Meeker had worked for Horace Greeley before coming to Colorado to lead the utopian Union Colony on the eastern plains. Unfortunately, things got a little more "Western" than Meeker probably had in mind.

He quickly decided that hunting, fishing, racing ponies, and generally enjoying life just wouldn't do for Utes. In modern jargon, he had no respect for the Utes' unique cultural or belief systems. Instead of free-roaming Indians, he wanted sedentary Christian farmers. The culture clash made conflict inevitable.

When he suggested that a good place to start the "civilizing" process was to forget about racing ponies and plow up the racetrack, the Indians refused in a manner Meeker thought surly. He called for some troops. To the Utes, troops meant a massacre, so they ambushed the troops, killed and mutilated Meeker and all the men at the agency, kidnapped Meeker's wife and daughters, held them for a week, and then released them unharmed.

The politicians and public were outraged; the newspapers went nuts; and soon the women's kidnapping became a lurid tail of horror at the hands of the red man.

"The Utes must go," became the cry of the day. And go they did, under army escort, and burning forests as they went, to reservations in Utah and southern Colorado on a trek they called the "Trip of Sorrow."

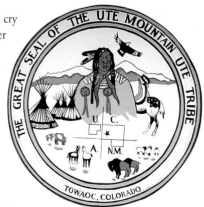

painting came from, why it was chosen, or how long it had actually been hanging in the treaty room, but it took a pointed "suggestion" from then-Congressman, Ben Nighthorse Campbell, himself a Native American, to get the offensive painting removed and replaced with other art.

Campbell, now a U.S. senator, is proof it doesn't hurt to have a Native American from a Colorado reservation stomping around Washington in cowboy boots and bolo tie. Campbell reminds his colleagues about places like Towaoc, and that when a treaty states "as long as the sun shall shine and the grasses grow," it means a very long time, indeed.

The Utes are still trying to hold the government to one of its oldest promises, made in 1902, when the government agreed to build the Animas–La Plata dam and diversion project to provide water for the Utes (among others). Finally, after a century of political and environmental wrangling, the federal government is preparing to make good on its promise.

The Utes, who long ago lost their faith in the government experts, brought their own lawyers, accountants, environmental experts, and congressman to the table. The complicated water fight reached a milestone in December 2000 when Campbell, despite protest from some Utes, helped assure the passage of a new round of amendments to the Colorado Ute Settlement Act. The law authorized the long-awaited water project, but it was a scaled-down version, referred to as "Animas–La Plata Lite," with construction slated to begin in earnest by 2003. The Utes were paid cash for some of their water rights and a new reservoir northwest of Durango and various pipelines and pumping stations were designed to deliver usable water to Utes in Colorado and Utah. Although the water project fell short of fulfilling the promises in the original 1902 agreement, the Utes grudgingly agreed to the compromise plan, settling for a glass half full of water instead of a glass full of empty promises.

The Utes' accountants and lawyers are also matching wits with the federal government and the energy companies. Just because much of the Four Corners region looks barren, there's no reason to think it is underneath; in fact, it's loaded with coal (which could be developed with Animas–La Plata water) and natural gas.

■ **SAN LUIS VALLEY** *map pages 176–177, B/C-6/7*

As you continue to drive east on U.S. 160, climb over the Continental Divide, and loop around the Rio Grande National Forest, you drop into another mysterious section of southern Colorado: the San Luis Valley. With its northern outpost of Saguache, the triangular valley stretches 50 miles in width and runs all the way to the border of New Mexico, making it one of the world's largest valley basins. The northwestern border is formed by the San Juan, La Garita, and Conjeos-Brazos Mountains, from which the Rio Grande River has its humble beginnings. Centuries-old Spanish land grants, immigrants, and the water from the Rio Grande and other mountain streams created the conditions for a farming culture with a long, deep taproot. With sufficient water to feed the valley's hay and potato farms, and generations of farming families working the land, the valley has long been a little emerald encircled by mountains. On the southeastern side, the inspiring Sangre de Cristo Mountains put an abrupt end to the flat valley floor. At sunrise or sunset, the sky turns a vibrant red around the range's peaks, making it easy to understand why the range's namers thought of the "blood of Christ."

In the valley itself, the small, isolated towns that have been influenced by the Indian, Spaniard, and white man are not only steeped in history, but radiate a friendliness and open-mindedness unequaled anywhere else in the state. The scenery is breathtaking as well, and the forests provide many nature-oriented diversions. The **Cumbres and Toltec Scenic Railway** (505-756-2151) runs from Antonito to Chama, New Mexico, and provides as authentic a narrow-gauge railroad trip as any in the state. The mountain scenery is unbeatable all along the route. Just the train ride makes it worth a trip through the area. (See "Historic Railroads," page 271.)

Alamosa, where U.S. 160, U.S. 285, and the Rio Grande meet, is the largest town in the valley, home to Adams State College and the gateway to the **Great Sand Dunes National Park,** 30 miles to the north. This huge pile of sand, sandwiched between flat farmland and mountain splendor, is a geological wonder and quite a playground—you can even ski on it. *Take U.S. 160 east from Alamosa. At Blanca turn onto Colorado 150 and drive north; 719-378-2312.*

The town of **Manassa,** off U.S. 285 on Colorado 142 south of Alamosa, has a small museum dedicated to the great boxer Jack Dempsey, also known as the "Manassa Mauler." East of Manassa, on Colorado 159, lies the town of **San Luis,** which in 1851 became Colorado's first "officially" incorporated town. It has the second-oldest "common" land—land open for use by all residents—in the United States, with the Boston Common being the first. Residents built a religious shrine for special Holy Week celebrations. (See "Religious Tradition," page 193.)

The San Luis Valley's abundant natural hot springs are as soothing as the famous springs in Glenwood, Ouray, or Steamboat, but they remain, for the most part, under-promoted and basically undeveloped. The surrounding mountains get hundreds of inches of pure Colorado champagne powder, perfect for skiing; they do contain small ski areas, but no mega-resorts typical of the central mountains.

■ SAN LUIS HISTORY

After the Mexican War of 1846, the United States gained the territory of New Mexico, which then included the San Luis Valley and its people, ranches, and communities. Trouble with raiding Indians forced the government to pay attention, and in 1852, little Fort Massachusetts was built in the hills above the San Luis Valley. It was abandoned six years later because it was too vulnerable to Indian attack. That logic set well with the Utes, but not with the white settlers of the valley. **Fort Garland** was built in 1858, and its strategic location at the head of the San Luis Valley and its accommodations for more than 100 soldiers provided a stronger sense of security. Assigning legendary frontiersman Kit Carson to command the fort in 1866 also improved morale. The fort, restored to its past glory, now operates as a living-history museum. *U.S. 160, 25 miles east of Alamosa; 719-379-3512.*

Kit Carson

■ RELIGIOUS TRADITION

The San Luis Valley did not draw its strength from muskets and men alone. For centuries the area's strength has also come from its common culture, a mixture of Spanish and Mexican, which took root long before the United States, New Mexico, or even Colorado itself existed. Faith in the time-tested credos of the Catholic religion also became a cornerstone upon which much of south-central Colorado was established, and it continues to inform the lives of the people in this area.

The Spanish explorers brought Catholic priests on their expeditions in an effort to at least lay claim to any lost souls they might encounter. For 300 years those priests found northern New Mexico and southern Colorado to

Life springs eternal, even on the great dunes of the San Luis Valley.

be fertile ground for soul searching (even if the Indians didn't think much of it).

The San Luis Valley was no exception. The church was the centerpiece of life in its small, isolated towns. Priests and sisters cared for the sick, taught the children, and sheltered the poor and homeless. If priests or nuns weren't available, the Penitentes, who were more widely known for their self-flagellation ceremonies during Holy Week, would step in to fill the void.

Work began in the late 1850s on what is believed to be the state's oldest surviving Catholic church, Our Lady of Guadalupe, in the town of Conejos. The church was officially dedicated by the bishop of Santa Fe in 1863. The town of San Luis hopes that a unique, newly created path through the Holy Week observances will not only be a spiritual experience for all Christians, but a positive economic experience for the small town.

An early Catholic church and mission. (Colorado Historical Society)

On a nearby mesa, the 800 residents of San Luis have carved a gravel trail, more than a mile long, that twists through the trees and cuts through the rocks. Lining the sinuous path are 15 bronze sculptures representing the 14 Stations of the Cross and the resurrection of Jesus Christ. The less-than-life-size sculptures make the whole project look more like a shrine than a piece of religious art.

The site serves several purposes. It gives the area's devoted residents a unique Holy Week celebration, letting them walk the trail on Good Friday and pay homage to the Stations of the Cross. The scale of the effort also attracts pilgrims, curious tourists, and others seeking a different Holy Week experience or spiritual renewal than can be had in an urban pew.

Those pilgrims and visitors provide a slight springtime boon for the small, isolated town and its artists and merchants. Although any such economic benefits are gladly accepted, the oldest town in Colorado endures regardless, having learned another lesson quite well:

By your endurance you will gain your lives.

—Luke 21:19

WILLA CATHER'S COLORADO

[In] Mexican Town...lived all the humbler citizens, the people who voted but did not run for office. The houses were little story-and-a-half cottages, with none of the fussy architectural efforts that marked those on Sylvester Street. They nestled modestly behind their cottonwoods and Virginia creeper; their occupants had no social pretensions to keep up. There were no half-glass front doors with doorbells, or formidable parlors behind closed shutters. Here the old women washed in the back yard, and the men sat in the front doorway and smoked their pipes. The people on Sylvester Street scarcely knew that this part of the town existed. Thea liked to...explore these quiet, shady streets, where the people never tried to have lawns or to grow elms and pine trees, but let the native timber have its way and spread in luxuriance. She had many friends there, old women who gave her a yellow rose or a spray of trumpet vine....

———

[Dr. Archie] took up a black leather case, put on his hat, and they went down the dark stairs into the street. The summer moon hung full in the sky. For the time being, it was the great fact in the world. Beyond the edge of the town the plain was so white that every clump of sage stood out distinct from the sand, and the dunes looked like a shining lake. The doctor took off his straw hat and carried it in his hand as they walked toward Mexican Town across the sand.

North of Pueblo, Mexican settlements were rare in Colorado then. This one had come about accidentally. Spanish Johnny was the first Mexican who came to Moonstone. He was a painter and decorator, and had been working in Trinidad, when Ray Kennedy told him there was a "boom" on in Moonstone, and a good many new buildings were going up. A year after Johnny settled in Moonstone, his cousin, Famos Serreños, came to work in the brickyard; then Serreños' cousins came to help him. During the strike, the master mechanic put a gang of Mexicans to work in the roundhouse. The Mexicans had arrived so quietly, with their blankets and musical instruments, that before Moonstone was awake to the fact, there was a Mexican quarter; a dozen families or more.

As Thea and the doctor approached the 'dobe houses, they heard a guitar, and a rich barytone voice—that of Famos Serreños—singing "La Golandrina." All the Mexican houses had neat little yards, with tamarisk hedges and flowers, and walks bordered with shells or whitewashed stones. Johnny's house was dark. His wife, Mrs. Tellamantez, was sitting on the doorstep, combing her long, blue-black hair. (Mexican women are like the Spartans; when they are in trouble, in love, under stress of any kind, they comb and comb their hair.) She rose without embarrassment or apology, comb in hand, and greeted the doctor.

"Good-evening; will you go in?" she asked in a low, musical voice. "He is in the back room. I will make a light." She followed them indoors, lit a candle and handed it to the doctor, pointing toward the bedroom. Then she went back and sat down on her doorstep.

Dr. Archie and Thea went into the bedroom, which was dark and quiet. There was a bed in the corner, and a man was lying on the clean sheets. On the table beside him was a glass pitcher, half-full of water. Spanish Johnny looked younger than his wife, and when he was in health he was very handsome: slender, gold-colored, with wavy black hair, a round, smooth throat, white teeth, and burning black eyes. His profile was strong and severe, like an Indian's.

What was termed his "wildness" showed itself only in his feverish eyes and in the color that burned on his tawny cheeks. That night he was a coppery green, and his eyes were like black holes. He opened them when the doctor held the candle before his face.

"*Mi testa!*" he muttered, "*mi testa*, doctor. *La fiebre!*" Seeing the doctor's companion at the foot of the bed, he attempted a smile. "*Muchacha!*" he exclaimed deprecatingly.

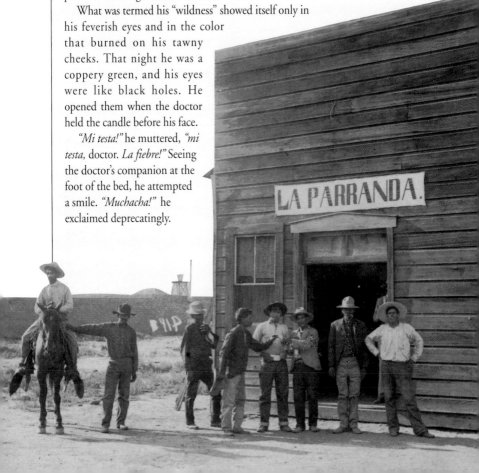

Dr. Archie stuck a thermometer into his mouth. "Now, Thea, you can run outside and wait for me."

Thea slipped noiselessly through the dark house and joined Mrs. Tellamantez. The somber Mexican woman did not seem inclined to talk, but her nod was friendly. Thea sat down on the warm sand, her back to the moon, facing Mrs. Tellamantez on her doorstep, and began to count the moonflowers on the vine that ran over the house. Mrs. Tellamantez was always considered a very homely woman. Her face was of a strongly marked type not sympathetic to Americans. Such long, oval faces, with a full chin, a large, mobile mouth, a high nose, are not uncommon in Spain. Mrs. Tellamantez could not write her name, and could read but little. Her strong nature lived upon itself. She was chiefly known in Moonstone for her forbearance with her incorrigible husband.

Nobody knew exactly what was the matter with Johnny, and everybody liked him. His popularity would have been unusual for a white man, for a Mexican it was unprecedented. His talents were his undoing. He had a high, uncertain tenor voice, and he played the mandolin with exceptional skill. Periodically he went crazy. There was no other way to explain his behavior. He was a clever workman, and, when he worked, as regular and faithful as a burro. Then some night he would fall in with a crowd at the saloon and begin to sing. He would go on until he had no voice left, until he wheezed and rasped. Then he would play his mandolin furiously, and drink until his eyes sank back into his head. At last, when he was put out of the saloon at closing time, and could get nobody to listen to him, he would run away—along the railroad track, straight across the desert. He always managed to get aboard a freight somewhere. Once beyond Denver, he played his way southward from saloon to saloon until he got across the border. He never wrote to his wife; but she would soon begin to get newspapers from La Junta, Albuquerque, Chihuahua, with marked paragraphs announcing that Juan Tellamantez and his wonderful mandolin could be heard at the Jack Rabbit Grill, or the Pearl of Cadiz Saloon. Mrs. Tellamantez waited and wept and combed her hair. When he was completely wrung out and burned up—all but destroyed—her Juan always came back to her to be taken care of—once with an ugly knife wound in the neck, once with a finger missing from his right hand—but he played just as well with three fingers as he had with four.

—Willa Cather, *The Song of the Lark,* 1915

(opposite) From stirrups to sombreros, Spanish and Mexican influences came north from Santa Fe into southern Colorado. (Colorado Historical Society)

■ TRINIDAD: WAR IN THE MINES *map pages 176–177, D-9*

The beginning of the 20th century saw unions and miners in the gold and coal mines agitating about hours, conditions, wages, scabs, and union representation. Violence by both the workers and the owners was common. The Western Federation of Miners (WFM) won recognition in Telluride in 1901, but that success was hard to repeat. In 1903, Cripple Creek became a battlefield, and when a WFM agitator blew up a trainload of scabs, killing 13 people, the public turned against the union. By 1904, the strike was over, the public was antiunion, and the miners were still complaining.

But the biggest collision between the workers and their corporate bosses—one that holds a place in union history—took place in 1914. It pitted coal miners and the United Mine Workers (UMW) against mine owners and the Colorado Fuel and Iron Company, run at the time by John D. Rockefeller Jr. The miners wanted an eight-hour day, better wages and safety controls, and the ability to choose their own housing. The miners were urged on by a personal visit by Mary Harris, better known as the famous socialist organizer "Mother Jones."

The strike in the Trinidad coal fields became official in September 1913. The owners tried to keep the mines open with nonunion workers; the strikers tried to keep the scabs out. Union men and their families set up tent cities near the mines and lived off union strike funds. Tensions heightened throughout the winter. The mine operators called for the state militia, which was promptly dispatched to protect the mines.

A scuffle between the militia and miners on April 20, 1914, touched off the explosive conflict at Ludlow Station, 18 miles south of Trinidad, after the militia tried to move the 900 miners and their families from their tent city. Five miners and one militiaman died in the violence, and the bodies of two women and 11 children were found afterward in the burned remains of the tent city. The confrontation became known as the "Ludlow Massacre."

Ten days of outright war erupted and President Woodrow Wilson dispatched the U.S. Army to the area. That settled the violence, and negotiations ended the strike in December 1914. It was only a partial victory for the union, because the UMW wasn't recognized as the miners' representative. Instead, a "company union" was created that was supposed to represent the workers. That plan was applauded at the time as a great compromise, but such "company unions" are one reason that even today in Colorado coal country you're likely to see baseball caps that read, "Guns, God, and Guts Made the UMW." A monument about 15 miles north of Trinidad off U.S. 25 commemorates the Ludlow Massacre.

Visitors to Trinidad will find a quiet town, with many well-kept 19th-century buildings and lovely parks. In the center of town is **Kit Carson Park,** where a larger-than-life bronze statue of Kit and his horse rides forever toward the Mountain Branch of the Santa Fe Trail.

The Colorado Historical Society operates the **Trinidad History Museum** (300 East Main Street; 719-846-7217) downtown, which includes the 1870 two-story Baca House, the 1882 brick Bloom House, and the fascinating Santa Fe Trail Museum.

■ HIGHWAY OF LEGENDS   *map pages 176–177, C/D-8/9*

If you've come to the San Luis Valley from the south, arriving at Trinidad on I-25, take the Highway of Legends (Colorado 12) on a drive through desert, mountain, and plain. Beginning at Trinidad, it loops around to the west through the towns of Segundo and Monument Park, over Cucharas Pass to Cuchara, in the San Isabel National Forest, then on to La Veta before arriving at Walsenburg farther north on I-25. (Needless to say, the drive is equally delightful if you're driving from Walsenburg south to Trinidad.)

GREAT OUTDOORS

Colorado's expansive wildlands, from desert to mountain to plain, offer almost too much to do, to see, to hear:

▸ The splash of color as a pheasant bursts from a row of yellow-dead corn and shoots into the sky.

▸ The solitude of an untouched mountain valley in full summer bloom, where the only sounds are the faint rattle of aspen leaves, feet crunching on the narrow path, and barely audible mumbles about finding God's country left the way He designed it.

▸ The crackles and small pops of a campfire and its glowing coals, sending a small circle of light into the surrounding wall of pine trees, beyond which is nothing but quiet darkness.

▸ The grunts and gulps of thin air needed to make a conquering yelp at the top of a 14,000-foot peak.

▸ The slight swish of fishing line as it slices the air and lands with a gentle plop in the middle of a rippling mountain trout stream.

▸ The sensation of softly treading through fall foliage in search of elusive deer and elk.

▸ The lapping of a seemingly gentle river against a raft that suddenly has to battle a torrent of tossing turns and shouted instructions as the water turns as white as the knuckles on the paddles.

▸ The sweet sweat of mountain bikers or cross-country skiers as they muscle their way over trails through desert and forest.

■ EXPLORING BY CAR

There are many ways to get into the backcountry. Some are as easy as driving to work, some require little more effort than shoveling snow off the sidewalk, and some are downright difficult. Let's start with the easy stuff.

A mule deer with felt-covered summertime antlers.

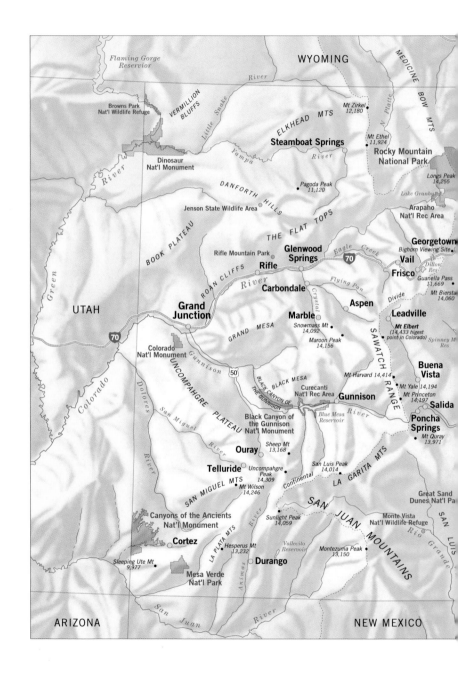

Flaming Gorge
Reservoir

WYOMING

MEDICINE BOW MTS

Browns Park
Nat'l Wildlife Refuge

VERMILLION BLUFFS

Little Snake River

River

ELKHEAD MTS

Mt Zirkel
12,180

Mt Ethel
11,924

Rocky Mountain
National Park

Steamboat Springs

Yampa River

Dinosaur
Nat'l Monument

Green River

DANFORTH HILLS

Pagoda Peak
11,120

Longs Peak
14,255

Jenson State Wildlife Area

Lake Granby

Arapaho
Nat'l Rec Area

THE FLAT TOPS

BOOK PLATEAU

Rifle Mountain Park

Glenwood
Springs

Eagle Creek

Georgetown
Bighorn Viewing Site

Vail

ROAN CLIFFS

Rifle

70

Dillon
Res.

Frisco

River

Flying Pan

Guanella Pass
11,669

UTAH

Grand
Junction

Carbondale

Crystal

Aspen

Divide

Mt Bierstadt
14,060

Leadville

Colorado
Nat'l Monument

GRAND MESA

Marble

Snowmass Mt
14,092

Maroon Peak
14,156

Mt Elbert
(14,433 higest
point in Colorado)

Spinney M
Res

70

Gunnison

SAWATCH RANGE

Green River

Colorado

Dolores

UNCOMPAHGRE

PLATEAU

50

BLACK MESA

BLACK CANYON OF
THE GUNNISON

Curecanti
Nat'l Rec Area

Gunnison

Mt Harvard 14,414

Buena
Vista

Mt Yale 14,194

Mt Princeton
14,197

Salida

San Miguel River

Black Canyon of
the Gunnison
Nat'l Monument

Blue Mesa
Reservoir

River

Poncha
Springs

Mt Quray
13,971

Sheep Mt
13,168

Ouray

Telluride

Uncompahgre
Peak
14,309

San Luis Peak
14,014

LA GARITA MTS

SAN MIGUEL MTS

Mt Wilson
14,246

Continental

Great Sand
Dunes Nat'l Pa

SAN

SAN LUIS

Canyons of the Ancients
Nat'l Monument

River

Sunlight Peak
14,059

JUAN

Monte Vista
Nat'l Wildlife Refuge

Rio Grande

Cortez

LA PLATA MTS

Hesperus Mt
13,232

Vallecito
Reservoir

Montezuma Peak
13,150

MOUNTAINS

Sleeping Ute Mt
9,977

Animas

Durango

Mesa Verde
Nat'l Park

ARIZONA

San Juan River

NEW MEXICO

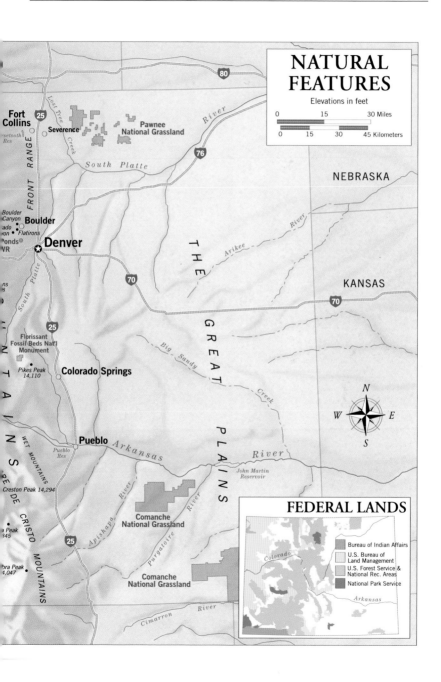

NATURAL FEATURES

Elevations in feet

0	15	30 Miles
0	15	30	45 Kilometers

Fort Collins

Severence

Pawnee National Grassland

River

80

76

South Platte

NEBRASKA

Boulder Canyon

Boulder

Flatirons

Denver

Arikee

River

FRONT RANGE

Lost Tree Creek

setooth Res

ado on

onds

NR

South Platte

70

KANSAS

70

Florissant Fossil Beds Nat'l Monument

25

Pikes Peak 14,110

Colorado Springs

THE GREAT PLAINS

Big Sandy Creek

N
W E
S

Pueblo

Pueblo Res

Arkansas

River

John Martin Reservoir

WET MOUNTAINS

Creston Peak 14,294

Apishapa River

Purgatoire River

Comanche National Grassland

a Peak 345

SANGRE DE CRISTO MOUNTAINS

25

Comanche National Grassland

bra Peak ,047

Cimarron River

FEDERAL LANDS

Colorado

Arkansas

- Bureau of Indian Affairs
- U.S. Bureau of Land Management
- U.S. Forest Service & National Rec. Areas
- National Park Service

Thanks to ranching, logging, and mining, four-wheel-drive and off-road vehicle roads lace, traverse, and loop through almost every national forest in Colorado. Because these roads don't get regular road-grader service, go to the local U.S. Forest Service or Bureau of Land Management office to pick up a map and find out which ones are still passable, and then get going. During the winter, these same thoroughfares become great snowmobile or cross-country skiing routes as well.

The best time of year for vehicle sightseeing has to be fall, when the aspen turn golden, the oak brush become copper, and the cottonwoods are converted into canopies of color, all set off by the dark green of the interspersed stands of evergreens and red-rock mountainsides.

Another tip about off-road access: you can't drive a motorized vehicle or mountain bike into any of the state's 21 designated wilderness areas. In many cases, though, you can cruise right up to the edge of the wilds and at least look in from the comfort of your rig, or maybe even open the door and take a few steps in.

National parks and monuments also have easy driving and hiking. Most have trails that allow you to get out of the car and tramp around for a couple of hours. You can get a glimpse of the scenery (Dinosaur) or take a stroll and learn something (Mesa Verde, Rocky Mountain).

■ EXPLORING ON FOOT, HORSEBACK, OR SKIS

Wilderness areas are the domain of the backpacker, horse camper, angler, and cross-country skier. You don't have to undertake a five-day outdoor expedition to enjoy a little wilderness wonderment, either. You can travel for an hour or so and watch all traces of civilization vanish in some of the state's lesser-known and less-traveled wildernesses. Or you can partake of the pedestrian-mall wilderness experience in, for instance, the Maroon Bells/Snowmass Wilderness Area outside Aspen.

Generally, the closer the wilderness is to resorts or towns, the heavier the traffic, so if it's solitude you seek, head for a wilderness area you've never heard of or one that hasn't been recommended by dozens of guidebooks and outdoor magazines. Mount Bierstadt (14,060 feet) is a good example. Go to Georgetown on I-70, drive past town to Guanella Pass, park the car, hop on the trail, and after two hours, 3 miles, and a 2,500-foot altitude gain, you are atop a 14,000-footer. "In shape" and "experienced" are key words when tackling such summits, so don't go wandering up any mountain with just a peanut-butter-and-jelly sandwich in your pocket. Get a map, bring food and water, bring a companion or two, and dress appropriately.

You shouldn't get the impression that finding a good hike is harder than the hike itself. Winter or summer, it's easy to find a trail. The national forests are laced with hiking trails, and almost without exception, every resort town has created or is creating some sort of hiking/pedestrian "experience" a stone's throw from your motel room.

Cross-country ski trails are produced when snow covers all the state's hiking trails and forest roads and trails. Most of the state's ski areas also have cross-country trails, fun in their own right and which also break the monotony of lift lines and allow skiers to stretch downhill muscles. (See "Skiing," page 222.)

Any mention of cross-country duty has to include the Tenth Mountain Hut and Trail System. Developed by members of the famed Tenth Mountain Division (of World War II), the trail and huts (actually comfy cabins) stretch from Aspen through the Leadville area, the division's old stomping grounds, and on to Vail. The trail offers a number of multiday treks through some of the most scenic mountains in the state. If you use the huts, you can ski for a day, then relax, eat a gourmet meal next to a warm wood stove, sleep in a real bed, and get up raring to go again the next day.

■ HIKING WITH KIDS

Colorado's mountains can look imposing when you have kids in tow. But there are many short, educational, and fun hikes where kids and parents can experience the outdoors together. Below are just a few of the options.

Great Sand Dunes National Park

You can turn a mountain hike into a day at the beach by frolicking in the 55 square miles of wind-swept sand dunes in the monument. Drive a little more than a mile past the park entrance and turn left into a parking lot right next to the sand. Then just let the kids romp. Remember to take plenty of water and sunscreen. *From Alamosa, drive 13 miles east on U.S. 116, then 16 miles north on U.S. 150.*

Hanging Lake Trail

This is a short, steep trail, just over a mile long. Take your time, because it's more than worth it when you reach the top. Hanging Lake is what its name implies: a body of water clinging to the mountainside. A wonderful waterfall feeds the turquoise lake. Behind that is Spouting Rock, where water shoots out of a rock. *Ten miles east of Glenwood Springs on I-70 in Glenwood Canyon.*

Molas Trail

In the heart of the San Juans, drive out of Silverton on U.S. 550 to the turn for Molas Lake and Trail, and pull into the parking lot. The trail meanders through high mountain meadows and has amazing views of such high points as the Needle Mountains. *In the San Juan Mountains.*

Petroglyph Point Trail

Almost 3 miles long, this loop trail starts about 20 miles inside the park at the museum parking area at Chapin Mesa. The trail circles a canyon and mesa that hold various ruins from the Anasazi Period, including a four-room cliff dwelling and the park's largest collection of petroglyphs (images carved into rock). *In Mesa Verde National Park; fee required.*

Ute Trail Tundra Walk

This trail starts at the top of Trail Ridge Road at the Alpine Visitors Center (see page 123) and travels up to 4 miles. This is high alpine tundra country, and it's as delicate as it is beautiful. The trail exposes hikers to the varieties of grasses, flowers, and trees growing "at the top of world"—almost 11,000 feet above sea level. *In Rocky Mountain National Park; fee required.*

■ MOUNTAIN BIKING

Mountain-bike riders also enjoy the state's trails: if you can drive it, horse it, or hike it, you can probably bike it. Anticipating the mountain-bike boom, Colorado pedaled into the craze ahead of the crowd. Volunteers and donations helped create two unique mountain-bike trail systems.

Kokopelli's Trail starts out with a taste of the best sandy desert biking experience and, for dessert, lands you in the alpine high country. The original trail was a 128-mile trek from Loma, near Grand Junction on the Western Slope, to Moab, Utah. Success spawned offshoots, more volunteers, and opportunities to tie into half a dozen other existing trails. Western Colorado and eastern Utah now have more than 1,000 miles of trails ready for knobby tires and tireless pedalers.

The Colorado Trail, on the other hand, will take you through the middle of the Rocky Mountains from Durango to Denver. You'll have to skirt some wilderness areas, and some sections are definitely not for amateurs, but with a map you can figure out how to take advantage of the trail for a quick ride or an all-out enduro.

Most of Colorado's towns are mountain-bike friendly.

A mountain-bike trek doesn't have to be an expedition, or even a dirt track experience in the high county. If you and your bike find yourselves taking a break along the Front Range there are plenty of urban bike trails that allow you to unload the bike and limber up the legs before you hit the high country.

Denver, Boulder, and Pueblo all have extensive trail systems within their city limits that take bikers along riverbanks and through parks. The state's mountain towns and resorts are also "bicycle friendly." In most resorts, mountain bikes are the preferred method of travel around town. Trail systems run along major roads and highways so you can get from here to there on your bike.

If you like long road rides, check out the trails along I-70 through the mountains. The trip up and down Vail Pass is exhilarating, and pedaling through Glenwood Canyon is breathtaking.

Oh, and remember those big hills you ski down in the winter? Some are open to mountain bikes in the summer.

For those who insist mountain bikes should only be ridden on trails in the mountains, here are a few suggested trails.

Animas Mountain Trail

Starts at the intersection of Second and Fourth Avenues in Durango and takes a moderately difficult route up the mountainside to a scenic viewpoint overlooking the Animas River Valley.

Bear Creek to Methodist Mountain

This is a tough 20-mile loop from Salida. Take County Road 108 out of town and peak out at around 9,000 feet above sea level before returning to Salida along the banks of Bear Creek and U.S. 50.

Bear Creek Road

A marked county road takes you on a gradual climb out of the middle of Telluride for 2 miles, with a lovely waterfall for your reward. Want something steeper? Try the 2.5-mile Judd Wibe Trail loop, which meanders around Cornet Creek and delivers beautiful views, and sore legs.

Boy Scout Trail

This trail in Glenwood Springs is aptly named: if you go, be prepared. The trail starts at the top of Eighth Street, just up the hill from downtown, and is a technically difficult jaunt to the top of Lookout Mountain.

Hunter Creek Trail

This trail, just outside of Aspen, is a local favorite. You can start up Smuggler Road and cut over into the Hunter Creek Valley, a sprawling expanse of national forest land that makes you forget the high-dollar glitter of Aspen.

Off the road and down a creek.

Lenhardy Cutoff

This route sends you on a smooth ride into the backcountry on County Road 371, which takes off from the town of Buena Vista. Not tough enough? Try the advanced Buena Vista to Mount Princeton loop. Take County Road 306 out of town to County Road 345, find the trail markers for the Colorado Trail, and get ready to climb more than 2,000 vertical feet before returning to town on County Road 321.

Peaks Trail

Linking Frisco to Breckenridge, this moderate climb through the hills starts at the intersection of Main Street and I-70 in Frisco and delivers you to the base of the Breckenridge Ski Area.

Tabeguache Trail

For a taste of high-desert biking, try this trail, which starts a couple of miles up the road to the Colorado National Monument. After some difficult pedaling, it leads you all the way to Montrose through desert scrub country.

Washout Road

This more relaxed trip starts north of Poncha Springs at the intersection of Colorado 285 and County Road 140. Turn up County Road 250 until you hit Forest Service Road 5630 (Washout Road), which leads you back to Colorado 285.

So, what are you waiting for? Grab your helmet and water bottle and hit the road.

■ CLIMBING

Colorado is full of mountains, so it's only natural that people will be climbing them. Although rock climbing has experienced a huge leap in popularity in the past few years, it's plain stupid to hop out of bed one morning, buy a rope, some carabiners, and rock bolts, and try to scale a cliff.

But if you want to get a good look at what serious rock climbing entails, Colorado has several spots where climbing is also a spectator sport. (Experienced rock climbers are a tight-knit community; I won't insult them by trying to describe Colorado's more challenging rock and ice routes.)

A quick trip outside of Boulder will lead you to some of the best, and most popular, rock-climbing areas in the state. The **Flatiron Mountains** are home to three renowned climbing areas: Boulder Canyon (a few miles west of town on

Colorado 19), Flagstaff Mountain (west on Baseline Road), and Eldorado Canyon (6 miles south of Boulder on Colorado 19, then 3 miles on Colorado 170).

At almost any time of day, when the weather is nice, you can watch climbers tackling routes up faces and around overhangs. The most spectacular ascents are long "traditional" climbs, where climbers use ropes, anchors, and belays to get up the rock.

Rifle Mountain Park has come into its own as one of the nation's top sport-climbing areas. It's located about 13 miles north of Rifle. The park has become so popular that many of the country's top climbers have moved to Rifle to take advantage of the area's seemingly endless number of challenging routes up rock walls and over boulders. *Take Colorado 13 north to the turnoff to Colorado 325.*

For those who think ice is nice, **Ouray** can't be beat. When winter descends on this high mountain town, ice climbers grab ice tools, strap on crampons, and ascend the numerous frozen waterfalls just minutes from town. Ouray throws a three-day **Ice Festival** (970-325-4981) and competition every January, which gives interested observers a chance to see top-notch ice jockeys chop and clomp their way up spectacular stretches of treacherous ice.

■ WHITEWATER RAFTING

Any river that runs high enough to float a good-size log probably also hosts some sort of raft, kayak, or canoe. All the rivers mentioned under "Reservoir Fishing and Boating" (see page 212) are regularly rafted and floated (and fished while floating) by individuals or by rafting companies that provide the raft, guide (complete with bad jokes), paddles, or any combination thereof. The following rivers go beyond just a quiet little float. They have either wet and wild whitewater rapids or serene scenery, or both, which makes a memorable trip.

Green River

In the northwestern corner of the state, the Green River affords a great view of Dinosaur National Monument from the bottom up. It's hard to believe there is a runable river anywhere near this high desert country. Once you get onto the river and peer up at the sheer dusty canyon walls, you forget the mesas and sink deep into the feeling of being surrounded by an amazing act of nature. You will have to go through federal floating-permit hassles, but the trip is worth it. *Call the local National Park Service office at 970-374-3000 for permit information.*

Heading out in a raft on Colorado's many rivers is often a thrill-a-minute experience, and kayaking them can be downright exhilarating.

Colorado River

For most of its run through Colorado, the Colorado River is pretty docile, if not downright mellow. There is one section, though, that gives you a good splash and stuns with startling scenery: where the Colorado follows I-70 and cuts through Glenwood Canyon. This amazing granite-lined, tree-sparkled slash in the earth reaches about 2,000 feet above the river. A Rocky Mountain bighorn sheep or startling peak view is a possible surprise around every twisting bend.

Gunnison River

You need to trust your guide or be a serious river rat to run the Gunnison River through the Black Canyon National Monument. The towering canyon walls are black granite, and you can lose yourself, your boat, and your booties as the river crashes down one of the steeper drops in the state. This is not a rookie's river. You can only get down to it or up out of it at a few points. Again, federal regulations rule, but getting the right to float is the easy part; staying afloat is the challenge.

Crystal River

Between Marble and Carbondale, the Crystal River rolls along as a docile little creek alongside Colorado 133 for ten months of the year. When spring runoff hits, however, the Crystal becomes one of the state's most exhilarating and challenging kayaking trips. It's fast, narrow, and full of whitewater that is more than enough of a skills test for the best boaters.

South Platte River

The small town of Fairplay, just over an hour's drive from Denver on Colorado 285, turns into rafting central every summer, thanks to the South Platte River. The South Platte winds its way in a grand loop, heading south, then east, then north, and provides miles of rafting and scenery. Other put-ins along the South Platte include Hartsel, Lake George, and Deckers, all strung out along the river on U.S. 24 and Colorado 67.

Arkansas River

Just over the Continental Divide from the South Platte, the Arkansas also has great whitewater and mountain scenery. Trips can start from Buena Vista, on U.S. 24, or Salida. From Salida, the river follows U.S. 50 through stunning canyon country all the way to the Royal Gorge, just outside of Cañon City.

■ RESERVOIR FISHING AND BOATING

Every sizeable Colorado stream or lake with ready access is ripe for fishing. The **Division of Wildlife** (303-297-1192) maintains fish hatcheries, which allow it to keep fresh loads of fish frolicking in wild waters. A slight dose of whirling disease, which comes from a bacterial parasite that deforms and kills small fingerling trout, has complicated the fish-stocking job, however; in some cases, it has reduced the number of fish stocked in various areas.

Although the Division of Wildlife is still supplanting existing stocks of fish with "stockers," it is also altering its regulations concerning bag limits or catch-and-release rules, sometimes on a stream-by-stream or lake-by-lake basis. Check with the Division of Wildlife for the latest regulations before heading out. Luckily, plenty of fish still lurk in the state's lakes and streams, so you don't have to worry much about whether you'll fish on your trip; just decide what kind of fish you want to catch and how you want to catch them.

Lake fishing has its followers, and it's easy to see why. Just bring your gear, a camp chair, and a cooler of beer, then cast your line, settle down, reel 'em in, go back to camp, and start lying.

All of the lakes listed below can accommodate some sort of floating craft, but there are two monster reservoirs that give you a chance to run your motor out of gas: Blue Mesa and Dillon Reservoirs. Check them out if driving is your thing.

Blue Mesa Reservoir
A short drive on U.S. 50 east of Gunnison, Blue Mesa is the biggest body of water in the state and, come winter, the biggest ice cube in the state. As with the other lakes mentioned, those with the proper gear (some say lack of intelligence is the most important) can brave the below-zero temperatures, dig holes in the ice, set up a camp chair or ice-fishing shack, unscrew the thermos of hot chocolate or other antifreeze, and begin.

Dillon Reservoir
Saddled between Dillon and Frisco on I-70, Dillon Reservoir offers all manner of motor- and sail-propelled boating.

Colorado fly-fishing.

Grand Mesa Mountain
There are hundreds of lakes, mostly small and unnamed, on the Grand Mesa just west of Grand Junction.

Horsetooth Reservoir
Just west of Fort Collins is Horsetooth Reservoir, with miles of shoreline and mountain views that might make you want to abandon your camp chair and cooler for a walk in the woods.

John Martin Reservoir
On the plains bordering U.S. 50 outside Las Animas, John Martin Reservoir has a long shoreline.

Pueblo Reservoir
Pueblo Reservoir is almost within the city limits.

Spinney Mountain Reservoir
A couple of hours of beautiful mountain driving to Hartsel from either Cañon City or Colorado Springs will deliver you to Middle Park and Spinney Mountain Reservoir, which yields some of the biggest fish in the state.

Steamboat Lake
Nestled up north right under Hahns Peak, and Lake Granby, Steamboat Lake is located at the edge of Rocky Mountain National Park.

Vallecito Reservoir
This is a good-size pond surrounded by pines and San Juan scenery west of Durango.

■ STREAM FISHING

This sport brings out anglers of a different cast, so to speak. Stream fishers actually prowl up and down a riverbank, fighting through cottonwood stands, willows, and oak brush to find the right ripple, the gentle swell, the slow rolling flat spot that might harbor the rainbow or brown trout they seek.

Gold-medal trout streams, on the other hand, were set aside for those who eschew such feeding frenzies and prefer the craft involved in tempting trout with merely a fly or lure. In these streams, respect for your prey is integral to the catch-and-release concept, which places the fish fight above the fish fry.

The catch-and-release policies in place on these gold-medal waters have the added benefit of sparing the populations of mature fish from the sometimes devastating effects of whirling disease, which generally only strikes baby fish. Once fish grow up in catch-and-release water, they can look forward to a long life, interrupted only by momentary tussles with anglers.

Because the streams are home to populations of full-grown trout, they continue to offer outstanding fishing; they feature stout trout that have matured over the years into hefty, "better take a picture or no one will believe me" behemoths.

Having said that, what all these rivers have in common is nearby access to less restrictive fishing, so you can drop off the fly-fishers, go a couple of miles, break out the marshmallows and camp chairs, and abide by regular river regulations. Thus, all types of fishing fans can hook up and wade into their preferred watery environment without having to break up families, end long-standing friendships, or otherwise turn the bait bunch against the fly and lure lovers.

Portions of 10 rivers in the state have received the gold-medal designation, and they're scattered all over the place; this is a regional sampling of gold medalists.

Colorado River

Before it becomes a wide slug of water, the Colorado River starts out as a pretty innocuous creek in Grand County. About 9 miles of the Colorado River is golden between Kremmling and Hot Sulphur Springs along U.S. 40.

Frying Pan River

You can hook two gold-medal streams in one day by visiting the Frying Pan River, golden from Ruedi Reservoir downstream through a narrow, red-rock canyon until it hits Basalt, and the Roaring Fork River, which turns gold as it comes out of Aspen along Colorado 82 and continues onward to Glenwood Springs.

Gunnison River

Tumbling out of Black Canyon and shifting gears into a gold-medal fishing playground, the Gunnison rolls and twists its way down to the North Fork.

North Platte River

Just west of Walden and accessible from Colorado 14 east or west, the North Platte runs golden all the way to Wyoming.

South Platte River
Down south a bit, a number of stretches of the South Platte are gold-medal material as the river makes its way from reservoir to reservoir. This is a favorite with Front Range urbanites. Traveling for an hour or so, you can go from being in a traffic jam to being knee-deep in a great fishing spot.

Rio Grande
In the San Luis Valley, the Rio Grande is designated gold medal for a couple of miles beyond its junction with the South Fork.

■ HUNTING

When fall arrives in Colorado, the state's mountains are transformed from brooding green giants into sparkling towers of red, orange, and yellow. But people who venture into the woods in the fall are also likely to see another color: blaze orange. This is the color worn by big-game hunters, who flock to the state by the thousands every fall to stalk deer, elk, antelope, black bear, and moose.

From August to November, big-game hunters are in the woods, armed with bows and arrows, rifles, and muzzleloaders. Hunting seasons vary according to the species, the weapon in hand, and the location of the hunt. Generally speaking, the state's national forests are home to herds of deer and elk and more than a few black bears. Antelope tend to cluster in the northern regions and the Piceance Basin, in Colorado's northwestern corner.

A number of areas consistently draw hunters in large numbers because the hunting is consistently good—sometimes trophy class. The San Juan Mountains, from Durango north through the Rio Grande and Uncompahgre National Forests, have produced more trophy deer and elk than any other region in the state.

The "Blaze Orange Corridor," which begins in the Gunnison area and runs northward through Glenwood Springs and Rifle and on to Meeker and Craig, draws the largest number of hunters. The White River National Forest, which stretches from the Flattops, just north of Glenwood Springs, to the edge of Meeker, is home to huge herds of both deer and elk. There are plenty of forest service roads, making access fairly easy, and there are campsites.

TR, BEARS, AND TEDDY BEARS

An April, 2, 1905, story on the front page of the *Denver Post* declared that "President Roosevelt is planning to eclipse his previous reputation for daring and will try to kill every bear he gets in Colorado on his coming trip with a hunting knife, instead of a rifle."

As it turned out, President Theodore Roosevelt did kill some black bears during his 1905 Colorado trip, but not with a hunting knife. And his love of big-game hunting was not the only reason for his visit. The forests through which Roosevelt trekked were at that time part of the White River National Land Reserve, created by President Benjamin Harrison in 1891, and Roosevelt wanted to include it in the system of national forests that remains one of the most appreciated legacies of his presidency.

As the president readied for the hunt, his staff saw to the installation of phone and telegraph lines, turning the elegant Hotel Colorado in Glenwood Springs into the "Little White House of the United States."

The president, meanwhile, picked out a nondescript Cayuse pony named Possum, climbed on a well-worn saddle, and let a scruffy hunting terrier named Skip follow alongside. Before long he was headed toward a tent camp pitched at elevation 9,000 feet in the forest south of Silt.

One member of Roosevelt's staff was then assigned the task of climbing on a horse every day at the Hotel Colorado, tracking down the president, and keeping him up to date on national and international affairs. On May 5, Roosevelt came out of the backcountry for a brief stay in the Hotel Colorado that, thanks to a rag-tag cloth bear, became almost as important as his hunting trip.

There are a couple of versions of the teddy-bear myth. One has it that Teddy's daughter Alice was admiring the bears brought back by the hunters and decided to name one Teddy. A second version claims that the maids at the Hotel Colorado stitched together a crude little stuffed bear named Teddy and presented it to the president. Anyhow, a little marketing and hype later, the teddy bear was enthroned as an indispensable children's toy—a position it still holds.

When he was finished, Roosevelt took back to Washington the dog, Skip, of whom he'd grown fond on the trip. He also brought back tales of having shot his first bear two days into the trip, and bragged that the rest of his entourage bagged 10 black bears and three lynx.

Meeker and Craig are good launching points for hunters trying their luck in the Piceance Basin, which contains some of the nation's largest mule deer and elk herds and a substantial population of antelope. A peek into the historic **Meeker Hotel** (560 Main Street) reveals the depth of the region's wild bounty; a veritable herd of big-game animal heads is mounted on its walls.

Bird hunters also flock to the state, shotguns in hand, to test their marksmanship against fast and high-flying targets. Waterfowl, primarily geese and colorful ducks, splash down on both sides of the Continental Divide. On the eastern side of the mountains, the Central Flyway is the waterfowl conduit. The Pacific Flyway keeps birds circling the Western Slope looking for a safe landing.

Game birds such as rails, quail, grouse, and pheasants are also scattered across the state. On the Western Slope, the fertile farmland around Delta, Olatha, Montrose, and Paonia has traditionally been good bird country, especially for pheasant. The eastern plains also provide good cover and food for game birds, with Fort Morgan and Sterling, in the far northeast corner of the state, offering a good chance for pheasant and quail.

Hunting in Colorado is governed by an extensive set of rules and regulations, which change almost yearly to manage herd sizes and otherwise optimize the health of big- and small-game populations. *Colorado Division of Wildlife; 303-297-1192.*

■ BIGHORN SHEEP

It's the quintessential Colorado wildlife scene, and one not soon forgotten by those fortunate enough to see it: hundreds of feet above a canyon floor, a group of Rocky Mountain bighorn sheep in single file delicately picks its way up the barren canyon wall. As the rams, ewes, and lambs scale a nearly vertical granite face, they alternate between gentle, precisely placed steps and adventurous, high-energy bounds, which send loose rocks clattering into the canyon below. The bighorns' climb looks impossible, because the human eye cannot detect the minuscule toeholds and ledges that form their uphill trail. When the group tops out, a mature ram stands still for a moment, his sturdy figure and curled horns appearing in silhouette against the skyline.

Such a scene delights wildlife enthusiasts, from hunters to photographers, but few would have the opportunity to see it today if not for man's "meddling" with nature. Originally plentiful, bighorns, like deer and elk, were decimated by the 1880s, victims of the influx of hungry miners, who availed themselves of every nook

These domestic sheep, being herded in the San Juan Mountains, are distant cousins of Colorado's famous bighorns.

and mountainous cranny. At the beginning of the 20th century, there were no sport-game hunting seasons in the state, and only one surviving bighorn herd, near Tarryall, west of Colorado Springs.

In 1945, Colorado launched an effort to reestablish bighorns throughout the state, trapping and moving about 1,800 Tarryall bighorns to several new areas. By 1953, because of transplants from the Tarryall herd, the state's population of bighorns had risen to about 3,000 animals, scattered in enough regions to allow for the first bighorn hunting season since 1887. Transplants, disease control, and other management techniques have enabled the current bighorn population to reach about 8,000.

Nearly 80 different bighorn herds are scattered throughout Colorado's high country, ranging from the 20-head group in Waterton Canyon, outside Denver, to the 300 bighorns roaming the Collegiate Range. Bighorns have also been reintroduced to Rocky Mountain National Park, Dinosaur National Park, Mesa Verde, and the Colorado National Monument.

As the number of bighorns has grown, so has the sale of bighorn hunting licenses. The fees for these go to support the transplant program.

As with most big-game animals, habitat loss and development pressure are serious threats to Colorado's bighorns. Because the animals usually roam above the timberline in generally inaccessible terrain during the summer, humankind's activities haven't had a significant impact on their summer range. The winter range in the lower elevations, though, is a different story. A herd of bighorns once wintered on the cliffs and among the apple orchards of the Vail Valley, for example. As soon as ski runs and condos started going up, most of the bighorns fled.

The bighorns' tight-knit social structure also makes them susceptible to devastating outbreaks of disease, such as lungworm and other bacterial infections. One such outbreak decimated the Tarryall herd, which fell from 3,000 animals to 150. Despite the various threats to Colorado's bighorn sheep, a combination of the transplant program, limited hunting, and consistent disease control should allow the state's bighorns to flourish.

■ WHERE TO WATCH WILDLIFE

A full range of Rocky Mountain wildlife can be seen throughout Colorado. Although most species hide from humans by inhabiting the state's millions of acres of national forests and parks, there are a number of places where, if you get out of your car, open your eyes, and look in the right direction, you'll have a pretty fair chance of seeing wildlife. Below are some of the most accessible areas for watching wildlife.

Georgetown, Rocky Mountains
Rocky Mountain bighorn sheep, the state animal, prance and parade among the rocky crags directly above I-70 near Georgetown, about 50 miles west of Denver. The Bighorn Viewing Site (Exit 228) is equipped with high-powered telescopes and information about these nimble cliff dwellers. A herd of about 200 animals can usually be seen all year.

Jensen State Wildlife Area, Western Slope
Between Meeker and Craig in northwestern Colorado, this wildlife area is home to elk, deer, blue grouse, red-tailed hawks, rabbits, coyotes, and pheasant, depending on the season.

Rocky Mountain Arsenal, Front Range
For decades, the U.S. Army manufactured nerve gases and other high-potency killing devices on a small portion of this huge federal reserve, in northwestern Denver. In 1992, all the land that wasn't part of the munitions manufacturing became the Two Ponds National Wildlife Refuge. The area supports hundreds of species, including deer, bald eagles and other birds, and dozens of other small animals. *Between Quebec Street and Buckley Road at 112 Rocky Mountain Arsenal; 303-289-0232.*

San Luis Valley, Southern Colorado
Twenty thousand sandhill cranes invade the Monte Vista National Wildlife Refuge during their spring migration through the San Luis Valley. Some endangered whooping cranes usually accompany them. Bus tours and other events mark the happening, which usually takes place in February and March.

Severence, Front Range
This town of just over a hundred people, about 10 miles north of Fort Collins, hosts as many as 50,000 snow and Canada geese for the winter. It's pretty easy to spot birds in the adjoining fields and farmlands.

S K I I N G

Here's a sure bet. After a day on the slopes, walk (or limp, if necessary) into the nearest bar. Settle down next to some likely looking locals and ask what contributions their particular town made to ski history. Then watch it fly. Odds are ten to one you will be snowed under with colorful tales, bits of truth, a little exaggeration, and some downright lies about how this place, or the ridge just down the road, is where it all started.

Out will come stories of miners on their "snowshoes," racing down a slope with a long pole behind them serving as a rudder. You'll hear a long list of people who "first" thought that Colorado's towering mountains were the perfect ski hills. Technologically speaking, there will be reminders of how an ingenious rope/pulley system was used to lug people up an infant ski hill; or how early ski lift towers were built by muscle and guts; or how someone tore the engine out of a Buick and jury-rigged it to primitive cable lifts to create the first modern ski lift.

Listen intently, nod your head a lot, laugh now and then, and agree wholeheartedly that other towns' claims are a load of baloney, and you might end up drinking for free all night.

■ EARLY DAYS

So, who's telling the truth about the beginning of Colorado's huge, internationally famous ski industry? Well, actually, almost everyone.

Let's start with God—or, rather, a messenger of God named Father John Dyer, who strapped on a pair of skis and figured out how to operate them well enough to avoid meeting his maker. By 1864, the Methodist minister was delivering the Word and the mail to the hardscrabble mining camps in South Park and the soon-to-boom town of Leadville.

It's hard to refute any story about half-drunk gold or silver miners strapping barrel staves to their feet and scooting across the snow. It was probably more fun than dancing to the pounding of a pickled pianist with the few well-worn women in town. Many of Colorado's mining camps and towns created ski clubs in the late 1800s.

Primitive skis also came in handy for cowboys, miners, and mail carriers who couldn't let snow deter them from their rounds, even in the late 1800s. Anywhere

Colorado skiing has come a long way since its primitive days.

snow measured belly deep to a tall mule, skis were part of the Colorado gold and silver scene. From then on, though, things get a little harder to nail down. The definition of "skiing development" is loose enough to include skiing with fellow miners, cutting down a few trees that were in the way of early skiers, developing specialized machinery, and designating entire mountains just for skiing.

The following is a cursory glance at the start of recreational skiing in Colorado. Remember, though, that it's not comprehensive enough to base a bar brawl on. Just keep smiling and nodding your head.

The first star of Colorado skiing was Norseman Carl Howelsen, a champion ski jumper who eventually landed in Steamboat Springs. In 1914, Howelsen organized a winter festival (which survives to this day), constructed a ski jump on Howelsen Hill, and demonstrated his talents to the awed locals. The **Steamboat Winter Carnival** (970-879-0882) remains a celebratory reminder of the town's skiing history and of Carl Howelsen, the man who put Steamboat on the skiing map.

At about the same time, the scene shifted to an unlikely ski town, Denver, and an unusual ski hill, Genesee Mountain. A number of ski clubs decided that trips into the mountains were as risky as actually skiing, so they brought the skiing closer to home on Genesee Mountain, just west of town. They cut a skinny little ski run from the trees, built a jump for the adventuresome, and, just like that, Denver became a pioneer ski town. Throughout the first 20 years of the 20th century, ski clubs in Boulder and Colorado Springs also trekked to the nearest snow-covered hill and plowed down the thing.

Ironically, the Depression was when skiing really went commercial. With the economy in tatters, spending a Rocky Mountain winter day with sticks strapped to your feet, being dragged up a mountain by a rope, and then heading downhill (often falling face-first into the snow) was one hell of a good time. At least that's what people thought in Aspen, Breckenridge, Steamboat Springs, Wolf Creek Pass, Monarch Pass, Glenwood Springs, Estes Park, Allenspark, Grand Lake, Creede, Cumbres Pass, Berthoud Pass (which installed the state's first rope tow, in 1937), Hot Sulphur Springs, and Glen Cove. All had some sort of rudimentary ski area operating before World War II.

But those efforts all paled in comparison with what was happening at Winter Park, which was destined to become the state's first truly commercial ski area.

When the Moffatt Tunnel was completed in 1927, the Denver and Rio Grande Railroad ran right past some very enticing ski hills. In 1938, the city of Denver annexed the area and developed the unnamed trails into the Winter Park Ski Area.

THE FIRST SKIERS

So far as anyone can find out, skiing came into being in Norway. A cave drawing from about 2000 BC, near the Arctic Circle in that land, shows a man skiing down hill on twelve-foot skis with a balance pole, knees slightly bent. The oldest surviving pieces of skis are 4,500 years old. The pragmatic purpose of the ski, obviously, was to enable people to move efficiently and quickly through snow-covered country impassable, or nearly so, to the unaided human foot. Skis allowed snowbound country folk to visit neighbors in the dead of winter or to go to the nearest village for company, supplies, a mug of brew, the latest news or, maybe, some romancing with a lusty town wench (women's lib was late coming to the harsh winter climates of Scandinavia). And, more important, skis endowed the wintertime hunter with a mobility as magical as jet airplanes to modern man, potentially as lethal as the horse to footbound soldiers. However, though people in several parts of our world have been using skis for transportation, sport and, alas, war for more than a hundred years, the human beast is a fun-loving creature who eventually discovered how to turn a cheap, simple tool into an expensive, complex toy.

Skiing emigrated to both Europe and America about 1850, but around 1960 its expansion took off with a rush, changing this sporting activity into a social event with economic and political implications as far removed from moving efficiently through snow as snow is from smog.

—Dick Dorworth, "The Ski. The Tool," *Mountain Gazette,* 1978

Miners, cabin fever, and "snowshoes" got Colorado skiing going downhill. (Colorado Historical Society)

Using donations, city and federal funds, and volunteers and laborers from Depression-era government agencies, work went quickly. The new T-bar lift was a quantum leap over the old rope tows. By 1941, runs, lifts, buildings, and skiers were all over the place, thanks in part to the famous "ski trains" that delivered skiers right to the slopes. The **Winter Park Ski Train** (303-296-4754) still operates today.

■ CHOOSING A SKI RESORT

Skiers can sample three distinct skiing experiences in Colorado: mega-resorts, historic hideaways, and hometown hills. They can also decide, by their choice of resort, whether seared ahi or tuna salad will be on the bill of fare.

Proximity to the urbanites in Denver and along the Front Range made the eastern slope of the Rockies the logical place to build mega-resorts. These resorts run the gamut, from full-scale, planned-resort complexes that can accommodate a

(above) Skiers in the late 1940s disembark from the ski train at Winter Park. (Colorado Historical Society) (opposite) Cross-country skiing in the present tense.

destination skier flying in from Tulsa to the great ski hills with parking lots to accommodate the Denver accountant who moved from Tulsa to be an hour's drive from great skiing.

Scattered deeper throughout the Rockies and farther from Denver are the historic hideaways. These ski resorts mix their mining heritage with champagne powder to entice destination skiers. Flung far and wide, from north to south and everyplace in between, are the hometown hills. These unpretentious ski areas, usually miles from the nearest town, feel like mom-and-pop operations compared with the big resorts, but you may fall in love with their simplicity, friendliness, and miles of uncrowded ski runs, which give most people a skiing day just as challenging, diverse, and delightful as you'd find anywhere else.

Probably the best way to start planning your ski vacation is with a copy of the ski guide published by Colorado Ski Country USA. The group is a nonprofit skiing promotional outfit and the guide will provide an avalanche of good information about all the ski areas and amenities they offer. *Colorado Ski Country USA, 1507 Blake Street, Denver, CO 80202; 303-837-0793; www.skicolorado.com.*

Ticket price ranges are listed in this book as:
inexpensive = under $35; **moderate** = $35–$50; **expensive** = over $50.

■ VAIL: THE ULTIMATE MEGA-RESORT

The Irish Baron Lord Gore's hunting party probably peeked into the Vail Valley in the 1850s. All they saw were deer, elk, and buffalo, which they killed in prodigious numbers and left to rot. It would take more discerning eyes and about 110 years to see the valley's potential as king of the "planned unit development" approach to Colorado ski areas.

The eyes in question belonged to Earl Eaton, a uranium prospector, and Pete Seibert, a former Tenth Mountain vet, who needed only one look at the valley's mountains to envision a great ski area. By the late 1950s and early 1960s, ski areas were cropping up almost as fast as the gold camps of a century earlier, so the two got crafty. Instead of shouting to the rooftops about this mother lode, they quietly applied for a forest area ski permit, formed the innocent-sounding Trans Montane Rod and Gun Club, and started buying land.

There was nothing at the base of the mountain, so Vail was planned and created with a historic aura. Victorian mining towns were a dime a dozen, so the architects went further back into history and drew up tidy plans based on European resorts:

Olympic medalist Billy Kidd plows through powder at Steamboat Springs.

the whole place was done in Tyrolean style. With plans stipulating the location for every tree, park bench, and ski rack, the entire resort was built in one year. Vail opened in 1962, with the snowless curse that seems to afflict many new ski resorts. Never fear. A Ute medicine man was called; once he arrived and did his dance, chants, and gyrations, the snow came. Strange, but true.

Vail then set out to become the Rockies' most famous resort, by means of a mega-promotional campaign that, by some estimates, cost more than the construction of the resort itself. It worked. Then came the clincher: the resignation of President Richard Nixon. Vailites forgot politics and jumped for joy: one of their own, Gerald Ford, was now president. As a congressman, Ford had vacationed in Vail for years. Now he was the big cheese and Vail was his Western White House. The whole town basked in the presidential glow.

Vail's success drew corporate attention. Ralston, Quaker Oats, Federated Stores, Sears Roebuck, Gillette Holdings, and other corporate giants have all owned a piece of Vail, making the resort a part of corporate skullduggery elsewhere.

Corporate cash covered every inch of the valley with golf courses and condos, and made Vail a year-round resort; summers were full of enticing events in a town surrounded by millions of acres of national forest. **Beaver Creek,** the exclusive ski mountain and development just down the road, repeated the success. Again, every shrub and condo was placed by design (except for the trailer court you pass on the way to the slopes).

A bit of reality arrived in the late 1980s, when the town of Vail discovered a glaring omission: no cemetery, presumably because the planners didn't think people would want to be planted permanently in a town with no roots. The roots have grown, though. The town of Vail (not Vail Inc.) has plotted the new cemetery, which is open to both long-time residents and condo owners seeking eternal rest under the snow they loved.

■ **VAIL TODAY**

You can't miss Vail if you're driving on I-70. The town, with its original Tyrolean-style core, has been supplemented by bigger and newer hotels and commercial areas. The ski runs are right off the road. Indeed, the hardest part of a Vail vacation may just be the two-hour drive from Denver. Once you get off the highway, the town and its businesses take over. Park your car in the parking garages and prepare to be shuttled to and fro. You can ride from motel to ski lift to restaurant to shopping areas, and back again, day and night.

The place works. The snow gets plowed; the trash gets dumped; the shuttles run on time. It's clean. The lifts are fast and plentiful. The people are friendly. Then there's the snow: standard-issue Colorado white gold, especially in the back bowls, which hold more runs than you can cover in a three-day weekend. Vail/Beaver Creek remains the first, and still probably one of the best, of the planned ski resorts.

Vail Mountain

Box 7, Vail, CO 81658; 970-476-5601 or 800-427-8216; snow report, 800-427-8216. 100 miles west of Denver on I-70.

Terrain: 193 trails on 5,289 acres: Front side: 32% beginner, 36% intermediate, 32% advanced; Backside bowls: intermediate and expert only.

Lifts: One gondola, 14 high-speed quad chairs, one fixed-grip quad chair, three triple chairs, five double chairs, nine surface lifts.

Snowmaking: 380 acres.

Vertical drop: 3,450 feet (1,052 meters).

Ticket prices: Expensive.

Facilities: Rental equipment and lessons; child care; disabled skiing, call 970-479-3264.

Dining: Fourteen restaurants, ranging from full service to hot-dog shacks, strewn across the mountain and at base facilities.

Accommodations: Vail central reservations, 800-525-2257.

Snowboard facilities: Two terrain parks, two halfpipes, numerous snowboard-only runs.

Cross-country skiing: 19 miles (30 kilometers) of groomed trails.

Beaver Creek

Box 7, Vail, CO 81658; 970-949-5750 or 800-859-8242; snow report, 800-427-8216.

Terrain: 146 trails on 1,625 acres: 23% beginner, 43% intermediate, 34% advanced.

Lifts: Six high-speed quads, three triple chairs, four double chairs, one surface lift.

Snowmaking: 550 acres.

Vertical drop: 4,040 feet (1,232 meters).

Ticket prices: Expensive.

Facilities: Rental equipment and lessons; child care; snowcat excursions.

Dining: Five restaurants, ranging from cafeteria to gourmet, on the mountain and at base lodges.

Accommodations: See Vail, above.

Snowboard facilities: three terrain parks, three halfpipes.

Cross-country skiing: 19 miles (30 kilometers) of groomed trails on Beaver Creek Mountain.

■ ASPEN

In 1938, Elizabeth Paepke visited Aspen and fell in love with the charming, if somewhat dilapidated, old buildings that survived the silver boom. People were being hauled up Ajax Mountain in "the Roche," a 3,000-foot boat tow designed by famed Swiss mountaineer Andre Roche. The mountain was already hosting a number of regional and national ski races.

The war put everything on hold, but in 1945, Elizabeth brought her husband, Walter, to Aspen. He looked at the ski hill and Victorian town, and decided this was the place for a world-class resort. Unlike many other skiing visionaries, Paepke had the money, education, and drive to make it happen. He started buying land, gave away paint to spruce up the town, and tapped Austrian-born skier Friedl Pfeifer and distinguished architect Herbert Bayer to turn his plans into reality.

Paepke's Container Corporation of America, which revolutionized the cardboard box business, made him a wealthy man. But he still needed some investors, and they signed on gladly: hotel magnate Conrad Hilton; Paul Nitze, Paepke's brother-in-law and later secretary of the Navy; and D. R. C. (Darcy) Brown, a local who retained extensive family holdings in the area. The Forest Service quickly finished the paperwork, two lifts were built, Ajax was renamed Aspen Mountain, and in 1946 the locals held the first Roche Cup on their new ski hill.

The January 11, 1947, grand opening included the U.S. Army Band, the governor, the Tenth Mountain Division Color Guard, dozens of notables—and, unfortunately, no snow in Aspen itself. Luckily, there was plenty of snow at 11,300 feet, where the lifts topped out, and the celebration was a success.

In 1950, Aspen claimed its place among the world's best ski hills when it hosted the Federation Internationale de Ski biennial world championships. The world's best ski racers descended on Aspen for the event and proclaimed Aspen Mountain one helluva ride. Aspen the ski town was on its way.

But Paepke, with his classical education at Chicago's Latin School and Yale, wanted more than a ski resort. The Athenian ideal of a fit body and cultivated mind was the ultimate goal. Skiing pretty much took care of the body, so in 1949 Paepke went to work on the mind. That year was the 200th birthday of the German poet, philosopher, and statesman Johann Wolfgang von Goethe, and Paepke planned to celebrate that birthday in Aspen. He invited the world's foremost philosophers and thinkers to town for "contemplation of the noblest works of man," in Paepke's words. He convinced the noted humanitarian Albert Schweitzer to attend, along with pianist and composer Arthur Rubenstein, opera singer Dorothy Maynor, philosopher Mortimer Adler, and conductor Dimitri Mitropoulos and his Minneapolis Symphony. The event was stimulating, to say the least, and put Aspen on the world's cultural map.

Ski developments and the town kept pace with the intellectual rampage. New runs and lifts were added, making Aspen one of the most challenging ski hills in the

Skiers descend between tall evergreen trees on the Face of Bell on Aspen Mountain.

nation. The once-deserted streets started to fill, the 19th-century miners' cottages were restored, businesses and motels opened up, and Aspen's second boom started.

But a mountain that challenges international racers can also scare beginners or casual skiers, so Friedl Pfeifer turned to **Buttermilk Mountain** in the 1960s to create a teaching hill for beginners and those seeking a more casual skiing experience.

Developer "Whip" Jones then built **Aspen Highlands,** which took on the aura of an unpretentious, home-town ski hill. Finally, the Aspen Ski Corporation made the big jump to Snowmass Valley, south of town, and built a brand new ski area with modern lifts, challenging runs, and a complete ski village that existed only to serve the skier.

Even though many of the state's ski areas have tried to duplicate the Aspen example, there still remains just one Aspen, because no other ski area has all the Aspen elements—Victorian mining-town history, pioneering ski efforts, fantastic terrain, a learning hill, a completely planned ski area and town built just for skiing, and a heady dose of culture, philosophy, and music to stimulate the mind.

■ SKIING ASPEN

To get to Aspen, take I-70 to Glenwood Springs and start up Colorado 82's four lanes, which turn to two not-so-safe lanes just past Carbondale to reach Aspen. (The road is called "Killer 82" because of the many collisions, including car/deer wrecks.) Go slow, enjoy the scenery—wide-open ranch land squeezed between mountains—and don't pass; you'll get there soon enough.

Woody Creek, on the left across from the Snowmass Ski Area, is interesting. Stuck in the middle of a trailer park full of Aspenites who actually work is the **Woody Creek Tavern** (970-923-4585). This earthy and infamous hangout is owned by gonzo journalist Hunter S. Thompson; his spread is farther up the road, where his target practice—with weapons ranging from typewriters to submachine guns—won't disturb the neighbors.

You can see the runs on Snowmass Mountain from the highway, particularly The Burn—a huge swath of ski hill that is a powder-hound, tree-bashing delight. Past the airport rests Buttermilk Mountain and then, when you're on the edge of town, comes a glimpse of Highlands Ski Area.

As you enter town, bear left at the Y intersection to find Intellectual Alley, officially named the Aspen Meadows—home to the Aspen Institute for Humanistic Studies, the International Design Conference, the Aspen Center for Physics, and the Aspen Music Festival, where students from around the world come for a summer of instruction. This area is also the famed West End, packed with the huge, generally empty, and almost always lavish second homes of movie stars, moguls, and the idle rich who "need" a home in Aspen. The same breed has covered Red Mountain with similar residences.

If you instead take a right at the Y, and then a big bending left, you'll be on Main Street. This is still Colorado 82, which will lead you over Independence Pass in the summer but is closed in the winter. Funky old Aspen fades the closer you get to the middle of town, at Mill and Main Streets. This corner is occupied by the **Hotel Jerome** (330 East Main Street; 970-920-1000), an 1889 jewel built during the Aspen silver boom. Aspen Mountain's famous runs are visible anytime you look up. As you head toward the hill, you'll pass salons, restaurants, bars, and boutiques—some in 19th-century buildings, a few in 1960s–'70s-style leftovers, and some in brand new efforts. This mix is also apparent in the pedestrian mall two blocks from the ski lifts.

If you're staying for a few days or if you fly in, forget about a car. Reliable bus service will deliver you all over town and to all the ski hills, and it's the cheapest ticket you'll buy during your stay. *Ruby Park bus station, 430 East Durant Avenue; 970-925-8484.*

Aspen Mountain

Aspen Skiing Company, Box 1248, Aspen, CO 81612; 970-925-1220 or 800-525-6200; snow report, 970-925-1221 or 888-277-3676. Off Colorado 82; call for directions.

Terrain: 76 trails on 675 acres: 70% intermediate, 30% advanced.

Lifts: One high-speed six-passenger gondola, one quad SuperChair, two quad chairs, four double lifts.

Snowmaking: 210 acres.

Vertical drop: 3,267 feet (996 meters).

Ticket prices: Expensive.

Facilities: Rental equipment and lessons. Challenge Aspen offers some of the best services for disabled skiers; 970-923-0578.

Dining: Six on-mountain restaurants, at the base, middle, and top.

Accommodations: Aspen central reservations, 970-925-9000 or 888-452-2409.

Snowboard facilities: One terrain park.

Cross-country skiing: There are 50 miles (80 kilometers) of cross-country trails, both heading into the backcountry and making quick loops around Aspen. Contact Snowmass Touring Center; 970-923-3148, or Aspen Touring Center; 970-925-2145.

Buttermilk Mountain

Aspen Skiing Company (see address and phone numbers, above).

Terrain: 43 trails on 420 acres: 35% beginner, 65% intermediate.

Lifts: One high-speed quad, five double chairs, one surface lift.

Snowmaking: 108 acres.

Vertical drop: 2,030 feet (619 meters).

Ticket prices: Expensive.

Facilities: Rental equipment and lessons; child care; Fort Frog for children; activities for the disabled.

Dining: Two on-mountain restaurants.

Accommodations: See Aspen Mountain, above.

Snowboard facilities: A 2-mile-long terrain park, one halfpipe, and boarder-cross course.

Cross-country skiing: See Aspen Mountain, above.

Snowmass

Aspen Skiing Company (see address and phone numbers, above).

Terrain: 84 trails on 3,010 acres: 9% beginner, 69% intermediate, 22% expert.

Lifts: Seven quad SuperChairs, two triple chairs, six double chairs, five surface lifts.

Snowmaking: 160 acres.

Vertical drop: 4,406 feet (1,344 meters).

Ticket prices: Expensive.

Facilities: Rental equipment and lessons; child care; disabled skiing (see Aspen Mountain, above).

Dining: Ten on-mountain restaurants.

Accommodations: In Aspen call Aspen central reservations, 888-452-2409; in Snowmass Village, 800-332-3245.

Snowboard facilities: Three terrain parks, one halfpipe.

Cross-country skiing: See Aspen Mountain, above.

Aspen Highlands

Aspen Skiing Company (see address and phone numbers, above).

Terrain: 112 trails on 714 acres: 19% beginner, 29% intermediate, 52% advanced.

Lifts: Three high-speed quads and one triple.

Snowmaking: 110 acres.

Vertical drop: 3,635 feet (1,108 meters).

Ticket prices: Expensive.

Facilities: Rental equipment and lessons.

Dining: Two on-mountain restaurants.

Accommodations: See Aspen Mountain and Snowmass, above.

Cross-country skiing: See Aspen Mountain, above.

■ MEGA-RESORTS NEAR DENVER

Developers paid attention to Vail and quickly bunched a batch of resorts within easy driving distance (less than two hours) of Denver or other large population centers in Colorado. They learned their lessons well. These resorts get their skiers

A ski patrol maneuvers through deep powder near Breckenridge Ski Area.

on the hill as quickly and painlessly as possible. And the mountains happen to contain some of the best skiable terrain in the United States. The following resorts are strategically placed to accommodate either a day trip from Denver or a week of skiing fantasies.

■ BRECKENRIDGE

Eighty-five miles west of Denver on I-70 and Colorado 9, Breckenridge is a hybrid, combining a gold-mining past with a planned-ski-resort future. The town mined gold from 1859 to 1948, decayed, and was revived in 1961 by the Breckenridge Ski Area, now one of the biggest in the state, with four mountains plus back bowls. It's sort of strange to walk down the main drag, lined with restored and "new" Victorians, and then visit the back streets and historical displays and get a dose of dilapidated 19th-century mining history.

Breckenridge Ski Area
Box 1058, Breckenridge, CO 80424; 970-453-5000 or 800-789-7669; snow report, 970-453-6118. On Colorado 9, south from I-70.
Terrain: 139 trails on 2,043 acres: 20% beginner, 31% intermediate, 49% advanced.
Lifts: One six-pack (six people on one chair), five SuperChair quads, one triple, seven doubles, and nine surface lifts.
Snowmaking: 504 acres.
Vertical drop: 3,398 feet (1,036 meters).
Ticket prices: Expensive.
Facilities: Rental equipment and lessons; child care; Kid's Castle on Peak 8 (a child-friendly section of mountain, with a restaurant). Facilities available for disabled skiers; 970-453-6422 or 800-383-2632.
Dining: Five on-mountain restaurants, two at the base.
Accommodations: Breckenridge central reservations; 970-453-2918 (in Colorado) or 800-221-1091 (nationwide).
Snowboard facilities: Two terrain parks, one halfpipe.
Cross-country skiing: 31 miles (50 kilometers) of groomed, double-set trails.

■ COPPER MOUNTAIN

Even closer to Denver than is Breckenridge, the Copper Mountain area has sprouted into a real resort, complete with condos, restaurants, and other amenities at the base of a great ski complex designed to get you out of your car and onto the mountain as quickly as possible.

Copper Mountain Resort
Box 3001, Copper Mountain, CO 80443; 970-968-2882 or 800-458-8386; snow report, 800-789-7609. On I-70 about 75 miles west of Denver.
Terrain: 125 trails on 2,433 acres, 350 acres are set aside for guided extreme skiing: 25% beginner, 40% intermediate, 35% advanced.
Lifts: One six-pack, four quad chairs, five triple chairs, five double chairs, and six surface lifts.
Snowmaking: 380 acres.
Vertical drop: 2,601 feet (793 meters).
Ticket prices: Moderate.
Facilities: Rental equipment and lessons; day care; 30-acre portion of Union Creek set aside for families and children.

Accommodations: Copper Mountain central reservations, 800-458-8386.
Snowboard facilities: One terrain park, two halfpipes.
Cross-country skiing: 16 miles (25 kilometers) of groomed trails.

■ KEYSTONE, NORTH PEAK, AND ARAPAHOE BASIN
These are three fine hills lurking just over 70 miles from Denver on I-70. You'll
pass through the town of Silverthorne before arriving at the ski hills and Keystone
Village, which is constantly adding new restaurants, shops, and condos and other
places to stay. Keystone is keyed to the beginning and intermediate skier, but
North Peak and the Outback are preferred by experts. Arapahoe Basin caters to
snowboarders with a halfpipe for performing acts of aerial derring-do.

KEYSTONE MOUNTAIN/NORTH PEAK/ARAPAHOE BASIN

Box 38, Keystone, CO 80435; general information, 970-468-2316 or 800-222-
0188; accommodations/reservations, 800-239-1639; snow report, 970-468-4111.
Off I-70 about 70 miles west of Denver. Ticket prices are expensive and tickets are
interchangeable at Vail, Beaver Creek, and Breckenridge.

Keystone Mountain
Terrain: 116 trails on 1,861 acres: 32% beginner, 57% intermediate, 11%
advanced.
Lifts: Two gondolas, five high-speed quad chairs, one quad, two triples, five double
chairs, seven surface lifts.
Snowmaking: 849 acres.
Vertical drop: 2,900 feet (884 meters).
Facilities: Night skiing; rental equipment and lessons; child care.
Dining: Three restaurants on Keystone Mountain and numerous others at base.
Accommodations: Central reservations for Keystone Village and Silverthorne;
800-239-1639.
Snowboard facilities: One terrain park, two halfpipes.
Cross-country skiing: 11 miles (18 kilometers) of groomed and packed trails near
the four resorts, 57 miles (91 kilometers) of backcountry trails.

LEGACY OF THE TENTH MOUNTAIN DIVISION

Colorado's role in providing a training ground for a special force of World War II fighters was arguably the single most important event to spur the post-war development of the ski industry here. The state's unique contribution to the war effort involved a sprawling high-altitude training camp in the heart of the Rockies, in a valley just west of Tennessee Pass, near Leadville. That remote mountain valley was transformed into Camp Hale and became home to the Tenth Mountain Division, a fighting unit made up of soldiers on skis.

The idea for the division arose after the Scandinavians, outmanned and outgunned, deployed ranks of soldiers who could climb mountains, ski, and fight all at the same time. The skiing soldiers held off the Nazi onslaught for longer than anyone imagined during a brutal winter campaign.

Recruits for the Tenth Mountain Division came from the ranks of professional ski patrols, college ski teams, adventuresome mountaineers, and a cadre of experienced skiers and ski instructors from the United States and Europe. Volunteers for the division, which numbered about 10,000 men by the time the war was over, underwent a thorough screening process before they were accepted in the elite corps.

The raw recruits were greeted by some raw training conditions—freezing temperatures, and miles and miles of snowy mountain peaks on which they could learn how to ski and maneuver, and then fight a battle in the dead of winter. The army cleared a ski run and built a T-bar lift on Cooper Mountain so the troops would have a place to practice skiing on their wide, wooden skis, which were used for both cross-country and downhill skiing. The skis were white to go with the outfit's white camouflage uniforms. There were close-order drills in freezing temperatures, during which skiers wielded ski poles and a rifle while toting a backpack full of mountaineering gear.

Learning to ski and march was the easy part. To hone their mountaineering skills, the troops were sent to scale the surrounding peaks. On other training treks they lived in the untracked mountains for days at a time. One of the tougher training runs involved climbing over the Continental Divide to ski to Aspen and back.

When the call to combat came in 1944, the men of the Tenth put their training to use in a string of deadly battles in the Italian Alps, culminating in the decisive battle that put the Po River Valley in Allied hands. The rightfully famous assault on Riva Ridge—in which troops scaled the rocky ridge at night and routed the surprised enemy the next morning—proved the pluck and valor of the division.

After the war, the army ordered the slow dismantling of Camp Hale. About all that is left today to mark what was once a bustling training grounds are some of the foundations for the barracks. Tenth Mountain veterans erected a monument that overlooks the vacant valley on Tennessee Pass Road and gives a brief history of Camp Hale and the division, and lists the nearly 1,000 men of the Tenth who fell in combat. Although Camp Hale is now gone, the Tenth Mountain Division is still part of America's fighting force and has seen action from Korea to Afghanistan.

The Tenth Mountain Division's impact on Colorado skiing after the war, though, was far more permanent than was Camp Hale. Many of the troops fell in love with the Colorado mountains and the state's supply of soft powder. Pete Siebert, who died in 2002, returned to Colorado to become the force behind the creation of Vail. Friedl Pfeifer, an Austrian skier who became a citizen during his stint with the Tenth, played a critical role in developing Aspen's famous ski hills and ski schools. Gerry Cunningham founded Gerry's Mountain Sports, which developed one of the first lines of ski clothes and equipment. Merrill Hastings founded *Ski Magazine* in Denver to promote the sport.

But just as importantly, men from the Tenth Mountain Division spread out across the state and put their experience and love of skiing to work as ski instructors, mountain managers, and advisors. In addition to having key roles at Aspen and Vail, Tenth Mountain veterans made substantial contributions to Winter Park, Ski Broadmore, Powderhorn, Breckenridge, Steamboat, and Arapahoe Basin, to name just a few.

Tenth Mountain Division soldiers, training to fight the Nazis. (Denver Public Library)

North Peak

Terrain: 19 trails on 249 acres: 10% beginner, 37% intermediate, 53% advanced.
Lifts: One gondola, one quad, one triple.
Snowmaking: 150 acres.
Vertical drop: 1,620 feet (494 meters).
Dining: Two on-mountain restaurants.

Arapahoe Basin

Box 8787, Arapahoe Basin Resort, CO 80453; 970-468-0718 or 888-272-7246.
Terrain: 61 trails on 490 acres: 10% beginner, 50% intermediate,
40% advanced.
Lifts: One triple chair, four double chairs.
Vertical drop: 2,270 feet (692 meters).
Dining: One on-mountain restaurant, one at the base.

The Outback

Terrain: 17 trails on 899 acres: 67% intermediate, 33% advanced.
Lifts: One high-speed quad.
Vertical drop: 1,520 feet (463 meters).
Snowmaking: 100 acres.
Night skiing: Terrain and lifts variable depending on conditions.
Ticket prices: Inexpensive.

■ **WINTER PARK/MARY JANE**

Once no more than a ski hill and some railroad workers' shacks, this area was one of the state's first ski areas. After more than a half-century it's still going downhill, which in this case is good. Paresenn Bowl has become a favorite for intermediate skiers yearning for the challenge, but not the terror, of ungroomed fresh powder. Families can also take advantage of lower lift prices when they ski Mini Mountain and Galloping Goose. The **Ski Train** (303-296-4754), which has become an institution as well as a means of transportation, will deliver you to the area's 112 trails and resort trimmings.

Winter Park/Mary Jane

Box 36, Winter Park, CO 80482; 970-726-5514 or 800-729-5813 (outside Colorado). On U.S. 40, north from I-70, about 70 miles from Denver.

Terrain: 134 trails on 2,886 acres: 25% beginner, 51% intermediate, 24% advanced.

Lifts: Eight high-speed quad chairs, four triple chairs, seven double chairs, three surface lifts.

Snowmaking: 294 acres.

Vertical drop: 3,060 feet (933 meters).

Ticket prices: Moderate.

Facilities: Rental equipment and lessons; child care; home to the National Sports Center for the disabled, the largest facility of its kind in the nation.

Dining: Twelve restaurants scattered on the mountains and at base lodges, from full-service dining to cafeterias and pizza. Bar service.

Accommodations: Winter Park central reservations handles bookings for the entire Fraser Valley, 800-453-2525.

Snowboard facilities: Three terrain parks, one halfpipe.

■ Historic Hideaways

Scattered throughout the central Rockies are a number of resorts with a historical flavor. With the exception of Crested Butte, detailed below, these towns are described here mainly in terms of skiing. To read more of their history see "Rocky Mountains," page 80, and "San Juan Mountains," page 128.

■ Crested Butte

Thirty miles north of Gunnison, Crested Butte has had its share of gold and silver miners, gunslingers, coal miners, and skiers; and when it comes to Colorado history, Crested Butte has tasted more than a smattering of it all. Although it wasn't a gold or silver boomtown, its location just north of Gunnison made it the logical supply center for the surrounding mining camps.

The town didn't die when the mining camps did; instead, it turned into a mining town itself, thanks to the huge vein of high-grade coal at its back door and the 1881 arrival of the Denver and Rio Grande Railroad. By 1884 Crested Butte had become one of Colorado Fuel & Iron's company towns, under the compassionate hand of CF&I owner John Cleveland Osgood.

Then there are the outlaw legends.

First came Butch Cassidy and the Sundance Kid, *sans* Wild Bunch. In 1902, so the story goes, the pair entered a local saloon for a few cold beers. A few were all they got, because a batch of men with badges came right after them. The pair left town running, and kept one foot ahead of the law.

The famous James brothers, Frank and Jesse, are also said to have been short-term visitors, hiding out for a while in Parlin, outside of Crested Butte, and creating no mischief. More trouble, however, was Billy the Kid, who allegedly worked in an outlying sawmill, got fired, held up the next passing stage, and continued down the road into legend.

Dashing downhill or traipsing through the trees: Colorado skiing offers it all.

The Big Mine kept Crested Butte an honest-to-goodness Colorado mining town, prosperous if not exactly booming, until 1953. When the Big Mine shut down, everyone expected Crested Butte to join the ghost town parade. Skiing came to the rescue, however. Rozeman Hill had been hosting skiers since 1951, but it wasn't until 1963 that Crested Butte Mountain opened, creating a unique attraction by linking a historical town to a nearby ski area. (Crested Butte Mountain and its attendant planned village and amenities are a couple of miles north of the town of Crested Butte.) The new ski area was an immediate hit with students from Western State College in Gunnison, and helped create the college's unofficial slogan: "Ski Western State and pick up a degree in your spare time."

There's a splash of modern action at the entrance to Crested Butte, but once you turn left onto Elk Avenue and start to explore the town's few back streets, things start to look old and settled, ready for the region's famed harsh winters.

Crested Butte has retained its Victorian charm and the influences left by the southern European immigrants who worked its coal mines. It feels like a Victorian mining town that has managed to keep up with the modern world. It's not full of condos; not every building has been painted or remodeled to appeal to the second-home market; and it didn't pave most of its streets until the 1980s. It just happens to have a great ski mountain right up the road.

Mount Crested Butte
Box 5700, Mount Crested Butte, CO 81225; 970-349-2333 or 800-810-7669; snow report, 888-442-8883. On Colorado 135; call for directions.
Terrain: 85 trails on 1,434 acres, including 550 acres of ungroomed terrain called the "Extreme Limits": 13% beginner, 30% intermediate, 57% advanced.
Lifts: Three high-speed quads, three triple chairs, three doubles, six surface lifts.
Snowmaking: 300 acres.
Vertical drop: 3,062 feet (933 meters).
Ticket prices: Moderate.
Facilities: Rental equipment and lessons; child care for infants to three-year-olds.
Dining: Three on-mountain restaurants, three at the base.
Accommodations: Either at the ski area or in the town of Crested Butte; call 800-544-8448.
Snowboard facilities: One terrain park, one halfpipe, numerous snowboard-only runs.
Cross-country skiing: 19 miles (30 kilometers) of groomed track.

■ SKI COOPER

The famed Tenth Mountain Division trained here, just 10 miles from Leadville, the king of the silver cities, with its Victorian allures. Ski Cooper has kept up with the times and now features Chicago Ridge, an 1,800-acre back bowl just for powder junkies. The ski area is a pretty long 100 miles from Denver by way of I-70, Colorado 91, or U.S. 24.

Ski Cooper

Box 896, Leadville, CO 80461; reservations, 719-486-3684; snow report, 719-486-2277. On U.S. 24, south from I-70.

Terrain: 26 trails on 400 acres: 30% beginner, 70% intermediate.

Lifts: One triple chair, one double chair, two surface lifts.

Skiing Genessee Mountain in the old days.
(Denver Public Library)

Vertical drop: 1,200 feet (366 meters).

Ticket prices: Inexpensive.

Facilities: Rental equipment and lessons; child care.

Dining: Cafeteria at the base lodge.

Accommodations: The closest accommodations are in Leadville, 719-486-3900 or 800-933-3901.

Cross-country skiing: 15 miles (24 kilometers) of groomed track; snowcat tours to Chicago Ridge and other backcountry powder hot spots.

■ STEAMBOAT SPRINGS

Way up in the north-central part of the state, 160 miles from Denver via I-70 and U.S. 40, Steamboat Springs was a skiing pioneer, but its main business was as a regional retail center for local ranchers and coal miners. The skiing boom didn't destroy those roots; it just led to the present mixture of skiers and real cowboys the town loves to tout. If you want to be cool, ski in a cowboy hat.

Skiers with lit torches gracefully slide down a mountain during the Winter Carnival in Steamboat Springs.

Steamboat

2305 Mount Werner Circle, Steamboat Springs, CO 80487; 800-922-2722; snow report, 970-879-7300. On U.S. 40, north from I-70.

Terrain: 142 trails on 2,939 acres: 15% beginner, 54% intermediate, 31% advanced.

Lifts: One gondola, four high-speed quads, one quad, six triple chairs, six double chairs, two surface lifts.

Snowmaking: 438 acres.

Vertical drop: 3,668 feet (1,118 meters).

Ticket prices: Moderate.

Facilities: Rental equipment and lessons; child care; instruction for the physically and developmentally disabled, call 970-879-6111, Ext. 531.

Dining: Six restaurants ranging from cafeteria to barbecue to gourmet on the mountain and at the base.

Accommodations: Call Steamboat's central reservations, 970-879-6111 or 800-922-2722.

Cross-country skiing: 19 miles (30 kilometers) of groomed trails; call for rates.

Howelsen Hill

Box 775088, Steamboat Springs, CO 80477; 970-879-4300. On U.S. 40, north from I-70.

Terrain: 19 trails on 100 acres: 100% intermediate.

Lifts: Two surface, one double.

Vertical drop: 440 feet (134 meters).

Ticket prices: Inexpensive.

Facilities: Night skiing; 4,200-foot (1,281-meter) bobsled track, open day and night; 5- and 90-meter ski jumps.

Dining: Snack bar at base lodge.

Accommodations: See Steamboat, above.

Cross-country skiing: 6 miles (10 kilometers) of groomed trails, 1.6 miles (2.5 kilometers) open at night; free.

Snowboarder on Telluride Mountain.

■ TELLURIDE

This picturesque town in the San Juan Mountains boomed long enough to get a good shot of Victorian-era buildings. The Telluride Ski Area was created in 1971 and has since expanded to both sides of Coonskin Mountain, with a modern, planned resort on the backside, so you can choose from Victorian gingerbread or chrome-and-glass accommodations.

Telluride
65 Mountain Village Boulevard, Telluride, CO 81435; 970-728-6900 or 888-288-7360; general info, 970-728-4431; snow report, 970-728-7425. On Colorado 145; call for directions.
Terrain: 85 trails on 1,700 acres: 21% beginner, 47% intermediate, 32% advanced.
Lifts: Two gondolas, seven high-speed quad chairs, two triple chairs, two double chairs, two surface lifts.
Snowmaking: 155 acres.
Vertical drop: 3,535 feet (1,078 meters).

Ticket prices: Moderate.

Facilities: Rental equipment and lessons; child care; facilities for disabled.

Dining: Seven restaurants scattered on the mountain and at the base lodges.

Accommodations: Telluride central reservations, 800-525-3455.

Snowboard facilities: 20-acre terrain park with a 1,000-foot (305-meter) vertical drop, one halfpipe.

Cross-country skiing: More than 31 miles (50 kilometers) of groomed trails.

■ ABOUT HOMETOWN SKI HILLS

Most people would be surprised to learn that not every Colorado ski area falls into the mega-resort or historic category. Hometown ski areas range in size from mere hills with a couple of creaky old lifts to fairly good-size mountains with lifts and amenities just a notch or two below the big hills. Tucked into the mountains here and there are small ski areas with plenty of great skiing, but without the glitz, promotional muscle, history, and massive mountain operations of the "big guys."

In visiting them, you'll enjoy the following:

▶ Being able to ski down the hill without carving turns around other skiers or tearing up the slope as if you were a steroid-crazed halfback executing an open-field punt return.

▶ Not having to fear being run over by someone skiing like a steroid-crazed halfback executing an open-field punt return.

▶ Lift lines that don't give you the chance to read a chunk of *War and Peace* before heading up the hill.

▶ Lift ticket prices that don't require notes from your banker.

▶ Being able to eat and afford some good old American food in the base lodge, instead of wandering into a fern-infested "grille" where lunch costs as much as a good pair of ski poles.

▶ The feeling that, by the end of the day, the lift operator is almost family and the rest of the hill's crew really does like having you around.

■ LITTLE HILLS CLOSE TO BIG CITIES

■ ELDORA

Boulder's hometown hill, Eldora, is less than an hour from Denver—and the 21-mile drive through Boulder Canyon on Colorado 119 is a great drive in itself.

Eldora Mountain Resort

Box 1697, Nederland, CO 80466; reservations, 303-440-8700, from Denver 303-258-7082; snow report, 303-440-8700. On Colorado 119; call for directions.

Terrain: 53 trails on 680 acres, with 16 trails (covering 91 acres) available for night skiing: 15% beginner, 85% intermediate.

Lifts: Four double chairs, two quads, two triple chairs, four surface lifts.

Snowmaking: 320 acres.

Vertical drop: 1,400 feet (427 meters).

Ticket prices: Inexpensive.

Facilities: Rental equipment and lessons.

Dining: One on-mountain restaurant, one at base lodge.

Accommodations: The closest are in the town of Eldora; 800-422-4629.

Snowboard facilities: Three terrain parks, one halfpipe.

Cross-country skiing: 28 miles (45 kilometers) of groomed and backcountry trails.

■ LOVELAND BASIN

Just 56 miles west of Denver, on I-70 before the Eisenhower Tunnel, is one of Colorado's original ski areas. The area's devotees routinely cross-country ski into the deep powder bowls above timberline.

Loveland Basin

Box 899, Georgetown, CO 80444; 800-736-3754; reservations, 303-571-5580; snow report, 303-571-5554.

Terrain: 70 trails on 1,365 acres: 25% beginner, 48% intermediate, 27% advanced.

Lifts: Three quads, two triple chairs, four double chairs, one surface lift, one Mighty-Mite for the ski-school kids.

Snowmaking: 159 acres.

Vertical drop: 2,410 feet (735 meters).

Ticket prices: Inexpensive to moderate.

Facilities: Rental equipment and lessons.
Dining: Two cafeterias and three restaurants at the base area.
Accommodations: The closest are in Georgetown, 12 miles away; 800-225-5683.
Snowboard facilities: One terrain park.

■ **SILVER CREEK**

Seventy-eight miles from Denver on I-70 and U.S. 40, or just 15 minutes north of Winter Park, SolVista teaches families how to have fun on skis, and gears its two hills to the student, with one of the state's best instructional programs.

SolVista Golf & Ski Ranch

Box 1110, Granby, CO 80446; 970-887-5143; snow report, 800-754-7458.
Terrain: 33 trails on 287 acres: 30% beginner, 50% intermediate, 20% advanced.
Lifts: One triple chair, one high-speed quad, one double chair, two surface lifts.
Snowmaking: 170 acres.
Vertical drop: 1,000 feet (305 meters).
Ticket prices: Inexpensive.
Facilities: Rental equipment and lessons a specialty; child care.
Dining: Cafeteria at the base lodge.
Accommodations: Ski-in/ski-out condos, hotel and motel rooms, and nearby guest ranches are in the surrounding communities of Granby, Winter Park, and Grand Lake; 970-726-9421.
Cross-country skiing: 25 miles (40 kilometers) groomed track.

■ **LITTLE HILLS SCATTERED ALL OVER THE PLACE**

■ **ARROWHEAD**

Just west of Vail on I-70, Arrowhead is now part of the Vail/Beaver Creek ski area.

Arrowhead Ski Area

Box 69, Edwards, CO 81632; 800-427-8216 (see Vail Mountain for more contact information).
Terrain: 13 trails on 178 acres: 30% beginner, 50% intermediate, 20% advanced.
Lifts: One high-speed quad chair and one tow.
Snowmaking: 80 acres.
Vertical drop: 1,700 feet (518 meters).
Ticket prices: Expensive.

Facilities: Rental equipment and lessons.
Dining: One restaurant at the base area and one on the mountain.
Accommodations: At the ski area, call 970-926-8300; or in Vail/Beaver Creek Valley, call the Vail Resort Association, 800-525-3875.
Backcountry skiing: Private lessons and equipment rental available through Paragon Guides, 970-926-5299.

■ CUCHARA VALLEY

On the east side of San Luis Valley, this resort is only about 75 miles from Pueblo on I-25 and U.S. 160. This small ski area is generally geared to beginners and intermediates, although there are a few runs that can give an expert a thrill. Lift lines are unheard of.

Cuchara Ski Valley
946 Penadero Avenue, Cuchara, CO 81050; 719-742-3163 or 877-282-4272.
Terrain: 28 trails on 230 acres: 25% beginner; 75% intermediate.
Snowmaking: 196 acres.
Lifts: One triple chair, three double chairs, one surface lift.
Vertical drop: 1,562 feet (475 meters).
Ticket Prices: Inexpensive.
Facilities: Rental equipment and lessons.
Dining: On-mountain restaurant.
Accommodations: Limited at the ski area; closest lodge is 2 miles away.

■ HESPERUS SKI AREA

A modest little hill north of Durango on U.S. 160.

Hesperus Ski Area
9848 U.S. 160, Durango, CO 81301; 970-382-0164.
Terrain: 13 trails on 80 acres: 30% beginner; 50% intermediate, 20% expert.
Lifts: Two surface lifts.
Vertical drop: 700 feet (214 meters).
Ticket Prices: Inexpensive.
Facilities: Base area.
Accommodations: Available in Durango; 800-525-0892.

Telluride looks even more picturesque from mid-air.

■ MONARCH

Set between Gunnison and Salida on U.S. 50, this resort gets mountains of snow and—thanks to all that soft and dry powder snow, a warm welcome mat, and the bang for the skiing buck—draws skiers from all over south-central Colorado.

Monarch Ski and Snowboard Area

23715 U.S. 50, Monarch, CO 81227; 719-539-3573 or 888-996-7669; snow report, 800-228-7943.

Terrain: 54 trails on 670 acres: 28% beginner, 46% intermediate, 26% advanced.

Lifts: Four double chairs, one quad.

Snowmaking: Who needs it when you average 350 inches of snow a year?

Vertical drop: 1,170 feet (357 meters).

Ticket prices: Inexpensive.

Facilities: Equipment rental and lessons; child care.

Dining: Cafeteria at the base lodge and a snack bar on the mountain.

Accommodations: The 100-room Monarch Lodge is the only lodge at the ski area; call 800-332-3668, or call the local chamber of commerce, 719-539-2068, for information on rooms in Gunnison and Salida.

Snowboard facilities: One terrain park.
Cross-country skiing: 2 miles (3 kilometers) of track skiing.
Snowcat skiing: Great Divide Snow Tours, from $20–80 per day.

■ POWDERHORN

About 35 miles from Grand Junction on I-70 and Colorado 65, Powderhorn sits on the flanks of the Grand Mesa, a huge flat-topped mountain, and receives a steady downpour of light powder. The area draws skiers from across the Western Slope. Excellent cross-country skiing and snowmobiling can be found in the national forest surrounding the mountain.

Powderhorn Ski Resort
Box 370, Mesa, CO 81643; 970-268-5700.
Terrain: 27 trails on 510 acres: 20% beginner, 80% intermediate.
Snowmaking: 50 acres.
Lifts: One quad, two double chairs, one surface lift.
Vertical drop: 1,650 feet (503 meters).
Ticket prices: Inexpensive.
Facilities: Rental equipment and lessons; child care.
Dining: Restaurant, bar, and cafeteria at the base lodge.
Accommodations: Limited lodging at the ski area, 970-268-5170; or call 970-242-3214 for lodging information in Grand Junction and nearby towns.
Cross-country skiing: 7.5 miles (12 kilometers) of trails.

■ PURGATORY/DURANGO

Perched in the mountain, 50 miles north of Durango on U.S. 550, this is the prime ski area and resort for the entire Four Corners region and has a well-earned reputation as a challenging, fun place to ski. It is both a self-contained resort, offering lodging, dining, and shopping, as well as a day trip for many in the outlying area.

Durango Mountain Resort
945 Main Street, Durango, CO 81301; 970-247-9000 or 800-315-7401.
Terrain: 75 trails on 1,200 acres: 20% beginner, 50% intermediate, 30% advanced.
Lifts: One six-pack, one high-speed quad, four triple chairs, three double chairs, two surface lifts.
Snowmaking: Over 245 acres.

Vertical drop: 2,029 feet (618 meters).
Ticket prices: Moderate.
Facilities: Rental equipment and lessons; child care.
Dining: Six restaurants at the ski area, ranging from cafeteria to gourmet.
Accommodations: Eight condo complexes at the ski area; extensive lodging in Durango, 888-442-4222.
Cross-country skiing: 10 miles (16 kilometers) of groomed trails.

■ **SILVERTON MOUNTAIN**

This recent addition to Colorado's ski hills is perched in the high-altitude valley 6 miles above Silverton. The owners want to re-create the old days of Colorado skiing, with a minimum of glitz and perks and a maximum of untracked powder skiing. To accomplish this experiment, the number of skiers and boarders is limited every day. After riding the lift, snow riders are encouraged to hike farther up the hill for more fun. The area opened in 2002, offering guided trips into the steep and deep terrain. There's no trail grooming or avalanche control, so you're pretty much at the mercy of the snow and wind—which means a guide, avalanche beacon, shovel, and probe pole are also part of the experience. The snow, however, gets great reviews. Skiers and riders call the experience more of a backcountry adventure, a poor man's helicopter skiing experience.

Silverton Mountain
Box 654, Silverton, CO 81433; 970-387-5706.
Terrain: 1,600 acres of powder where you make your own trails. For expert skiers and snowboarders only.
Lifts: One double chair.
Vertical drop: 3,000 feet (915 meters).
Ticket Prices: The $99 daily ticket includes the services of a guide. Reservations are strongly recommended.
Facilities: Bare minimum.
Accommodations: Available in Durango, 800-525-0892, and Ouray, 970-325-4981.

■ **SUNLIGHT MOUNTAIN RESORT**

About 16 miles from Glenwood Springs is my hometown hill. Here's how she works: you take a leisurely drive on a two-lane county road, passing a subdivision or two, several ranches, and great mountain scenery. You arrive at the ski area and

park. A set of condos is up the hill, a hotel with restaurant and lounge just off to the side. You go to the main lodge, walk up and buy your lift ticket, get on the lift, ride the lift, get off the lift, and start skiing. If you want to dawdle, you can get a cup of hot chocolate in the cafeteria or stash something in a locker, or talk shop at the ski shop. Good skiing, no frenzy, light on the wallet, easy duty.

Sunlight Mountain Resort

10901 County Road 117, Glenwood Springs, CO 81601; 970-945-7491 or 800-445-7931. Off I-70; call for directions.

Terrain: 66 trails on 460 acres: 20% beginner, 58% intermediate, 22% advanced.

Lifts: One triple chair, two double chairs, one surface lift.

Snowmaking: 21 acres.

Vertical drop: 2,010 feet (613 meters).

Ticket prices: Inexpensive.

Facilities: Rental equipment and lessons; child care.

Dining: Cafeteria at the base lodge.

Accommodations: Limited number of condos at the ski area, 800-445-7931. Full range of lodging in Glenwood Springs, 800-221-0098 (in Colorado) or 888-445-3696.

Cross-country skiing: 15 miles (24 kilometers) of groomed trails.

■ WOLF CREEK

Set atop the Continental Divide near Wolf Creek Pass, between Pagosa Springs and Del Norte on U.S. 160 in the south of the state, this resort gets more snow than any other ski area in Colorado.

Wolf Creek

Box 2800, Pagosa Springs, CO 81147; 970-264-5639; snow report, 970-264-5629.

Terrain: 112 trails on 1,600 acres: 20% beginner, 60% intermediate, 20% expert.

Lifts: Two triple chairs, two double chairs, two surface lifts.

Vertical drop: 1,425 feet (434 meters).

Ticket prices: Inexpensive.

Facilities: Rental equipment and lessons.

Dining: Two cafeterias.

Accommodations: The closest lodging is in Pagosa Springs; 970-264-5629.

Over the (frozen) river and through the woods, cross-country style.

■ SKIING ADVENTURES

■ CROSS-COUNTRY HUTS

Spending days in the backcountry on snowshoes or cross-country skis, surrounded by nothing more than the beauty of snow-covered scenery, is the prime allure of cross-country hut systems. Colorado is home to two of the best hut systems in the nation, which allow you and a few friends to trek away your days in splendid forested silence, with only the sounds of your skis and the winter world around you.

The Alfred A. Braun Hut System
Colorado's original hut system offers six huts in the Elk Mountains, connecting Aspen to Crested Butte. The huts sleep anywhere from seven to 14 skiers.
Alfred A. Braun Hut System, Box 7937, Aspen, CO 81612; 970-925-5775 for reservations.
Price: $17.50 per person, four-person minimum.

Tenth Mountain Trail
Commemorating the historic Tenth Mountain Division, this hut system links Aspen to Vail and Leadville with a string of comfortable huts through some of Colorado's most striking mountains and valleys. The huts sleep 16 skiers.
Tenth Mountain Division Hut Association, 1280 Ute Avenue, Aspen, CO 81612; reservations, 970-925-5775.
Price: $22 per person, no minimum.

■ HELICOPTER SKIING
Expert skiers can combine the thrill of cutting fresh tracks through wilderness powder with the ride of a lifetime via chopper skiing.

Telluride Helitrax
Guides take you into the heart of the San Juan Mountains stretching in all directions from Telluride.
Telluride Helitrax, Box 1560, Telluride, CO 81435; 970-728-3895.
Price: Call for prices and reservations.

■ SNOWCAT SKIING

Those who like to get to the wild and uncut, yet stay a little closer to the ground, can take a snowcat into untouched skiing terrain.

Chicago Ridge Snowcat Tours

Ride into the heart of more than 1,600 acres of Chicago Ridge, atop the Continental Divide, and plunge into powder you usually only dream about. The views alone are worth the ride.

Chicago Ridge Snowcat Tours/Ski Cooper, Box 896, Leadville, CO 80461; 719-486-2277.

Prices: Call for prices and advanced reservations for full- and half-day rides.

Great Divide Snow Tours

Ride into more than 600 acres of untouched terrain that has some of the deepest and longest-lasting powder in the state.

Great Divide Snow Tours/Monarch Ski Resort, 23715 U.S. 50, Monarch, CO 81227; 719-539-3573 or 888-996-7669.

Steamboat Powder Cats

Travel into the woods 2 miles north of the Steamboat ski area for unmatched powder skiing. Intermediate skiers are welcome and a deluxe overnight trip to a charming mountain cabin can also be arranged.

Steamboat Powder Cats, Box 2468, Steamboat Springs, CO 80477; 970-879-5188.

Prices: Call for prices, reservations required.

PRACTICAL INFORMATION

■ AREA CODES AND TIME ZONES

All of Colorado is safely within the Mountain Standard Time Zone—one hour ahead of the Pacific Timers, one hour behind those in the Central Time Zone, and two hours behind the folks in the Eastern Time Zone.

Although Colorado takes up plenty of space on the map, phone callers only have to contend with four area codes. Most of the phone numbers in the Denver metro area have a 303 area code, but a growing population has prompted the phone company to start assigning newer numbers with a 720 area code. For our purposes, the Denver metro area includes Boulder and goes from Castle Rock in the south, Idaho Springs to the west, Aurora and Brighton to the east, and Longmont and Fort Lupton to the north. The 719 area code covers the southern reaches of the state, from the Kansas border through Colorado Springs and Pueblo and into the San Luis Valley. Everyone else gets a 970 area code. That includes the folks in Sterling and Fort Morgan, the state's northeastern corner, northern towns such as Fort Collins and Greeley, and the entire Western Slope, home to most of the state's ski areas and mountain resorts.

■ CLIMATE AND CLOTHING

"If you don't like the weather in Colorado, wait five minutes and it will change." That sarcastic snatch of local wisdom contains words to live by. Weather forecasting in Colorado is called "vague guessing" by most locals. This is especially true in the mountains; it can be snowing in Telluride, for instance, while the sun is shining just over the ridge in Ouray.

Here are the general weather trends for Colorado, along with some recommendations on what to wear.

Denver's huge international airport, which opened in the 1990s, has increased access to Colorado from all over the world. The main terminal's unique architecture has pleased some and confounded others.

■ EASTERN PLAINS

Eastern plains weather resembles that of the Midwest. Spring is tornado season, but it's also when the plains start to turn green. Fall harvest season is pleasant and temperate. Winter is snowy and windy, but mild by Midwestern standards. Summer can be hot (80 to 90 degrees Fahrenheit), but verdant land on all sides makes travel cooler.

The weather can turn on a cornstalk in the plains, so it's a good idea to have some extra clothes on hand: a rain jacket for spring and summer squalls, or a hefty jacket and gloves for unpredictable fall weather. During winter, gear up. The wind can chill you to the bone, so a heavy coat, gloves, and boots are in order.

■ MOUNTAINS

In the mountains, summers are made to order—not too hot in the day (70 to 80 degrees) and cool at night (40 to 50 degrees). However, as soon as the sun goes down, so does the mercury. Fall, with its fantastic colors, is a bit unpredictable but not that much cooler than summer. Winter, of course, is cold and snowy, but that's why the Rockies have such great skiing.

Since a crisp fall day can turn downright bitter and cold rain can turn to snow, it's best to bring along a warm jacket, preferably waterproof, or at least a good heavy sweater to keep the evening chill at bay. Sunny winter days can be deceiving. They look warmer than they are, and in the shade you can find yourself with chattering teeth. The key to comfort is layering. Bring sweaters, a light jacket, long underwear, and a parka so you can shed and add layers to match the conditions.

■ WESTERN SLOPE

The Western Slope is a high mountain desert, but it's not Death Valley. Summer temperatures can be in the high 90s and up, but as soon as the sun drops the mercury plunges to 60 or 70 degrees. Fall and spring are just a bit cooler all the way around, making them the preferred seasons for the locals. Winter is milder than in the mountains, but things still freeze and snow still falls; it just melts faster.

Still, the weather can surprise you at any time of the year, so be prepared for the worst and hope for the best. A good rule of thumb is to take more warm clothes than you think you'll need. You wouldn't want a surprise summer rainstorm, a drastic fall temperature swing, or a truly nasty blast of winter weather to spoil your excursions.

■ SOUTHERN COLORADO

The extreme south, along the border with New Mexico, can generally be hotter and drier than the northern regions. But this is still Colorado. Winter storms can hit with freezing ferocity, so be sure to bring your cold-weather gear. The same cautions about the Western Slope apply here: bringing too many clothes is better than not bringing enough, regardless of the time of year.

■ ALTITUDE

"Rocky Mountain High" takes on a whole new meaning when it applies to altitude sickness. Since most of Colorado is about a mile above sea level, the thin air can affect everything from your stamina to your golf game. Those arriving in Colorado from around sea level may experience a bout of minor altitude sickness, especially if your trip takes you to the mountain towns and resorts perched anywhere from 6,000 to 9,000 feet. Symptoms include headaches, lethargy, sleep disturbance, and, in extreme cases, nausea. There is no miracle cure. All you can do is take it easy for the first day or two while your body adjusts to the thin air being sucked into your lungs. The altitude can cut down on your stamina as your heart and lungs work overtime to get oxygen-filled blood to all your body parts. That extra blood flow also means alcohol goes to your head faster, so take care when imbibing at bars and bistros. On the plus side, your duffer drives on the golf course will fly through the thin air like rocket shots.

■ GETTING THERE AND AROUND

Whether you prefer to go by car, train, or plane, Colorado can accommodate your type of travel.

■ BY CAR

Colorado is bisected by two interstate highways that cut right through many of the state's major attractions. Interstate 25 runs north and south along the Front Range, and delivers drivers to the off-ramps for all the state's major cities, from Pueblo to Fort Collins. Interstate 70 lets you roar across the Great Plains from the east; sends you through Denver; takes you through the Rockies, where it serves as the main highway for many of the state's ski areas; and then sends you into the Utah desert, on the western side of the state.

For those who love highway construction and design, I-70 is an educational trip. You actually go under the Continental Divide, at 10,000 feet above sea level, as you cruise through the Eisenhower Tunnel—quite an engineering feat. Then you get to drive over Vail Pass, enjoying one of the more environmentally sensitive stretches of interstate in the land. Finally, there's Glenwood Canyon, a 12-mile stretch of highway that has been proclaimed an engineering and environmental masterpiece. The four-lane road is tucked into a narrow canyon along the Colorado River, with the sheer canyon walls reaching almost 2,000 feet overhead. This stretch of the interstate, which cost more than $500 million to build, moves back and forth across the river via bridges, tunnels, and chunks of road carved out of sheer rock. The road's environmental credentials include a solar-powered rest stop with a composting toilet (no kidding).

For those looking for roads less traveled, U.S. 50 is a nice southern route through the state. It runs from Lamar on the eastern plains through Pueblo, and on to the mountain towns of Salida and Gunnison, before linking up with I-70 in Grand Junction. Heading north, U.S. 40 provides a scenic route starting west of Denver and going to Steamboat Springs before heading across the Piceance Basin toward Dinosaur National Monument.

Winter driving in Colorado can be a bit of an adventure, especially if you aren't prepared. First off, expect snow anytime and anywhere, especially on the mountain passes. When a good storm hits, only cars with snow tires or chains are allowed over the passes. Even if you have a four-wheel-drive SUV, without the right tread you will be forced to park at the bottom and wait. Rental cars usually don't come equipped with snow tires or chains. You might want to pick up some cheap chains before you head into the hills; the closer you get to the snow, the more expensive the tire chains become. The best advice for driving in the snow is to go slow. Don't rush or try anything tricky. It's better to get where you're going late than not at all.

Every few winters, a monster storm will settle in over the state and bring all travel to a virtual standstill. It may snow so fast and hard you can barely see your hood ornament, much less the road. Don't freak out. Chill out. If you're in the mountains and the passes are closed, just toss another log on the fire, snuggle up to a warm body and get ready for a great powder day on the slopes.

Drifting and blowing snow on the eastern plains can be treacherous, and can prompt road closures. Don't worry, though; the folks in the towns along the highway know the drill. They quickly transform the local gym into a makeshift hotel, throw an impromptu slumber party, and make sure stranded travelers get a warm reception while the storm blows itself out. If the snow is so thick you can't see the road, pull off the road and wait for emergency personnel to find you. In the spring, tornadoes can sweep across the eastern plains with little warning. If you are driving and see any sort of funnel cloud, twister, or tornado, head for a town or find some sort of shelter and hunker down.

The most up-to-date information on road conditions, including restrictions and closures, comes right from the **Colorado State Patrol.** *700 Kipling Street, Denver; 970-245-8800 or 303-639-1111; csp.state.co.us.*

■ BY TRAIN
Colorado has daily passenger rail service, courtesy of **Amtrak's California Zephyr.** The train trip, whether you're going east or west, is timed to make sure passengers pass over the Continental Divide and through Colorado's mountains in the daytime, giving riders a moving view of some of the state's spectacular mountain scenery. The route also assures a good chance to spot wildlife, from bald eagles to deer, elk, and bighorn sheep. *800-872-7245.*

See Historic Railroads, pages 271–274, for information about train trips back to the past.

■ BY PLANE
Denver International Airport (DIA) is a major airline hub, with thousands of flights coming and going every day. Thanks to the airport's runway configuration and other design elements, it can handle nasty weather, which allows flights to land and take off even in the worst of conditions. *8400 Peña Boulevard, Denver; 303-342-2000; www.flydenver.com.*

The **Colorado Springs Airport** (COS) has also seen significant growth as an alternative gateway for flyers who want to avoid the on-the-ground hassles of sprawling Denver International. *7770 Drennan Road, Colorado Springs; 719-550-1900; www.springsgov.com.*

The **Eagle County Regional Airport** (EGE) is the biggest and busiest of the "little" mountain airports. It serves the Vail Valley and also offers an alternative route for folks heading to Aspen, which is just a 60-mile drive away. *1193 Cooley Mesa Road, Gypsum; 970-524-9490; www.eagle-county.com/regional_airport.*

The **Yampa Valley Regional Airport** (HDN) serves the Steamboat Springs area. *East of Hayden on U.S. 40; 970-276-3669; www.co.routt.co.us.*

The **Gunnison County Airport** (GUC) will get you an hour away from Crested Butte. *711 West Rio Grande; 970-641-2304.*

A number of smaller airports in the mountains handle daily flights either from DIA or directly from major cities across the United States. The number of flights and carriers varies from year to year, so check with your airline or travel agent.

■ **BY BUS**

You can take the big dog to Colorado by hopping on a **Greyhound Bus.** Greyhound not only serves the state's larger cities and resorts, but also stops in many smaller towns. *800-231-2222; www.greyhound.com.*

Colorado's cities and resorts also offer handy in-town bus service—from the massive big-city bus operation in Denver, the **Regional Transportation District** (RTD), which includes a mix of buses and light rail service, to the free skier shuttles and town-wide bus services running in most major resort areas. *RTD: Colfax Avenue and Broadway, or Market Street and 16th Avenue; 303-299-6000.*

■ **RESTAURANTS**

Wherever you venture in Colorado—high into the mountains to world-renowned ski resorts, off the beaten path to the unspoiled towns scattered around the eastern plains, through the fertile farm and ranch land of the Western Slope, or into burgeoning Front Range cities—you'll find ample opportunities to indulge your taste buds at an endless selection of eateries.

Although Colorado restaurants have long been known for hearty, "mountain-style" cooking ("Rocky Mountain oysters," anyone?), the past few years have brought a new vitality to the state's cuisine, thanks to an influx of high-caliber chefs and restaurateurs. Undaunted by short growing seasons and the challenge of importing hard-to-find ingredients, these culinary pioneers often go to great lengths to get the products they need for their dishes. (FedEx is enjoying a booming business flying in fresh seafood and other goodies from around the world to appease vacationing foodies.) As a result, menus around the state are as likely to include pan-seared snapper with cider glaze as barbecued ribs slathered with sauce.

■ ACCOMMODATIONS

In Colorado, you will never be too far from basic accommodations. Towns along every interstate and major highway, as well as those near ski resorts or any sort of tourist attraction, contain rows of Best Westerns and other chain properties, stands of condos, and mom-and-pop operations.

■ CHAIN HOTELS AND MOTELS

Adam's Mark. *800-444-2326; www.adamsmark.com*
Best Western. *800-528-1234; www.bestwestern.com*
Days Inn. *800-325-2525; www.daysinn.com*
Delta Hotels. *800-268-1133; www.deltahotels.com*
Doubletree. *800-222-8733; www.doubletree.com*
Four Seasons Hotels and Resorts. *800-819-5053; www.fourseasons.com*
Hilton Hotels. *800-445-8667; www.hilton.com*
Holiday Inn. *800-465-4329; www.6c.com*
Hyatt Hotels. *800-233-1234; www.hyatt.com*
La Quinta. *800-531-5900; www.laquinta.com*
Marriott Hotels. *800-228-9290; www.marriott.com*
Quality Inns. *800-228-5151; www.qualityinn.com*
Radisson. *800-333-3333; www.radisson.com*
Ramada Inns. *800-272-6232; www.ramada.com*
Sheraton. *800-325-3535; www.starwood.com*
Stouffers. *800-468-3571; www.marriott.com*
Westin Hotels. *800-228-3000; www.westin.com*

■ CAMPING

With several thousand public, easily accessible campsites scattered across the state, you can generally find the right campsite to match the camping experience you are seeking. Whether you prefer a primitive wide spot along a wilderness trail; a more sophisticated setup for car camping, complete with running water; or a full-service operation that will accommodate everything from a water-skiing boat to an RV, there is a Colorado campsite out there waiting for you.

The U.S. Forest Service (see below) and the **Colorado State Park Headquarters** (303-866-3437) manage the most extensive campground operations. The Forest Service operates 400 campgrounds, with 8,000 spots to pitch your tent in a national forest or recreation area. The Colorado State Park system includes about 40 public parks, lakes, and recreation areas, with camping available at 26 locations.

The **Bureau of Land Management** (303-239-3600) also manages hundreds of thousands of acres of public land in the state and oversees a growing group of recreation areas open to campers. A word to the wise: Before making your camping reservation, it's usually a good idea to also call for specific information about the area you want to visit.

Fees are required at most of these campsites, and the state charges a fee for every vehicle entering a state park or recreation area. Although most campsites operate on a first-come, first-served basis, you can make reservations in advance by calling 800-283-2267, and thus avoid driving all day to arrive and find out you are last-come, not served.

■ U.S. FOREST SERVICE

Probably the quickest way to get a one-stop overview of what's up in the woods is to call the forest service supervisor's office for each specific forest. The staffers at these offices can provide up-to-the-minute information about the pluses and minuses of the campsites in their neck of the forest, as well as information on road closures, fire danger, the best and worst times to visit, easy access points, and maybe some attractions you aren't aware of.

In addition, the forest service folks work closely with their counterparts at the state and Bureau of Land Management, so they can offer information and advice about most of the outdoor action in the area. The following is a list of U.S. Forest Service headquarters:

Rocky Mountain Region Headquarters, U.S. Forest Service. *Denver; 303-275-5350.*

Arapahoe and Roosevelt National Forests and **Arapahoe National Recreation Area.** *Fort Collins; 970-498-1100.*

Grand Mesa, Uncompahgre, and Gunnison National Forests. *Delta; 970-874-6600.*

Pike and San Isabel National Forests. *Pueblo; 719-545-8737.*

Rio Grande National Forest. *Monte Vista; 719-852-5941.*

Routt National Forest. *Steamboat Springs; 970-879-1870.*
San Juan National Forest. *Durango; 970-247-4847.*
White River National Forest. *Glenwood Springs; 970-945-2521.*

■ NATIONAL PARK SERVICE

The National Park Service oversees Colorado's eight national parks, monuments, and historic sites, which host about 500,000 overnight visitors a year—from backpackers to campers to recreational-vehicle fans.

It is probably a good idea to make reservations at national parks and monuments well in advance of your visit by calling the National Park Service Regional Headquarters. *303-969-2000.*

Again, for the latest information about each specific site, it's best to contact the people on the ground, not in the regional office:

Bent's Old Fort National Historic Site. *719-383-5010.*
Black Canyon of the Gunnison National Park. *970-641-2337.*
Colorado National Monument. *970-858-3617.*
Curecanti National Recreation Area. *970-641-2337.*
Dinosaur National Monument. *970-374-3000.*
Florissant Fossil Beds National Monument. *719-748-3253.*
Great Sand Dunes National Park. *719-378-2312.*
Hovenweep National Monument. *970-529-4464.*
Mesa Verde National Park. *970-529-4465.*
Rocky Mountain National Park. *970-586-1206.*

■ HISTORIC RAILROADS

Narrow-gauge tracks laid precariously along mountainsides, over trestles, or through rolling forests still carry sturdy steam locomotives, reminding visitors what the world was like before the automobile and freeway. Plumes of steam spew from the smokestack, and sparks and soot spray the summer air with their unique smell to mark the passage of Colorado's most famous, scenic, and delightful historic train rides.

Cumbres & Toltec Scenic Railroad

The longest and highest narrow-gauge line in North America stretches 64 miles from Antonito, Colorado, to Chama, New Mexico. From Antonito, the train starts a slow chug up the rolling high country, passing through the dramatic Toltec

Gorge of the Los Piños River before cresting out at a heady 10,015 feet atop Cumbres Pass. Then it's all downhill, at a four-percent grade, into Chama. The trip along rivers and over mountains has made many agree that the Cumbres & Toltec was one of the most spectacular feats of mountain railroad-building ever undertaken. Winding as it does along Colorado's isolated border with New Mexico, the train is well off the beaten track, but it's well worth a trip. If you're coming from Colorado, take U.S. 285 south from Denver through Alamosa to the Antonito station. From Santa Fe, hit U.S. 285 north to Espanola, then U.S. 84 to the Chama station. The enclosed coaches have windows that can be opened or closed, and a completely open sightseeing coach is available to all, with on-train refreshments. Cars are not heated, so bring your own warmth. The train stops for lunch in Osier, where you can hop off and head back to where you started. *June to mid-October. Antonito Depot, Box 668, Antonito, CO 81120; Chama Depot, Box 789, Chama, NM 87520; 505-756-2151.*

Cripple Creek/Victor Narrow Gauge Railroad

Take a 4-mile round-trip through the gold town of Cripple Creek. *Memorial Day until mid-October. Box 459, Cripple Creek, CO 80813; 719-689-2640.*

Durango & Silverton Narrow Gauge Railroad

This train takes you 45 miles through the heart of southwestern Colorado's stunning San Juan National Forest, passing remnants of the state's mining past and living reminders of its mining present. Over $300 million in gold and silver were hauled on the narrow-gauge tracks in mining's heyday, which can be relived in a number of ways on the current train. A choice of authentically restored 1880 passenger cars is available, including the opulent private Cinco Animas car (for charter only), a standard covered coach, and an open-air gondola car. Refreshments are served in the Alamosa Parlor Car. Along the way you will hear the shriek of the steam whistle and see abandoned mine sites and miles of roadless, virgin forest, making it an unforgettable journey.

The entire trip from Durango to Silverton takes most of a day, so many visitors opt for staying the night in Silverton, which started as and remains a mining town, and returning to Durango the next day. Reservations are strongly recommended. Call for an order form/brochure and then pick up your tickets in advance, especially if you are planning to view the spectacular fall foliage. *May to late October, depending on the length of trip. 479 Main Avenue, Durango, CO 81301; 970-247-2733 or 888-872-4607.*

Georgetown Loop Railroad

This hour-long, steam-powered ride winds its way back to the glory days of Colorado's gold boom. Starting from Georgetown, the narrow-gauge tracks cross the 95-foot-high Devil's Gate Bridge (called the Eighth Wonder of the World when it was completed in 1888), then take 14 twisting turns before hitting Silver Plume. A brief rest and you're back aboard for the return trip, which closes the loop. The rolling stock, engines, and restored passenger cars, some of which are open to the mountain air (so bring a jacket), are immaculate, and the crews are helpful and enthusiastic. You can take the **Lebanon Mill Tour** and delve deep into the golden era by going inside an old mine and mill accessible only by train. Be sure to bring a jacket (the mine is a constant 44 degrees) and walking shoes for this hour-and-a-half tour. You can board at either Georgetown, an hour's drive west from Denver on I-70, or Silver Plume, another half-hour away on the interstate. *Late May to early October, Box 217, Georgetown, CO 80444; 303-569-2403.*

Leadville Colorado and Southern Railroad

This railroad runs from Leadville to the Climax Mine, giving riders a panoramic view of this once-booming valley of silver. *326 East Seventh Street, Leadville, CO 80461; 719-486-3936.*

Manitou & Pikes Peak Cog Railway

This modern people-mover makes a three-hour round trip from Manitou Springs to the top of Pikes Peak, gaining 8,000 feet in altitude during the 9-mile journey through aspens and pines to timberline. Once atop the peak you can see the purple mountains' majesty and amber waves of grain that inspired Katherine Lee Bates to pen "America the Beautiful." *May through October with hourly departures during peak seasons. Cog Road Depot, 515 Ruxton Avenue, Manitou Springs, CO 80829; 719-685-5401, or Box 1329, Colorado Springs, CO 80901.*

Royal Gorge Scenic Railway

Snake along the top of the imposing Royal Gorge in modern, open-air cars. The train will stop for peeks over the edge that make you want to get back in your seat. *Box 1387, Cañon City, CO 81212; 719-275-5485.*

Royal Gorge Aerial Tram and the Royal Gorge Incline Railway

A ride on either of these conveyances provides stunning views of the gorge, which is spanned by the world's highest suspension bridge. Up to 35 passengers without a fear of heights can look down 1,200 feet into the bottom of the gorge from the safety of the comfortable tram cars that chug across the top. For those who want to take a closer look, the railway, the steepest in the world, takes you right to the bottom. Open year-round, weather permitting. *Royal Gorge Bridge Co., Box 594, Cañon City, CO 81212; 719-275-7507.*

The Ski Train
This is not a narrow-gauge railroad, but it is historic. Since 1941 it's been delivering skiers from Denver to the base of the Winter Park slopes. *Saturdays and Sundays, mid-December through mid-April, and Fridays as well mid-February, P.O. Box 481234, Denver, CO, 80248; 303-296-4754.*

■ Golf Courses

Most Colorado towns and resorts have at least a nine-hole golf course nearby. The following, however, are 18-hole layouts offering good golfing, fabulous views, or both. Most of the resort courses in the middle of the Rockies open in May, with those in the west and south—and even Front Range courses—offering almost year-round golfing.

Arrowhead Golf Club. Seventy-six sand traps and six lakes, not to mention scrub oak and the rock formations of Roxborough Park, make this course a dandy. Designer Robert Trent Jones Jr. has said that this course is among his favorites. Reservations are suggested. *10850 West Sundown Trail, Littleton; 303-973-9614.*

Aspen Golf Course. This beautiful course has great views and a challenging layout that incorporates a slew of hidden ditches and lakes. *39551 Colorado 82, Aspen; 970-925-2145.*

Beaver Creek Resort Golf Club. There are limited public tee times, but it's worth the wait to tackle this rolling, sand-trapped terror at the base of the Beaver Creek ski hill. Reservations are advised. *Beaver Creek; 970-845-5775.*

Breckenridge Golf Club. This public course was designed by golfing great Jack Nicklaus. It plays through the natural terrain, even passing a beaver pond, and has lots of pesky trees. Reservations are suggested. *200 Clubhouse Drive, Breckenridge; 970-453-9104.*

Broadmoor Golf Club. One of the most popular places to play in the region, and one of the oldest, Broadmoor is a challenging course amid a beautiful setting. *1 Lake Circle, Colorado Springs; 719-577-5790.*

Castle Pines Golf Club. Home of the PGA International Golf Tournament, the course challenges the pros, so you can imagine what it does to the rest of us. *1000 Hummingbird Lane, Castle Rock; 303-688-6000.*

Copper Creek Golf Club. A Perry Dye design, the course has the highest altitude of any PGA course in the nation and great views of the Tenmile Range. Reservations are suggested. *122 Wheeler Place, Copper Mountain; 970-968-2882.*

Flatirons Golf Course. Not only popular, but scenic and challenging, thanks to lots of lakes and trees. Call for tee times. *5706 East Arapahoe Road, Boulder; 303-442-7851.*

Grand Lake Golf Course. On the western edge of Colorado National Park, the course has tight fairways and tons of trees, so you have to keep it on the straight and narrow or bring lots of balls. But at an altitude of 8,400 feet, things really fly. *1415 County Road 48, Grand Lake; 970-627-8008.*

Hillcrest Golf Course. Located on the Fort Lewis College Mesa, the view is of the La Plata Mountains, and the course offers some good mountain golfing. *2300 Rim Drive, Durango; 970-247-1499.*

Meadow Hills Golf Course. The course is not as challenging or expensive as some of the others listed, but it is still a good play, with mature trees and geese creating most of the obstacles. *3609 South Dawson Street, Aurora; 303-690-2500.*

Patty Jewett Golf Club. Built in 1898, this was the first golf course west of the Mississippi. Today, the course has 27 holes. *900 East Espanola Street, Colorado Springs; 719-385-6934.*

Pueblo West Golf Club. The second-highest-rated course in the state is a good test of all your golfing skills, cursing included. *251 South McClulloch Boulevard, Pueblo; 719-547-2280.*

Rifle Creek Golf Course. The greens are located at the base of Rifle Gap, where artist Christo hung a short-lived red curtain from rim to rim. The 18-hole layout is short, but steep and tricky. *3004 Colorado 325, Rifle; 970-625-1093.*

Skyland Country Club. The fact that it is tucked into the base of Mount Crested Butte and surrounded by high-country scenery helps keep your mind off the battle its 18-hole layout presents. *385 Country Club Drive, Crested Butte; 970-349-7541.*

Snowmass Lodge and Club. More expensive and less challenging than the Aspen 18, but the setting is stunning. *239 Snowmass Club Circle, Snowmass Village; 970-923-5600.*

Steamboat Golf Club. Designed by Robert Trent Jones Jr., the course is one of the toughest in the state, and offers views of Mount Werner and the Yampa River Valley. Reservations are suggested. *West U.S. 40, Steamboat Springs; 970-879-4295.*
Tiara Golf Course. A young tough near the Colorado National Monument entrance assures nice views. *2063 South Broadway, Grand Junction; 970-245-8085.*
Vail Golf Club. This municipal course is flank to shank with the Gore River and Vail Mountain. *1778 East Vail Valley Drive, Vail; 970-479-2260.*
Wellshire Golf Course. Even though it is full of trees and very long (over 6,500 yards), at a mile high you can slash away and hope for altitude assistance to improve your score. *3333 South Colorado Boulevard, Denver; 303-757-1352.*

■ OFFICIAL TOURISM INFORMATION

■ STATEWIDE INFORMATION
Colorado Ski Country USA is the promotional association for all of the state's ski areas. It produces a slick, 100-page magazine describing every ski area, how to get there, and has listings of accommodations and other nearby amenities. *303-837-0793; www.coloradoski.com.*
  Colorado Travel and Tourism Authority will send you the official state vacation guide. Included in the guide are phone numbers and addresses for everything from government offices to all the state's chambers of commerce and national parks and recreation areas. *303-892-3885 or 800-265-6723; www.colorado.com.*
  Weather Reports/Road Conditions Statewide. *303-639-1111 or 303-639-1234; csp.state.co.us.*

■ OUTDOOR RECREATION ORGANIZATIONS
Colorado Association of Campgrounds, Cabins, and Lodges. *Cañon City; www.campcolorado.com.*
Colorado Dude and Guest Ranch Association. *Tabernash; 970-887-3128; www.coloradoranch.com.*
Colorado Golf Association. *Denver; 303-366-4653; www.golfhousecolorado.org.*
Colorado Reservation Service. *800-777-6880; www.coloradoreservationservice.com.*
Colorado River Outfitters Association. *Thorton; 303-280-2554; www.croa.org.*
Colorado Tennis Association. *Denver; 303-695-4116; www.coloradotennis.com.*

■ HUNTING AND FISHING INFORMATION

The **Colorado Division of Wildlife** (DOW) produces a number of comprehensive brochures that outline in detail every aspect of the state's hunting and fishing regulations and rules. The DOW also publishes *Colorado Outdoors,* a bimonthly, full-color magazine "dedicated to the conservation and enjoyment of Colorado outdoors—its animals, fish, soil, forests, prairies, and waters." *For a subscription, write to Colorado Outdoors, 6060 Broadway, Denver, CO 80216, or call 303-291-7469. For general information, call 303-297-1192, and for information on wildlife watching, call 303-291-7520; wildlife.state.co.us.*

■ USEFUL WEB SITES

Colorado Tourism Office. The state's official tourism Web site has links to accommodations, ski resorts, calendar of events, camping and general information for every region in the state. *www.colorado.com*

Colorado Avalanche Information Center. This great site has weather advisories, hotline numbers, and avalanche photos. *www.geosurvey.co.us/avalanche*

Colorado Ski Country USA. Pages on the site describe the state's ski areas, have links to ski resorts, and provide snow reports, skiing-related news, and information about lift-ticket prices and discounts, along with travel tips and accommodations options. This is a good place to check for travel packages. *www.coloradoski.com*

Denver Post and **Rocky Mountain News.** Denver's two daily newspapers both have Web sites packed with local information and news. *www.denverpost.com* and *www.rockymountainnews.com*

National Park Service. The site provides up-to-date information on fees and accommodations at the national parks and monuments, recreation areas, and historical sites in Colorado. *www.nps.gov*

Recreation.Gov. A good site with information about every type of recreational opportunity on federal, state, or local public lands, ranging from skiing to wind surfing to backpacking. *www.recreation.gov*

SkiColorado.com. This private site has links to all the state's ski areas and information about travel packages, lodging, snow conditions, lift ticket prices, and discount deals. *www.skicolorado.com*

State of Colorado. The state's Web site provides links to every town, county and chamber of commerce, in addition to links to the Division of Wildlife (for hunting and fishing information), the state's park system, museums, historic sites, road and travel information, and information on fees and other charges for state-run attractions. *www.colorado.gov*

U.S. Forest Service. This helpful site provides information about the recreational offerings in national forests and other federally controlled public lands. *www.fs.fed.us.com*

■ FESTIVALS AND EVENTS

More than 2,000 festivals and events take place annually in the state of Colorado. Below is a selection of some of the more famous and well attended of these. For a complete list and more detailed information, get a copy of the **Colorado Calendar of Events,** published by Ricky Clifton. *303-759-4257.*

■ JANUARY

Aspen: Aspen/Snowmass Winterskol. This five-day extravaganza includes fireworks, parades, all manner of ski races, and an impressive torchlight descent down Aspen Mountain. *970-925-1940.*

Breckenridge: Ullrfest and World Cup
Ullr, the Norse god of snow, is honored with a parade, fireworks, and the best pro freestyle skiers in the nation. *970-453-6018.*

Denver: National Western Stock Show
Visit the largest stock show in the United States, with 23 days of rodeos and a month's worth of all the cow-town ambiance you can handle. *303-295-1660.*

Meeker: Meeker Massacre Sled Dog Race and White River Rendezvous Devil's Hole Hill Climb
The town honors two types of snow travel, sled dog and snowmobile. *970-878-5510.*

■ FEBRUARY

Breckenridge: Fat Tuesday
Mardi Gras comes to the mountains. *970-453-5579.*

Delta: North Fork Snowmobile Races and Snowdeo
This event has all the snowmobiling fun you can imagine. *970-874-8621.*

Denver: Grand Ball
The traditional gala begins the opera season. *303-674-8110.*

Steamboat Springs: Winter Carnival
The oldest winter carnival west of the Mississippi features a band on skis, ski jumping, ski jouring (skiers being pulled by horses), and more. *970-879-0882.*

Walsenburg: Ground Hog Brunch
The Walsenburg golf course lets you munch while watching for a certain furry shadow. *719-738-1065.*

■ MARCH

Craig: Greek Festival
This northeastern Colorado town dines on souvlaki, dolmas, and baklava before dancing Greek folk dances. *970-824-5689.*

Denver: Colorado Ballet
The performances run for one month at the Denver Performing Arts Complex. *303-986-8742.*

Denver: St. Patrick's Day Parade
This parade is allegedly the second longest in the nation, due in part to the 5,000 horses. *303-534-8500.*

Monte Vista: Monte Vista Crane Festival
The town welcomes whooping and sandhill cranes returning to the valley for spring. Guided wildlife tours and lectures are featured. *719-852-3552.*

San Luis: Stations of the Cross
A Good Friday observance of the traditional Stations of the Cross, which are represented by sculptures along a trail outside of town. *719-672-3685.*

Springfield: Spring Equinox Festival
During the spring and autumn equinoxes, the sun turns Crack Cave into Colorado's version of Stonehenge, shining into the cave to reveal the ancient Ogam calendar and writings linked to Celtic runes in 4th-century Eire. *719-523-4061.*

Vail/Beaver Creek: American Ski Classic
This event highlights the Legends of Skiing Competition, honoring past national and world champs. *970-949-1999.*

■ APRIL

Colorado Springs: Easter Sunrise Service
The service is held at the Garden of the Gods. *719-635-1551.*

Copper Mountain: The Hot Shot Eenie Weenie Bikini Ski Contest
Both men and women strip down to the least amount of clothing weather will allow for one final race down the slopes. *970-968-2882.*

Kit Carson: Mountain Man Rendezvous
Period dress, black-powder shooting, and displays of the cooking and crafts of yesteryear allow you to go back in time to the days when men matched the mountains. *719-962-3532.*

■ MAY

Antonito: Cumbres & Toltec Scenic Railroad Season Opening
This historic steam-powered train makes a scenic 64-mile loop over the mountains from Antonito to Chama, New Mexico. *719-376-5488.*

Boulder: Bolder Boulder 10K
This is one of the nation's premier 10-kilometer road races. *303-444-7223.*

Boulder: Kinetic Conveyance Sculpture Race
This race features the weirdest human-powered vehicles ever to traverse land and water. *303-444-5600.*

Cortez Indian Dances
From mid-May through Labor Day, the Cortez Cultural Center hosts evening dances by members of the Navajo and Ute tribes with occasional guest appearances by the Hopi. *970-565-1151.*

Many Colorado festivals revolve around skiing.

Cuchara: Cuchara Valley Cowboy Arts
Celebrate all things cowboy, from the rustic to the artistic. *719-742-3676.*

Denver: Cinco de Mayo
Civic Center Park changes into a Mexican fiesta, with food, dance, and costumes. *303-534-8342.*

Durango: Annual Iron Horse Bicycle Classic
More than 2,000 mountain bikers and road racers compete in three intense days of pedaling. *970-259-4621.*

Fort Garland: Rendezvous of Cultures
This party reunites the Hispanic, Indian, and Anglo influences in the San Luis Valley. *719-589-3681.*

Ignacio: Annual Bear Dance
The three-day spring celebration marks traditional Ute dancing, costumes, singing, and ceremonies. *970-563-0100.*

Telluride: Telluride Mountain Film Festival
This event showcases outdoor, adventure, and mountain films. *970-728-4123.*

■ JUNE

Aspen: Music Festival and School
Opera, jazz, and symphony performances run for nine weeks in the Wheeler Opera House and the Music Tent. *970-925-9042.*

Central City: Lou Bunch Day
In honor of the town's last madam, festivities include bed races and a formal costume ball. *303-582-5251.*

Cortez: Four Corners Arts & Crafts Fiesta
Native American and other artists from throughout the Southwest display and sell their wares. *970-565-3414.*

Cripple Creek: Donkey Derby Days
Donkey races and a greased-pig chase are a few of the festivities. *719-689-2169.*

Denver: Capitol Hill People's Fair
More than 500 arts and crafts booths are set up in Civic Center Park, and entertainment unfolds on multiple stages. *303-830-1651.*

Glenwood Springs: Strawberry Days
The state's oldest civic celebration offers arts and crafts booths, entertainment, a parade, and free strawberries and ice cream. *970-945-6589.*

Julesburg: Pony Express Re-Ride
Aerobic pony express riders change horses in a heartbeat, hold on to the mail pouch, and keep on going without missing a step. *970-474-3504.*

Larkspur: Colorado Renaissance Festival
This 16th-century revival, complete with jousting, is held on weekends in June and July. *303-688-6010.*

Salida: FibArk Boat Races
The longest and oldest downriver kayak race in America has raft races and other entertainment tossed in. *719-539-7997.*

Steamboat Springs: Rodeo
Cowboys and broncos tango every Friday and Saturday night for a 13-week run. *970-879-0880.*

Telluride: Bluegrass Festival
A weekend of fiddling, fun, and fandangos. *800-624-2422.*

Trinidad: Santa Fe Trail Festival
A two-day celebration of history and art. *719-846-9285.*

■ JULY

Aspen: Aspen Dance Festival
A six-week run of performances by nationally known dance companies, ranging from ballet to modern to avant-garde. *970-925-7175.*

Boulder: Colorado Shakespeare Festival
One of the nation's top three Bard bashes is performed under the stars. Dance and music festivals also fill the month. *303-492-0554.*

Breckenridge: Breckenridge Music Festival
Classical concerts and workshops run from July to August. *970-453-2120.*

Carbondale: Carbondale Mountain Fair
Food, entertainment, and a juried selection of fine professional art and handmade crafts abound. *970-963-1890.*

Central City: Opera Festival
Held in the restored opera house, the performances run through August with classic operas performed in English. *303-292-6700.*

Florissant: Hornbek Homestead Days
This festival is held at the Florissant Fossil Beds National Monument. *719-748-3253.*

Greeley: Denver Broncos Training Camp
It's fun to watch the fanatics, er, fans, who flock to watch their heroes prepare for the upcoming season. *970-351-2007.*

Greeley: Independence Stampede
The largest Fourth of July rodeo is preceded by a week's worth of barbecues and parades. *970-356-2855.*

Idaho Springs: Gold Rush Days
Watch mucking and drilling contests and try your hand at panning gold. *303-567-4382.*

La Junta: Bent's Old Fort Fourth of July
Relive the excitement of the fur-trapping era in an authentically restored fort. *719-384-2800.*

Lake City: Alferd Packer Trial
Watch the trial of the famed Colorado cannibal as presented by the Western State College Drama Department. *970-944-2527.*

Las Animas: Silly Homemade River Raft Race
Crowds of whimsically decorated handmade rafts float along the Arkansas River. Month varies from year to year, so call ahead. *719-456-0453.*

Manitou Springs: Pikes Peak International Hill Climb
More than 60 professional race car drivers twist up the 12 miles of gravel to the top of Pikes Peak in this Race to the Clouds. *719-685-4400.*

Vail Valley: Bravo Colorado Music Festival
Chamber, orchestral, and jazz music are performed in various locations throughout Vail and Beaver Creek. *970-827-5700.*

Winter Park: Jazz Festival
Headline jazz artists play outdoors among food and crafts booths. *800-903-7275.*

■ AUGUST

Castle Rock: International Golf Tournament
Castle Pines Golf Club hosts the PGA's only Colorado stop. *303-688-4597.*

Central City: Summer Fest Music Festival
Performances by some of the most talented jazz and classical musicians in Colorado and the country. *303-582-5251.*

Grand Junction: Palisade Peach Festival
A fun celebration of the area's famous peaches. *970-464-7458.*

Leadville: Boom Days
Celebrate the silver boom with a drilling contest and a 22-mile pack burro race over a 13,000-foot mountain. *719-486-3900.*

Leadville: Leadville Trail 100
Competitors run or bike 100 miles at 10,000 feet above sea level. Spectators free; runners insane. *719-486-3900.*

Montrose: Annual Black Canyon Horse and Mule Race Meet
Yes, mules can run, proving burros aren't the only four-legged Colorado athletes. Some years the race is held in July. *970-249-5000.*

Pueblo: Colorado State Fair
About two weeks of agricultural ecstasy, in which strawberry preserves and peaches vie for blue ribbons. Parades, a professional rodeo, big-name country-western artists, and nights of carnival lights make this the best fair in the state. *719-561-8484.*

■ SEPTEMBER

Aspen: Ruggerfest
International rugby teams hit town in this three-day bash. *970-925-5370.*

Beecher's Island: Beecher's Island Reunion
This remembrance of the battle, one of the last between whites and Native Americans, includes a black-powder shoot, crafts, and games. *970-332-5063.*

Denver: A Taste of Colorado
Every Labor Day weekend this Taste of Colorado is a great excuse to gorge yourself on every type of food imaginable. *303-295-6330.*

Estes Park: Annual Scottish-Irish Highland Festival
Celebration of Scottish and Irish heritage includes authentic Celtic music, athletic competitions, and kilts. *970-586-4431.*

Grand Junction: Renaissance Fair
Period costumes, artists, food, and entertainment. *970-242-3214.*

Ignacio: Southern Ute Tribal Fair
Traditional games, exhibits, and ceremonies. *970-563-0100.*

La Junta: Early Settlers' Day
One of the most popular events in southeast Colorado, with many arts and crafts booths, a beer garden, fiddling contests, and a barbecue. *719-384-7411.*

Leadville: St. Patrick's Day Practice Parade
A great excuse for green beer. *719-486-3900.*

Meeker Classic Sheepdog Championship Trials
The world's best sheepdogs and handlers attempt to corral ornery Colorado sheep. *970-878-5510.*

Steamboat Springs: Classic Labor Day Weekend
This event includes a vintage airplane fly-in, professional bull riding, a free outdoor concert, and more. *970-879-0882.*

Telluride: Film Festival
Premieres, retrospectives, and classics are screened during Labor Day weekend. *603-433-9202.*

Yuma: Old Threshers Day
Demonstrations of old wheat threshers, corn huskers, and other farm equipment and activities trace the history of farming. *970-848-0407.*

■ OCTOBER

Durango: Durango Cowboy Gathering
Lectures and demonstrations of cowboy skills, and readings from contemporary cowboy poets. *970-247-0312.*

■ DECEMBER

Denver: Parade of Lights
Brightly lit floats and bands converge on the downtown Civic Center, and the Denver City and County Building is set aglow with colored light in every nook and cupola. *303-534-6161.*

La Junta: Bent's Old Fort Christmas 1846
A frontier Christmas celebration. *719-384-5010.*

Pueblo: Posada
A processional with a living nativity scene and music and song. *719-542-1704.*

San Luis: Fiesta de Nuestra Señora de Guadalupe
Music and prayer. *719-672-3685.*

San Luis: Las Posadas
A two-week reenactment of the journey of Mary and Joseph in search of a room for the Christ child. *719-672-3685.*

RECOMMENDED READING

■ History

Borland, Hal. *High, Wide, and Lonesome.* Philadelphia, New York: J.B. Lippincott Company, 1956.

Fay, Abbott. *Ski Tracks in the Rockies: A History of Skiing in Colorado.* Evergreen, Colorado: Cordillera Press, Inc., 1984.

Fradkin, Philip L. *A River No More: The Colorado River and the West.* Tucson: University of Arizona Press, 1984.

Neihardt, John G. *Black Elk Speaks.* New York: William Morrow & Co., 1932.

Parkman, Francis. *The California and Oregon Trail.* New York: Thomas Y. Crowell & Co., 1849.

Ubbelohde, Carl, Maxine Benson, and Duane A. Smith. *A Colorado History,* 6th ed. Boulder: Pruett Publishing Co., 1988.

Vandenbusche, Duane. *A Land Alone, Colorado's Western Slope.* Boulder: Pruett Publishing Co., 1980

■ Fiction

Abbey, Edward. *The Monkey Wrench Gang.* Philadelphia: J. B. Lippincott Co., 1975. The seminal work on acting out the West's eco-outrage.

Cather, Willa. *Song of the Lark.* Boston and New York: Houghton Mifflin Co., 1932.

Guthrie, A.B., Jr. *The Big Sky.* Foreword by Wallace Stegner. Boston: Houghton Mifflin Co., 1952. The best novel written about Mountain Men, their way of life, and the mountains that provided their livelihood.

Michener, James A. *Centennial.* New York: Random House, Inc., 1974. Michener applies his exacting research and storytelling gifts to Colorado's vibrant past.

INDEX

COMPASS AMERICAN GUIDES

Alaska	Las Vegas	San Francisco
American Southwest	Maine	Santa Fe
Arizona	Manhattan	South Carolina
Boston	Michigan	South Dakota
Chicago	Minnesota	Southern New England
Coastal California	Montana	Tennessee
Colorado	Nevada	Texas
Florida	New Hampshire	Utah
Georgia	New Mexico	Vermont
Gulf South: Louisiana, Alabama, Mississippi	New Orleans	Virginia
	North Carolina	Wine Country
Hawaii	Oregon	Wisconsin
Idaho	Pacific Northwest	Wyoming
Kentucky	Pennsylvania	

Compass American Guides are available at special discounts for bulk purchases for sales promotions or premiums. Special editions, including personalized covers, excerpts of existing guides, and corporate imprints, can be created in large quantities for special needs. For more information, contact your local bookseller or write to Special Markets, Fodor's Travel Publications, 1745 Broadway, New York, NY 10019. Inquiries from Canada should be directed to your local Canadian bookseller or sent to Random House of Canada, Ltd., Marketing Department, 2775 Matheson Boulevard East, Mississauga, Ontario L4W 4P7. Inquiries from the United Kingdom should be sent to Fodor's Travel Publications, 20 Vauxhall Bridge Road, London, England SW1V 2SA.

ACKNOWLEDGMENTS

All photographs in this book are by Paul Chesley unless otherwise noted below.

Compass American Guides acknowledges the following institutions and individuals for the use of their photographs and/or illustrations: **Center of Southwest Studies, Fort Lewis College, Durango,** p. 187; **Colorado Historical Society,** pp. 19 (WPA378), 22 (F44346), 33 (F32696), 57 (F31, 851 BPF), 86 (F6643 BPF), 89, 96 (WPA461/F19395), 102 (WPA193 BPF and F163 BPF), 137 (WHJ1399), 142 (F3823 BPF), 172 (F23307), 194 (F40267), 196 (F43442), 225 (F3069), 226 (F26970); **Copper Mountain Resort,** p. 223 (©Nate Abbott/Copper Mountain Resort); **Crested Butte Mountain Resort,** p. 258 (photo by Tom Stillo); **Denver Metro Convention and Visitors Bureau,** p. 44; **Denver Public Library, Western History Collection,** pp. 117, 169 (photo by H.S. Poley), 170, 192, 241, 247; **Durango & Silverton Narrow Gauge Railroad,** p. 139 (photo by Darel Crawford); **Getty Images,** p. 63 (photo by Tom Cooper); **Grand Junction Visitor & Convention Bureau,** pp. 161, 165; **Museum of New Mexico,** p. 184 (13667); **Museum of Western Art,** pp. 23, 25, 92–93, 168; **Pueblo City-County Library District,** p. 76; **Peabody Museum of Natural History, Yale University, New Haven, Connecticut,** pp. 152–153 (© 1966, 1975, 1985, 1989). **TK, Inc.,** p. 157.

Compass American Guides also wishes to thank Mark Goodwin of the U.C. Berkeley Museum of Paleontology, who contributed the essay on page 151.

The author acknowledges the staffs at the many chambers of commerce across Colorado whose information helped immeasurably in the preparation of this book. Additional thanks to Abbott Fay, a former history professor, who participated in my initial brainstorming and read the finished manuscript. The staffs at the Colorado Historical Society; Denver Public Library, Western History Collection; Museum of Western Art; and Colorado Ski Museum were most accommodating, as was the crew at the Glenwood Springs Branch of the Garfield County Library.

■ ABOUT THE AUTHOR

Jon Klusmire was born in Aspen and raised in towns up and down the Roaring Fork and Colorado River Valleys. He received a history degree from Western State College in Gunnison, Colorado, and started his journalism career as a reporter for the *Weekly Newspaper* in Glenwood Springs, later becoming its editor. After writing a regular column for the *Aspen Times* for several years, he took the position of senior editor at that newspaper. Later, he was the editor of the *Glenwood Independent* daily newspaper in Glenwood Springs. His work has appeared in the *High Country News,* the *Los Angeles Times,* the *National Catholic Reporter,* and other publications.

■ ABOUT THE PHOTOGRAPHER

Paul Chesley has been a freelance photographer with the National Geographic Society since 1975, traveling throughout Europe and Asia. His work was included in the Society's first major exhibition, *The Art of Photography at* National Geographic*: A 100-Year Retrospective,* at the Corcoran Gallery of Art in Washington, D.C. Solo exhibitions of his work have been mounted in museums in London, Tokyo, and New York, and his photographic essays have been published in *LIFE, Fortune, Bunte, Paris Match, Connoisseur,* and other magazines. He has participated in 10 *Day in the Life* projects. He lives in Aspen.